Investigating Sexual Harassment in Law Enforcement and Nontraditional Fields for Women

Investigating Sexual Harassment in Law Enforcement and Nontraditional Fields for Women

PENNY E. HARRINGTON
Former Chief of Police, Portland, Oregon
Founding Director, National Center for Women & Policing

KIMBERLY A. LONSWAY, Ph.D.
Research Director, End Violence Against Women International

PEARSON
Prentice
Hall

Upper Saddle River, New Jersey 07458

Library of Congress Cataloging-in-Publication Data

Harrington, Penny
    Investigating sexual harassment in law enforcement and nontraditional fields for women/
Penny E. Harrington, Kimberly A. Lonsway.
      p. cm.
    Includes bibliographical references and index.
    ISBN 0-13-118519-5
    1. Sexual harassment in law enforcement—United States.   2. Sexual harassment of women—United States.
3. Sexual harassment—Investigation—United States.   4. Sex role in the work environment—United States.
I. Lonsway, Kimberly A. (Kimberly Ann)   II. Title.
   HV8141.H297 2007
   363.2'2—dc22
                                                                     2005052317

Executive Editor: Frank Mortimer, Jr.
Assistant Editor: Mayda Bosco
Marketing Manager: Adam Kloza
**Director of Manufacturing
  and Production:** Bruce Johnson
Managing Editor: Mary Carnis
Production Liaison: Brian Hyland
Production Editor: Janet Bolton
Manufacturing Manager: Ilene Sanford

Manufacturing Buyer: Cathleen Petersen
Design Director: Cheryl Asherman
Cover Design: Solid State Design
Cover Art: © Karen Beard, Getty Images, Inc.—
  Stone Allstock
Composition: Integra
Printing and Binding: R.R. Donnelley, Harrisonburg
Copy Editor/Proofreader: Maine Proofreading
  Services

Pearson Education LTD.
Pearson Education Australia PTY, Limited
Pearson Education Singapore, Pte. Ltd.
Pearson Education North Asia Ltd.
Pearson Education Canada, Ltd.
Pearson Educacion de Mexico, S.A. de C.V.
Pearson Education—Japan
Pearson Education Malaysia, Pte. Ltd.
Pearson Education, Upper Saddle River, New Jersey

10 9 8 7 6 5 4 3 2 1
ISBN 0-13-118519-5

Contents

Preface   xi

About the Authors   xv

CHAPTER 1

Introduction   1

Purpose of This Book   1

Sexual Harassment Lawsuits   3

Guidance for Agencies Based on Earlier Sexual
    Harassment Lawsuits   6

CHAPTER 2

Understanding the Problem of Sexual Harassment   10

Sexual Harassment of Women in Nontraditional Fields   11

Impact on Victims   14

Realistic Dynamics of Sexual Harassment   17

CHAPTER 3

The Law and Sexual Harassment   23

Federal and State Laws   23

General Definition of Sexual Harassment   25

Summary of Employee Rights Under the Law   35

Summary of Employer Responsibilities Under
    the Law   36

CHAPTER 4
Gender Harassment and Discrimination   40

Harassment: Not Always Sexual   40
Gender Harassment/Discrimination in Policing
  and Firefighting   41
Role of Stereotypes in Gender Harassment/Discrimination   43
Investigation of Gender Harassment/Discrimination   43
For More Information   48
Mentors for Investigators   49

CHAPTER 5
Retaliation   51

Legal Protection Against Retaliation   51
Types of Retaliation   53
Triggers for Retaliation   55
Impact on Victims   55
Preventing and Responding to Retaliation   55

CHAPTER 6
Preventing Sexual Harassment   59

Men Who Sexually Harass   59
Perils of Not Preventing Sexual Harassment   61
Sexual Harassment Prevention   62

CHAPTER 7
Designing a Comprehensive Sexual Harassment Policy   68

Goals of a Sexual Harassment Policy   69
Elements of Inadequate Sexual Harassment
  Policies   70
Elements of a Comprehensive Sexual Harassment Policy   71
Elements *Not* to Include in a Sexual Harassment Policy   73
Dissemination of a Sexual Harassment Policy   75
Sexual Harassment Policy and Dating   76
Conclusion   77

CHAPTER 8

Developing an Effective Training Program Regarding Sexual Harassment   79

Challenges in Sexual Harassment Training   79

Content of a Comprehensive Sexual Harassment Training Program   81

Design of an Effective Sexual Harassment Training Program   83

Other Educational Efforts   86

Evaluation of Sexual Harassment Training   87

Results of Existing Evaluation Research   88

CHAPTER 9

Responsibilities of Supervisors and Managers Regarding Sexual Harassment   91

Definition of Supervisor or Manager   91

Supervisors' and Managers' Legal Responsibilities   91

Supervisors' and Managers' Sexual Harassment
   Prevention Strategies   92

Inappropriate Actions By Supervisors and Managers   93

Supervisors' and Managers' Responses to Sexual Harassment   95

Supervisors' and Managers' Prevention of Retaliation   96

Accusations of Harassment or Discrimination Against Supervisors
   and Managers   96

CHAPTER 10

Complaint Procedures   98

Formal versus Informal Complaint Procedures   98

Informal Complaint Procedures   100

Formal Complaint Procedures   103

Implementation of the Complaint Process   105

Responses to Complaints   106

CHAPTER 11

Selecting an Investigator   110

Requirements for a Successful Investigator   110

Selection, Screening, and Training of Investigators   111

Types of Investigators   113

CHAPTER 12
Beginning the Investigation   117

Problems in the Workplace   117

Planning the Investigation   118

Interviews with Complainant, Respondent, and Witnesses   119

Elements to Establish   120

Anonymous Complaints   121

Uniform Standards for the Investigation   122

Other Issues in the Investigation   124

Common Mistakes   124

CHAPTER 13
Employee Options for Responding to Sexual Harassment   126

Employee Responses to Sexual Harassment   126

Informal Response Strategies   126

Formal Complaint Procedures   129

CHAPTER 14
Preparing for the Complainant Interview   133

Common Challenges   133

Tips for Successful Interview with Complainant   140

CHAPTER 15
Interviewing the Complainant   143

Before the Interview   143

At the Start of the Interview   145

During the Interview   149

At the Conclusion of the Interview   157

CHAPTER 16
Interviewing the Respondent   160

Preparation for the Interview   160

Start of the Interview   162

During the Interview   165

Conclusion of the Interview   172

CHAPTER 17
Interviewing Witnesses   173

Types of Witnesses   173
Code of Silence   174
Interview Process   175

CHAPTER 18
Documenting the Investigation   181

Final Investigative Report   181
Investigative Case File   184
Confidentiality Issues   185

CHAPTER 19
Making a Determination and Imposing Discipline   187

Review Personnel Files   187
Weigh the Evidence   188
Make a Determination   191
Impose Appropriate Discipline   193
Follow Up with Complainants and Respondents   196

CHAPTER 20
Other Issues   198

Same-Gender Harassment   198
Harassment Based on Sexual Orientation   199
Harassment of Civilian Women Employees   200
Bystander Harassment   201
Harassment of Nonemployees   201
Harassment by Nonemployees   202
Harassment of People in Protected Classes   203
Use of Computers for Harassment   204

References   206
Index   213

Preface

A Few Words from Chief Penny Harrington

As the first female chief of a major metropolitan police department, I decided to write this book several years ago while serving as the Director of the National Center for Women & Policing. In that role, I would receive telephone calls nearly every day from women police officers who were experiencing sexual harassment and discrimination in the workplace. I would listen to their stories and then advise them of the options they had for dealing with the situation. As I listened, I was always amazed at how similar their situations were, regardless of the size of the department or its location in the United States.

I would also occasionally receive telephone calls from police chiefs, sheriffs, and other law enforcement executives who were trying to deal with sexual harassment complaints. As I did with the female officers, I listened to their stories and frustrations and offered advice on how to handle these situations. Sadly, many of these were chiefs of small agencies who did not have the training or experience they needed to deal with these situations. I would praise them for having the courage to reach out for help.

Then I became an expert witness and consultant on issues of gender and race discrimination. I reviewed cases from across the country in all types of law enforcement agencies, fire departments, and business corporations. Yet no matter how different the setting or geographic location, I still saw the same issues being confronted and the same mistakes being made time after time.

As a result of these experiences, it has become apparent to me that the women who contact me for help or who file lawsuits do not do so lightly; these women have typically suffered from harassment and discrimination for *years* and finally could not take it any longer. It has also become equally apparent to me that the managers in these organizations usually do not know how to handle these allegations and often strike back in anger, making the situation worse.

Of course, these reactions should not be surprising. In fact, sexual harassment is not an easy topic for most people to discuss because it deals with our innermost beliefs and feelings about sex as well as the appropriate roles for men and women. These beliefs are a part of us, beginning in our childhood and continuing throughout our lives. It is no wonder, then, that these issues can cause problems in the workplace, both for those involved in sexual harassment situations and for those with the responsibility to respond appropriately.

If I could summarize the attitudes of most complainants with whom I have worked, I would say that *they just want the behavior to stop*. They do not want to file complaints or lawsuits, but when the behavior continues to the degree that it is having a serious effect on their health, their family, and their work, they have to do something. That "something" is often to either leave the job or file a complaint.

If I could summarize the attitudes of most of the harassers with whom I have worked, I would say that they feel they have not done anything wrong and are very angry that they are being accused of harassment. They most often blame the victim for the situation, saying that she is too sensitive, she is incompetent, she is a safety hazard to him and others, or she has a personality defect. I have hardly ever seen a harasser admit that his actions were wrong.

Finally, if I could summarize the attitudes of most of the leaders who have to deal with these complaints, I find that they are upset that the situation has gotten to this point, they just want it to go away, and they do not want to have to deal with it. Unfortunately, the reactions of these leaders will set the tone for the agency and will determine whether the organization will be able to appropriately deal with the allegations and provide a fair and just outcome. The most crucial step, therefore, is to assign a competent investigator and conduct a thorough and unbiased investigation in a timely manner while protecting the complainant from retaliation.

In writing this book, I hope to convince supervisors, managers, and others that *it really is not that difficult to handle these complaints!* The hardest part is simply garnering the courage to do it right; as for the rest of the process, we can show you how. You've come to the right place.

A Few Words from Dr. Kim Lonsway

While this book is clearly the brainchild of Chief Harrington, I bring to it my own 15 years of experience as a psychologist working with the many complex issues of sexual victimization. As a researcher, I have conducted studies to better understand the many beliefs and attitudes our culture has regarding sexual harassment and rape. As an educator, I have used that research to guide the design and evaluation of programs to prevent sexual victimization on college campuses and in other settings. As a community member, I have volunteered in my local rape crisis center by staffing the hotline, providing various forms of advocacy, and accompanying sexual assault victims throughout the stressful procedures of the medical and legal systems. Through all these experiences, I have developed an extensive background in the issues of sexual victimization that informs my current work with sexual harassment in the workplace.

More recently, I have worked with Chief Harrington to address these issues of sexual victimization as they intersect with the world of law enforcement. We first worked together at the National Center for Women & Policing to address a number of issues regarding the law enforcement response to sexual victimization in the community. This included designing an innovative national training program for law enforcement professionals investigating crimes of acquaintance sexual assault. Now, we continue to work together at Harrington & Associates to address the problems of sexual victimization within the law enforcement organization itself. Working as expert witnesses and consultants, we review materials in sexual harassment cases involving female law enforcement officers and others. By working together, we believe that we bring different perspectives to the problem and hopefully provide a more comprehensive guide for the reader.

Our Ultimate Recommendations

We hope that this book will be helpful for supervisors, managers, and others who are faced with issues of sexual harassment. In writing the book, our goal was to help organizations identify the things they need to do to provide an atmosphere in which employees are treated with respect and they can be most productive. We will therefore begin by highlighting some of the most important things that management can do to prevent and resolve issues of sexual harassment in the workplace:

1. Develop a sexual harassment prevention policy, and update it annually.
2. Distribute the policy to everyone in the organization, and redistribute it regularly.
3. Train all employees about the policy; evaluate and retrain all employees frequently.
4. Set up a fair and effective process for receiving and investigating complaints.
5. Hold supervisors and managers responsible for monitoring the workplace to detect any violations of the policy.
6. If a complaint is made, take immediate steps to resolve it:
   a. Protect complainants from retaliation.
   b. Conduct a thorough, timely, and fair investigation.
   c. Impose any necessary discipline and/or implement remedial training.
   d. Follow up with complainants to make sure they are not experiencing any retaliation.

This is the process in a nutshell. While we have provided detailed guidance for each of these steps in this book, another guide, titled *Recruiting and Retaining Women: A Self-Assessment Guide for Law Enforcement,* is also available. This self-assessment guide addresses not only issues of sexual harassment but other gender issues that affect the recruitment, selection, training, promotion, and retention of women officers. It is available both online and in hard copy through the National Criminal Justice Reference Service (www.ncjrs.org). This self-assessment guide provides a wealth of valuable information as well as checklists for making sure that organizations are doing all they can to prevent various forms of harassment and discrimination.

Please feel free to contact us if we can be of assistance to you in dealing with these serious issues of harassment and discrimination. Thank you and good luck!

Acknowledgements

We would like to thank the following for reviewing *Investigating Sexual Harassment in Law Enforcement and Nontraditional Fields for Women*: Professor Melanie Deffendall, Delgado Community College, New Orleans, LA; Professor Ida Dupont, Pace University, New York, NY; Professor Patrick J. Faiella, Massasoit Community College, Brockton, MA; Professor Robert E. Kettlitz, Hastings College, Hasting NE; and Professor Daniel S. Murphy, Appalachain State University, Boone, NC.

Chief Penny Harrington
(chiefpenny@charter.net; www.pennyharrington.com)

Dr. Kim Lonsway
(klonsway@charter.net; www.kimlonsway.com)

About the Authors

Chief Penny E. Harrington started her career in the Portland, Oregon, Police Bureau in 1964 as a policewoman. Over the years, she was a detective, a sergeant, a lieutenant, and a captain and in 1985 was appointed Portland Chief of Police, the first woman in the nation to lead a major city police department. After leaving Portland, Chief Harrington became the Special Assistant to the Director of Investigations for the State Bar of California. In 1995, she became the Founding Director of the National Center for Women & Policing (NCWP), a division of the Feminist Majority Foundation. Upon her retirement in 2001, she became a consultant and expert witness for employment discrimination cases. She is the author of *Triumph of Spirit,* her autobiography, and is the principal author of *Recruiting & Retaining Women: A Self-Assessment Guide for Law Enforcement.* Chief Harrington has received many honors, including being named as *Ms.* magazine's Woman of the Year in 1986 and being inducted into the Wall of Fame at Michigan State University. For more information, see www.pennyharrington.com.

Dr. Kimberly A. Lonsway earned her Ph.D. in Psychology at the University of Illinois at Urbana-Champaign, during which time she took a leave of absence to complete the 40-hour course Basic Law Enforcement Training at the Illinois Police Training Institute. Dr. Lonsway then spent two years as a postdoctoral research fellow at the American Bar Foundation, where she conducted interdisciplinary research on psychology and law, particularly focusing on issues of policing, training, and sexual victimization. Since moving to California, Dr. Lonsway has served as the Research Director for the National Center for Women & Policing (NCWP), the Director of Research and Training for Harrington & Associates, and the Director of Research for End Violence Against Women (EVAW)

International. In all these positions, Lonsway's work has continued to focus on the ways in which sexual victimization intersects with policing. In addition, Dr. Lonsway occasionally teaches courses in psychology and statistical methods for the Department of Psychology and Child Development at California Polytechnic State University. Fore more information, see www.kimlonsway.com.

Investigating Sexual Harassment in Law Enforcement and Nontraditional Fields for Women

Chapter 1

Introduction

PURPOSE OF THIS BOOK

The purpose of this book is to help those in law enforcement, firefighting, and other fields that are nontraditional for women to better prevent, identify, investigate, and resolve problems of sexual harassment. None of these tasks is easy, but the cost of failure is simply too high to ignore. The costs of sexual harassment include not only the personal and professional toll that sexual harassment takes on individual victims but also the lost productivity, sick leave, and even turnover that often result. If the victim sues, the resulting lawsuit is extremely time-consuming and expensive, not to mention emotionally difficult for everyone involved. We have seen lawsuits that result in multi-million-dollar payouts to plaintiffs plus the costs of attorney fees awarded by the court. There are obviously many reasons to take this problem seriously. Therefore, this book is designed to help prevent and to effectively resolve any problems with sexual harassment that might arise in the workplace so that they don't lead to an expensive and painful lawsuit.

Fortunately, the rewards are also great for those organizations that effectively address the problem of sexual harassment. By taking this issue seriously and implementing successful actions, organizations can

- Protect employees from sexual harassment, a problem that has serious negative effects on both their personal and professional lives.

- Inform employees of their right to a workplace that is free of sexual harassment, and describe policies regarding reporting, investigation, and potential discipline.

1

- Offer employees the kind of concrete guidance that they need to avoid problems and to model appropriate workplace behavior.

- Provide clear information that will assist victims of sexual harassment in reporting the problem or otherwise responding effectively.

- Train supervisors and managers to appropriately respond and resolve these problems.

- Ensure that those responsible for investigating complaints of sexual harassment receive the training they need to conduct such a complex and sensitive task.

- Record information to track the incidence of sexual harassment, and identify employees, supervisors, and units with repeated problems.

- Evaluate the sexual harassment policy and training programs in an ongoing way both to better understand their effectiveness and to implement continuous improvements.

- Protect the department and the city, county, state, or federal agency from civil liability that could cost millions of dollars in a plaintiff's successful lawsuit.

Our Focus on Sexual Harassment

While this book primarily deals with the issues of sexual harassment (and other forms of gender discrimination), similar recommendations would apply to harassment based on race, sexual orientation, or other protected categories. This book focuses on the problems of sexual harassment for two reasons. First, this is our primary area of personal expertise. Second, statistics provided by the Equal Employment Opportunity Commission (EEOC) indicate that most of the complaints it receives are for sexual or gender-based harassment, with fewer harassment complaints based on race, national origin, and other protected categories, so another reason for this focus is that sexual harassment represents the most commonly litigated area of employment discrimination. Therefore, while we believe our focus on sexual harassment is appropriate, we nonetheless hope that the book is also useful for investigators looking into other forms of harassment and discrimination in the workplace.

Our Focus on Victim Dynamics

Readers will also notice that this book focuses extensively on the dynamics of those who are victimized by sexual harassment—how they respond to the situation and what this means for the investigative process.[1] While there are other books and materials that are available to provide information on investigating complaints of sexual harassment, they often focus primarily on issues of policies, training, and general investigative processes, glossing over the nuts and bolts of actually doing the investigation (especially interviewing). We have tried to address this neglect by describing in detail *exactly how* to interview the parties, especially the complainant. We also provide the context for conducting these interviews by discussing what the research tells us about the dynamics of sexual harassment and its impact on victims. We believe it is critically important to understand how sexual harassment *really* operates to be able to conduct an effective investigation. For example, investigators must be aware of some of the most common dynamics of sexual harassment, such as the fact that most victims do not file a formal complaint and most of those who do file a report experience some form of retaliation for doing so.

Our Focus on Law Enforcement

The book is also based on our personal expertise in the field of law enforcement. For example, we will talk extensively about the unique aspects of police culture that contribute to the problem of sexual harassment, such as the concepts of "brotherhood" and "code of silence." However, we believe that many of the issues are similar in firefighting and other workplaces that are numerically dominated by men and traditionally defined as masculine. Therefore, in some cases we will provide information that is unique to policing, but the reader can otherwise assume that the recommendations apply to firefighting and other professions that are nontraditional for women.

SEXUAL HARASSMENT LAWSUITS

For the last several years, both of the authors have worked with Penny Harrington & Associates, L.L.C., a small private firm specializing in employment discrimination issues, particularly with respect to sexual harassment. During that time, we have reviewed numerous sexual harassment cases in law enforcement and other fields that are nontraditional for women. In these cases, the allegations have included many wide-ranging forms of sexual harassment:

- Derogatory comments about women's ability to do the job
- Specific comments designed to humiliate a particular woman
- Sexualized jokes, gestures, and cartoons
- Pornography (posted and/or distributed)
- Physical touching, grabbing, and fondling
- Threats of a physical and/or sexual nature
- Attempted and even completed sexual assaults
- Unfair practices for testing, promotion, and specialized assignments
- Unreasonable referrals for Fitness for Duty Evaluations
- Unwarranted discipline, demotion, and even termination

Typically, these female employees experienced severe retaliation after they filed a complaint of sexual harassment. To illustrate, some were

- Targeted with constant criticism and/or discipline.
- Denied opportunities for training, transfer, or promotion.

- Isolated or shunned in the workplace.
- Not provided with backup on emergency calls.
- Physically injured during a training exercise.
- Stalked or harassed both at work and at home.
- Threatened with a firearm.

In many cases, the retaliation extended to those who provided support to the complainant, such as family members or friends who were also in the department.

Sexual Harassment and Power

These lawsuits have taught us a number of things about sexual harassment, and one of the most important lessons is that it is fundamentally an issue of *power*. Unfortunately, those who have power, or who want to assert their power in the workplace, sometimes do so by forcing unwanted sexual or otherwise offensive conduct on others. Worse, this type of conduct can be perpetuated by some aspects of the unique culture in law enforcement agencies, fire departments, and other work environments that are traditionally masculine. For example, the brotherhood and the code of silence seen in policing can exacerbate the problem of sexual harassment by encouraging such behavior and ensuring that it is not reported or otherwise resolved.

It is therefore important for anyone trying to address the problem of sexual harassment to understand that sexual harassment is not typically the result of a misunderstanding or a bungled attempt at courtship. Yes, there are problems with sexual behavior in the workplace that are due to such miscommunication or misinterpreted social cues. For example, there are situations in which one employee repeatedly asks another employee out on a date. This kind of situation is often easily resolved because the conduct is relatively minor. However, even when the situation only involves one employee repeatedly asking out another, it may develop into stalking and sexual assault. Repeated requests for dates should therefore be viewed as sexual harassment and be taken seriously.

Nonetheless, such situations are likely to result in change on the part of the "harasser" without a full-scale investigation or a grievance procedure; in fact, they can often be resolved informally by a supervisor or someone else with relevant expertise, such as an employee in the Human Resources Department. (Of course, these situations still need to be recorded as a complaint of sexual harassment in case the situation repeats itself. We will discuss these procedures in detail throughout the book.)

In contrast, most forms of sexual harassment involve an abuse of power. In some cases, this may be blatant, such as a male supervisor implying that his female subordinate must sleep with him to keep her job. In police agencies, this is sometimes seen with probationary employees who experience subtle or blatant pressure to date or even sleep with their Field Training Officer. In this type of situation, the abuse of power is pretty clear; however, most cases of sexual harassment do not involve any effort to gain sexual favors. Rather, these cases typically involve behaviors that are designed to denigrate, degrade, and even humiliate women officers—to remind them that they are not wanted in the workplace and to "keep them in their place." For example, Dr. Louise Fitzgerald at the University of Illinois at Urbana-Champaign states that most sexual harassment is less about a "come-on" than a "put-down."

Common Misconception Regarding Sexual Harassment

Consent

To better understand sexual harassment, it is perhaps helpful to outline what it is *not*. For example, despite the common misconception, sexual harassment is not fundamentally an issue of consent. In other words, just because the complainant acquiesced to the sexual behavior does not necessarily mean that it is not harassment. Even employees who have "consented" (in other words, acquiesced) to sexual behavior with a colleague may have done so because of the dynamics of the situation. This is, of course, particularly true for employees who "consent" to participate in a sexual relationship with a supervisor or manager in their organization. For obvious reasons, employees often feel compelled to comply with the advances of employers who may have the power to determine their economic future. Yet the law protects employees even if they have complied with sexual demands as long as the demands were unwelcome. (Because it is so difficult to establish true consent in a situation in which one person has power over another in the workplace, many organizations seek to avoid this problem altogether by implementing policies prohibiting such relationships under any circumstances.)

Even in situations with sexualized comments, jokes, or pornographic materials in the workplace, the behavior can still constitute sexual harassment if complainants are seen as "consenting" because they do not verbally state their objections. In fact, the failure to verbally protest does not necessarily mean that the complainant welcomed such sexualized behavior. As in the previous situation, there can be a great deal of pressure to go along with sexualized behavior in the workplace even when it is considered extremely unwelcome. The burden is on those engaging in sexualized behavior to ensure that it is welcomed by all present, and their silence cannot necessarily be interpreted as consent.

Mutual Relationships

Another common misconception is that sexual harassment is really just about mutual relationships. Clearly, the law does not prohibit people from having friendships or mutual intimate relationships, even at work, as long as they are freely entered into by both parties without pressure (although some department policies do prohibit such relationships). Rather, the law prohibits *unwelcome* sexual relationships. Even in situations in which an employee has been in a mutual relationship with another employee that has ended, that employee still has the right to be free from harassment if he or she directly informs the other person that the relationship is no longer welcome. The fact that this employee previously engaged in a mutual relationship and consented to intimate behavior with another employee does not prohibit that person from seeking a remedy for sexual advances if they have now become unwelcome. However, the fact that the behavior is now unwelcome must be clearly communicated to the other person.

Harasser's Intentions

The lawsuits also teach us that despite the common misconception to the contrary, it is actually irrelevant whether or not the harasser *intends* for the behavior to be offensive; the courts have consistently ruled that the issue is the *impact* of the behavior on the victim. Yet research tells us that there is often a difference in the way such behaviors are perceived by men versus women in the workplace. For example, the extensive research literature in this area demonstrates that many men perceive sexual advances in the workplace as flattering or at least harmless, but many women perceive the same behaviors as intrusive, demeaning, or even threatening. Some researchers have attributed this gender difference to the threat of rape that is ever present in women's lives and that influences their perceptions of male sexual advances. Regardless, it is clear that the law does not take into account the perceptions or intentions of the person doing the harassing, only the one who is receiving it. The law thus prohibits sexual conduct in the workplace when the person receiving the sexual attention finds it unwelcome, regardless of how it was intended.

GUIDANCE FOR AGENCIES BASED ON EARLIER SEXUAL HARASSMENT LAWSUITS

Earlier lawsuits offer additional guidance in how agencies can successfully respond to the problem of sexual harassment. Typically, the individuals involved in these sexual harassment lawsuits complained to their agency in a variety of ways. They often complained informally to a supervisor and then formally through a departmental or external grievance procedure before filing the lawsuit. In most cases, the agency was thus clearly on notice that the behavior was occurring and that it was unwelcome or offensive. One example from our experience demonstrates this point:

> In one case, a female officer complained to her sergeant on many occasions about the behavior of one of her coworkers. This coworker would constantly talk about sex in the workplace, would continually ask her for a date, and would regularly leave sexually oriented material in her mailbox at work. When the behavior happened in front of the sergeant, he would sometimes tell the harasser to "knock it off." However, in response to the female officer's many complaints, the sergeant simply told her to ignore the behavior and that it was just the way that officer behaved. The female officer then filed a complaint through the chain of command, but it was sent back to her sergeant to investigate. Next, she went to Internal Affairs and filed a complaint, and she was subjected to severe retaliation in response. Finally, when all her efforts failed, she filed a lawsuit against the agency naming the officer, the sergeant, the chief, and others. She was awarded over $3 million by the jury.

We will talk in much greater detail about common problems with the agency response to sexual harassment and ways to design a more effective system for preventing, reporting, investigating, and resolving these difficult situations. For now, however, we simply want to make the point that most of the situations that result in litigation do so only after *multiple* failures on the part of the agency.

In our experience with sexual harassment lawsuits, agencies were typically well aware of what was going on and how the complainant felt about it. *The fundamental failure was therefore simply that the agency did not take the issue of sexual harassment seriously and decide to respond appropriately.* In the cases we have worked with, agencies have paid very dearly for that failure in terms of the costs for attorneys and employees to pursue the litigation and the settlement or damage awards that resulted.

The Bad News

To summarize, these lawsuits teach us that problems with handling sexual harassment usually occur in the following areas.

Policy

Although most law enforcement agencies have a sexual harassment policy, it often consists of language developed by the EEOC to describe prohibited workplace conduct. These policies may be legally adequate, but they are frequently not comprehensive enough to give guidance to employees on what is expected of their behavior in the workplace. In addition, most policies fail to recognize that harassment is frequently very subtle. For example, sexually explicit comments may be covered in the policy, but demeaning comments about women may not. In many agencies, discriminatory behavior persists despite an official policy against it because the written policy is inadequate, unpublicized, and unenforced.

Training

In one study of women in Florida law enforcement, over 50 percent said that their agency provided no formal training on sexual harassment (Robinson, 1993). Yet even when agencies do provide training about sexual harassment, it is often conducted by someone with a legal background who emphasizes the prohibitions and penalties against engaging in sexual harassment. Unfortunately, this type of training frequently results in employees becoming angry with their female coworkers instead of understanding the dynamics of sexual harassment and making a commitment to exhibit proper behavior in the workplace.

Reporting

Many employees are afraid to report sexual harassment that they are experiencing in the workplace, especially if supervisors or command staff witness the behavior and do nothing to stop it. Others decide not to report the behavior because the policy does not give them any options about where to report it. However, even when employees do report sexual harassment, the systems in law enforcement agencies seldom work to quickly and appropriately resolve their complaints, which results in litigation. For example, many agencies assign the investigation of sexual harassment complaints to Internal Affairs personnel without having adequately or appropriately trained those employees on how to conduct sexual harassment investigations.

Investigation

As described above, the task of investigating sexual harassment complaints is often assigned to personnel in Internal Affairs. Yet the functions and procedures of an Internal Affairs unit often preclude the fair treatment of sexual harassment victims in a number of ways. First, Internal Affairs investigators are rarely trained to understand the dynamics of sexual harassment, pertinent laws, or appropriate investigative techniques. Second, the standard of proof for Internal Affairs complaints is often inappropriately applied to complaints of sexual harassment. (For sexual harassment complaints, the appropriate standard of proof should be a "preponderance of the evidence," not "beyond a reasonable doubt.")

Third, most Internal Affairs investigators are male, which is a chilling factor for many females wishing to file a sexual harassment complaint. Fourth, Internal Affairs personnel typically use the general category of "misconduct" as the primary determination in an investigation, but this is inadequate to appropriately characterize and record complaints of sexual harassment. Because the documentation of sexual harassment complaints is then absorbed into the more general category of officer "misconduct" investigations, the agency then has no record of sexual harassment complaints, investigations, findings, or resolutions.

Fifth, serious breaches of confidentiality are all too common when Internal Affairs investigators handle sexual harassment complaints, perhaps because they are not trained to understand, prevent, and respond to such problems. As a result of these and other concerns, there is often a perception within law enforcement agencies that it is neither safe nor effective to report sexual harassment through the Internal Affairs process, either because it will not be taken seriously or, worse, because investigators themselves will retaliate against the complainant.

Retaliation

As described above, retaliation for filing sexual harassment complaints can be severe, often more severe than the sexually harassing behaviors that the person was originally reporting. Yet most police and fire departments do not have in place an adequate system for preventing or responding to retaliation. Making a complaint about sexual harassment is therefore typically a "career killer" within law enforcement, firefighting, and other professions that are nontraditional for women.

The Good News

The good news is that by reading this book, police and fire departments can go a long way toward preventing the nightmare of litigation. While it may sound trite, this actually is one of those win-win situations that people talk about. By taking the issue of sexual harassment seriously and redesigning the policies and procedures appropriately, agencies really *can* work toward preventing these problems. Of course, nothing can guarantee that sexual harassment will not occur in a police department, a fire department, or any other workplace environment; however, if an organization has implemented an effective system for reporting, investigating, and resolving these problems, employees are likely to be treated with the respect they deserve and employers are likely to avoid costly litigation.

ENDNOTES

1. Readers will notice that we typically use the term "complainant" to refer to someone who has filed a formal (or even informal) complaint of sexual harassment. However, we also refer to victims of sexual harassment who may or may not have filed any kind of complaint; in those situations, we use the term "victim."

Chapter 2

Understanding the Problem of Sexual Harassment

There are a number of common misconceptions about the problem of sexual harassment. This chapter is designed to provide general information about the prevalence and dynamics of sexual harassment in policing, firefighting, and other professions that are nontraditional for women. This information is absolutely essential for investigators because effective strategies for responding must be based on an accurate understanding of sexual harassment, its impact on victims, and the ways in which victims typically respond.

Sexual harassment is unwelcome behavior to which individuals in the workplace are subjected. This behavior is often sexual in nature and/or demeaning to women, and it interferes with an employee's ability to do his or her job.

For those who are victimized, sexual harassment can cause extreme anxiety, humiliation, and stress; it can lead to physical illness or loss of sleep. Yet despite these serious consequences, many employees are reluctant to report sexual harassment. Instead, they may request a shift change or a new supervisor without explaining that the request is a result of sexual harassment. Employees may even call in sick to avoid their harasser or may eventually quit their job when the harassment becomes unbearable. However, all employees have the right to work in a harassment-free environment. They are not obligated to modify their work conditions because they are being sexually harassed. Sexual harassment is, above all else, illegal under state and federal laws.

SEXUAL HARASSMENT OF WOMEN IN NONTRADITIONAL FIELDS

There is a great deal of research documenting the fact that women in nontraditional fields suffer from a higher rate of sexual harassment than their female counterparts in other fields (Gutek, 1985; Hesson-McInnis & Fitzgerald, 1997; Hunter-Williams, Fitzgerald, & Drasgow, 1999; Ilies, Hauserman, Schwochau, & Stibal, 2003; Koss et al., 1994; Lafontaine & Tredeau, 1986; U.S. Merit Systems Protection Board, 1981, 1987). Nontraditional fields are defined as those in which the majority of employees are male and the duties are traditionally defined as masculine.

Specifically, research indicates that 50–58 percent of women in the general workforce experience sexually harassing behaviors, in comparison with 69–77 percent in nontraditional fields such as policing, firefighting, and the military (Ilies, Hauserman, Schwochau, & Stibal, 2003; Lafontaine & Tredeau, 1986). Yet women in nontraditional workplaces are even less likely than women in other fields to indicate that they have been sexually harassed (Ilies, Hauserman, Schwochau, & Stibal, 2003). In sum, women in nontraditional fields are *more likely* to be sexually harassed but *less likely* to identify it as such. The research also finds that sexual harassment is particularly common in organizations with the following characteristics[1]:

- They have few or no women in the upper ranks.
- They have an unprofessional work environment that encourages casualness in dress, language, and relationships.
- They have a work environment in which sexual language, sexual joking, and sexual relationships are common.
- They do not have policies and procedures for responding to sexual harassment.
- They do not have managers in the upper ranks sending a strong message that sexual harassment will not be tolerated.
- They send messages, either explicitly or implicitly, that sexual harassment will be tolerated, that no one who is found guilty will be disciplined, and that anyone filing a complaint will be punished.

All of this has led some authors to conclude that sexual harassment is "an occupational hazard for women working in male-dominated occupations" (Rosell, Miller, & Barber, 1995, p. 339).

Law Enforcement

It is impossible to estimate the exact percentage of women who experience sexual harassment in policing. This is because of both the sensitivity of the issue and the differences in research methods used. Most importantly, the figures often differ based on whether female officers are asked about experiences with specific behaviors or whether they are asked if they have been "sexually harassed." When women are provided a list of sexually harassing behaviors, a rather high percentage indicate that they have experienced them on at least one occasion. Yet fewer women typically indicate that they have been "sexually harassed," and even fewer report the behavior to someone within their law enforcement agency. In fact, even when women officers are sexually harassed and experience psychological distress as a result, they tend to attribute the negative impact not to the sexual harassment but to other frustrations within the organization that are unrelated to gender (Brown, Campbell, & Fife-Schaw, 1995).

For example, Captain Robinson (1993) surveyed 1,269 female police officers throughout the state of Florida and found that 61 percent had experienced at least one of the specific behaviors listed on the questionnaire during the last six months. The most common behaviors were inappropriate gender comments (30 percent) and inappropriate sexual comments (28 percent). In fact, 43 percent of the women officers indicated that sexually oriented materials or sexually oriented jokes were a *daily occurrence*. Other behaviors experienced during the last six months included inappropriate touching (6 percent), letters/phone calls (3 percent), pressure for dates (4 percent), and pressure for sexual favors (3 percent).

Alarmingly, as many as 106 women officers (about 8 percent of the sample) stated that they had been offered a position, promotion, or other special consideration by a man in return for sexual favors. Yet many of the women officers who indicated that they experienced these behaviors did not suggest that they had been "sexually harassed" on the survey questionnaire. Rather, many stated that it is their plight to endure such behaviors to maintain a career in law enforcement. Only a small percentage of the women officers indicated that they had complained about the behavior to someone either inside (23 percent) or outside (15 percent) the agency (Robinson, 1993).

Other studies have reported similar conclusions, with estimates of women in policing experiencing sexually harassing behaviors ranging from 24 percent to 100 percent, but few of these women file a formal complaint. In those surveys, verbal harassment is the most common form of discrimination described. To illustrate, one survey of 541 women officers in nine states revealed that 24 percent experienced a "constant atmosphere of crude or subtle and snide jokes and comments toward police women" (Timmins & Hainsworth, 1989, p. 202). In another, 37 percent of the women officers experienced "unwanted and uninvited sexual attention from supervisors or coworkers" (Morris, 1996, p. 231). Other forms of harassment are also commonly described[2]:

- Touching and grabbing
- Insufficient instruction
- Coworker hostility
- Cursing
- Verbal and sexual teasing
- Practical jokes
- Silent treatment
- Excessive scrutiny and punitive supervision

- Lack of backup in emergencies
- Paternalistic overprotection
- Sexual propositions
- Pornographic material
- Unwanted sexual advances
- Sexual assault

When asked why they do not report these incidents, female officers commonly refer to the fear that "nothing would be done about it" or they would be "labeled by coworkers" (Nichols, 1995, p. 11).

In sum, the estimates for the prevalence of sexual harassment in policing differ based on those who are surveyed and what they are asked. Results range from a low of 24 percent of female police officers in one study saying that they experience a "constant atmosphere" of offensive remarks to 100 percent in another study describing at least one incident of sexually harrassing behavior. However, most of the research converges on a range of approximately 60–75 percent of American women in policing who are subjected to some form of sexually harassing behavior by their male coworkers, with sexual and/or sexist remarks being the most common by far. Particularly troubling is the small but significant number of female police officers who are sexually assaulted or denied backup in emergencies, as these situations can potentially be life-threatening.

Firefighting

As with law enforcement, women in firefighting are more likely than their female counterparts in the more general workplace to experience sexual harassment and other forms of gender discrimination. In a 1991 nationwide survey, over half of the women firefighters (58 percent) indicated that they had experienced sexual harassment, yet most of these women did not report the situation to a supervisor. As seen with women in other professions, many female firefighters in this survey indicated that they did not report because their supervisor already knew about the situation or was even involved in it personally. Not surprisingly, the women who had been sexually harassed experienced more stress than their female colleagues who had not (Rosell, Miller, & Barber, 1995).

There is also some evidence that sexual harassment is even more common among women of color within firefighting. For example, in a series of studies, researchers conducted interviews with 22 African-American women firefighters (Yoder & Aniakudo, 1995, 1996). They concluded that:

- 91 percent experienced unwanted sexual teasing, jokes, or remarks.
- 46 percent reported unwanted pressure for dates.
- 59 percent were exposed to unwanted letters, calls, or sexual materials.
- 68 percent experienced unwanted sexual looks or gestures.

- 64 percent reported unwanted deliberate touching.
- 23 percent were pressured for sexual favors.

Specifically, the women described situations "that were reminiscent of fraternity pranks: eggs and syrup in boots, short-sheeting beds, pails of water balanced precariously on doors and lockers, scattered gear, bursting into bathrooms, and flashing" (Yoder & Aniakudo, 1996, p. 257). The consequences of such behaviors can obviously be serious in a firefighting situation if critically important gear cannot be located or if practical jokes lead to injuries. Other behaviors described by the women included having "a man crawl into her bed while she was sleeping" and being "picked up and dangled by her feet; when she protested he simply dropped her on her head" (Yoder & Aniakudo, 1996, p. 258). Despite the seriousness of many of the situations described, only 77 percent of the women indicated that they had been "sexually harassed" as a firefighter (Yoder & Aniakudo, 1996, p. 257).

Unfortunately, the problems did not end with sexual harassment. These African-American women also described other experiences with gender discrimination and a generally inhospitable climate within the fire department. Pranks were seen as constant indicators that women in general—and these African-American women in particular—were not welcome in the field of firefighting (Yoder & Aniakudo, 1996). Other common experiences included being ignored or excluded, not having their accomplishments recognized, others focusing on their mistakes, holding them to a different standard for discipline and performance, being viewed as affirmative action hires, and having their physical needs neglected (e.g., ill-fitting gear or insufficient facilities for sleeping and restrooms).

Sadly, the women in this study said that they often could not tell whether the negative incidents they experienced were the result of their race or their gender, but the two seemed to be intertwined when it came to harassment and discrimination (Yoder & Aniakudo, 1996). Not surprisingly, the more negative behaviors that were experienced by the women, the less accepted they felt within their work environment and the less they valued their own contribution to the organization (Yoder & Aniakudo, 1996).

Clearly, there are differences between the fields of law enforcement and firefighting, but both share an increased prevalence of sexual harassment in comparison with other professions. Worse, the forms that sexual harassment can take in the unique work settings of law enforcement and firefighting can often be particularly dangerous, even life-threatening, for victims.

IMPACT ON VICTIMS

Despite their specific professions, it is important for everyone dealing with the issue of sexual harassment to understand the wide range of negative consequences that it has for victims. This type of harassment can affect both the victim's personal and professional life.

Personal Impact

On the personal side, sexual harassment can have a wide variety of well-documented negative effects on the victim's physical, psychological, and emotional well-being (for a review of this research, see Dansky & Kilpatrick, 1997; Sbraga & O'Donohue, 2000). These negative effects can include psychological problems: anxiety and nervousness, depression, irritability and tension, anger, decreased self-esteem, helplessness and vulnerability, difficulty trusting others, emotional numbing, shame, and uncontrolled crying.

Some victims of sexual harassment even experience symptoms of posttraumatic stress disorder, which can include emotional numbing, problems with eating and sleeping, nightmares, and flashbacks. In addition to these psychological symptoms, victims can also experience physical effects: headaches, fatigue, gastrointestinal problems, neck and back pain, nausea, and weight loss or gain.

Professional Impact

On the professional side, women who are targeted with sexual harassment (and who endure retaliation for reporting it) often feel that their career in the police or fire department is over. They may be passed over for promotion and desirable transfers, they may be denied training opportunities, and they are typically excluded from the informal social networks that colleagues use to gain information and mentoring to succeed in the organization. Many women who experience sexual harassment end up leaving policing or firefighting, and this is a loss for the agency, the community, and the field as a whole. Other professional consequences can include the following:

- Decreased job performance
- Decreased job satisfaction
- Decreased productivity
- Career disruptions and interruptions
- Problems in coworker relationships
- Decreased job commitment
- Decreased morale and motivation
- Increased time away from work
- Increased likelihood of quitting
- Decreased earning potential

The research also confirms that women who are sexually harassed typically hold management within their organization responsible for not preventing the problem (Stedham & Mitchell, 1998). Yet all of these professional problems have a negative effect not only on the victim but also on the employer, which must absorb the costs of decreased productivity, increased absenteeism and turnover, and medical and psychological health claims. The employer must also pay the costs of investigating, mediating, and possibly litigating the claim. The employer can even suffer more intangible losses, such as decreased recruitment of women, if it is known that sexual harassment is a problem in that organization.

Aggravating Factors

Not surprisingly, there are a number of factors that can aggravate or worsen the impact of sexual harassment on victims.

Frequency

Most obvious is the frequency: The more harassment a person experiences, the worse the effects are on her physical and psychological health. For example, we are aware of one situation where a civilian who was assigned to precinct desk duties was subjected to unwanted sexualized behavior from both a sergeant and lieutenant. On many occasions, the lieutenant would sit in her chair and when she returned to her desk, he would tell her that she could sit in his lap. The civilian was understandably embarrassed, so the lieutenant would get up and give the chair back to her. Then, however, the sergeant would walk by and see her in an upset state, so he would rub her shoulders to "ease her tension." This civilian was a very quiet woman who did not form friendships in the workplace. Yet one night, she went home and committed suicide by taking an overdose of sleeping pills. She left a note that she just could not take the harassment any more.

As this example illustrates, the consequences of frequent sexual harassment can be severe. However, despite what people often think, the behavior is *not* more damaging when the person labels it "sexual harassment." Rather, the negative impact that victims experience in terms of their psychological, physical, and professional well-being are the same, regardless of whether or not they label the behavior "sexual harassment" (Magley, Hulin, Fitzgerald, & DeNardo, 1999).

Thus, organizations should seek to prevent sexual harassment and correct ongoing problems to avoid the negative impact—both on the victims and on the agency. Organizations also need to train employees to appropriately identify sexual harassment so that they will avoid engaging in any prohibited behavior and will file a formal complaint if they experience it or observe it occurring.

Severity

Another factor that can worsen the impact of sexual harassment is the severity of the behaviors involved. Specifically, behaviors are often described as more severe if they are more frequent, last longer, and are more intense. Examples include the following (Fitzgerald, Swan, & Magley, 1997):

- Multiple harassers
- Exclusive focus on a single victim
- Physical rather than just verbal behaviors

- Harasser of high status in the organization
- Fewer possibilities to avoid or escape the harassment
- Multiple types of harassing behaviors

Of course, the severity of sexual harassment is ultimately in the eye of the beholder to some extent, because the same situation will be experienced differently by different people, depending on their background and personality characteristics.

Mitigating Factors

It is not surprising that the impact of sexual harassment on victims is determined in large part by the way in which the organization responds—whether the situation is taken seriously, whether the victim experiences retaliation for reporting, and whether the organization takes corrective action in response to the situation (Bergman, Langhout, Palmieri, Cortina, & Fitzgerald, 2002). Obviously, victims do better if the organization views the issue of sexual harassment as a serious problem and responds appropriately when an incident is reported. This book is designed to help managers in police and fire departments do just that.

REALISTIC DYNAMICS OF SEXUAL HARASSMENT

Gender

It is absolutely clear that women are more likely than men to become victims of sexual harassment, both in law enforcement and in other professions. To illustrate, research consistently documents that about half of all working women will experience some form of sexually harassing behavior during their lives (for a review, see Sbraga & O'Donohue, 2000). For men, the estimates are more in the range of 8–15 percent (Martindale, 1992; Reese & Lindenberg, 1999; U.S. Merit Systems Protection Board, 1981). Certainly, the vast majority of sexual harassment complaints are filed by women. For example, 2002 statistics from the Equal Employment Opportunity Commission (EEOC) reveal that 85 percent of the charges were filed by women and only 15 percent by men.[3] (However, the percentage of charges filed by men has steadily risen from 9 percent in 1992.) Some have even estimated that approximately 90 percent of all sexual harassment situations involve a male perpetrator and a female victim (Berdahl, Magley, & Waldo, 1996; Waldo, Berdahl, & Fitzgerald, 1998).

In addition, the negative impact of sexual harassment is far more serious for women than it is for men. While the research documents that sexual harassment can have similar negative effects on male and female victims, harassment in policing clearly does not lead to the same type of demands and distress among men as it does among women (Parker & Griffiin, 2002). On the one hand, women are more likely than men to be upset by any kind of sexual attention at work (Berdahl, Magley, & Waldo, 1996; Cochran, Frazier, & Olson, 1997; Stockdale, Visio, & Batra, 1999; Waldo, Berdahl, & Fitzgerald, 1998). In contrast, men are much more likely than women to indicate that they would be flattered by sexual attention they receive at work (Gutek, 1985; Reese &

Lindenberg, 1999). This gender difference may be at least partly attributable to the fact that women live with the threat of rape and men do not.

As a result, we will generally strive throughout this book to use gender-neutral language when describing the complainant and respondent (the person accused of committing sexual harassment in the complaint). However, it must be clear at the outset that the vast majority of sexual harassment is committed *by men against women*.

Incident Reporting

Most Victims Do Not Report.   Research reveals that only 5–25 percent of women in a range of professions file a formal complaint within their organization after experiencing sexual harassment (Cochran, Frazier, & Olson, 1997; Dansky & Kilpatrick, 1997; Sbraga & O'Donohue, 2000). In fact, confronting the harasser and reporting the behavior are the *least common* responses by sexual harassment victims. Even women who are sexually assaulted in the workplace typically do not report it or quit their jobs. One study of women who experienced an attempted or completed workplace rape found that only 21 percent filed a formal report and 19 percent quit (Schneider, 1993).

Why Don't Victims Report?   There is a myth in our culture that is commonly held that women *should* report sexual harassment, and if a woman *doesn't* report the incident, perhaps she is not telling the truth about it (Fitzgerald & Swan, 1995). For example, the research clearly documents that victims are viewed more negatively and their claim is evaluated with greater skepticism when they fail to report it immediately.

Yet the evidence is equally clear that very few women report any sexual harassment they experience, and this is with good reason. First, many victims of sexual harassment choose not to report the situation because they do not define the situation as sexual harassment or do not consider the situation serious enough to report. Second, filing a complaint of sexual harassment requires that employees first perceive themselves as having been sexually harassed (or at least as having experienced behaviors that are inappropriate for the workplace and/or against organizational policy). Unfortunately, the research demonstrates that people who experience behaviors they would describe as sexual harassment *in a hypothetical situation* typically do not identify it as such when they actually experience the behavior *in real life*. Researchers Reese and Lindenberg describe it this way:

> When asked to define sexual harassment, a respondent will likely agree that [unwelcome] touching is sexual harassment. On any given day, the same individual may be repeatedly touched by a colleague or supervisor in a manner that is unwelcome. The individual may or may not perceive that she or he is being sexually harassed. In short, much research has indicated that individuals experienced behaviors that meet legal parameters for sexual harassment and/or are defined by the individuals as sexual harassment but are not perceived as "sexual harassment." (1999, p. 41)

This reluctance to label an experience as "sexual harassment" goes a long way toward explaining why so few people file a formal complaint. However, it may also result from a breakdown at any one of a number of points in the complaint process. For example, an employee who experiences sexually harassing behavior

- May not be aware of the policy or procedure for reporting sexual harassment.
- May not understand the policy or procedure for reporting sexual harassment.
- May prefer to handle the situation informally, thereby, avoiding a formal complaint.
- May fear negative reactions or repercussions for reporting an incident.
- May know of others who had negative experiences after reporting an incident.
- May share a general perception that the policy or procedure is unfair.
- May not recognize the incident as sexual harassment.
- May not perceive any incidents as serious enough or frequent enough to file a formal complaint.

Any of these factors could explain why victims of sexual harassment do not either formally or informally report the behavior they are experiencing.

Victims' Fears of Retaliation Are Well Founded.   Additionally, many women who are sexually harassed decide not to file a formal complaint because they fear that it will do little or nothing to improve the situation and may even make things worse. Unfortunately, this fear is well founded. Research clearly documents that after confronting their harasser and/or reporting the situation, most victims continue to experience sexual harassment, as many as one-third of the victims see the harassment intensify, one-quarter of the victims experience retaliation as a result of reporting, and mental health and professional well-being often deteriorate.[4]

In firefighting, for example, there is evidence that many complaints of sexual harassment are not taken seriously and result in retaliation against the complainant. In one study of fire departments, only 35 percent indicated that they had received a formal complaint of sexual harassment, and 34 percent of those complaints resulted in discipline against the respondant. On the other hand, 10 percent of the complainants were disciplined for filing the complaint, 10 percent were told to ignore it, and 12 percent did not receive any response whatsoever (Rosell, Miller, & Barber, 1995).

Victims Use Indirect Strategies for Responding.   As a result of all these factors, it should not be surprising that so few women file a formal complaint in response to the sexual harassment they experience. Rather, victims of sexual harassment typically use more indirect strategies to improve the situation, such as[5]:

- Ignoring the behavior
- Changing the subject
- Joking about the behavior
- Hinting that the behavior is unwelcome
- Mentioning a boyfriend or husband

- Trying to appease the harasser
- Avoiding the harasser or even the workplace
- Leaving doors open during meetings with the harasser
- Including other workers in meetings with the harasser
- Sitting far away from the harasser
- Convincing themselves that nothing will change by reporting the behavior
- Trivializing the behavior
- Minimizing the situation
- Detaching themselves from the situation
- Thinking of the behavior as something other than harassment
- Blaming themselves for the situation
- Reminding themselves of the possibility of retaliation
- Quitting their job

While not all of these responses are particularly helpful or psychologically healthy for victims, they are nonetheless used to improve the situation. They are also used to avoid the kind of confrontation that is especially likely to provoke retaliation from the harasser and other coworkers. Therefore, anyone who works with sexual harassment victims must realize that even when they have not filed a formal complaint, they have typically taken a number of actions designed to stop the harassment and protect their own career, reputation, and well-being. These strategies may vary by social group (as defined by race, ethnicity, national origin, religion, etc.), and not all the strategies would be considered reasonable or appropriate by every social group. To illustrate, victims from certain cultural or religious groups may be particularly unlikely to directly protest or confront the harassment they experience. For example, in some Asian cultures, it is not acceptable for a woman to confront a male coworker directly, so she may be more likely to tell a trusted friend. Yet these alternative strategies for responding can be documented by a comprehensive investigation to demonstrate that the behaviors were nonetheless unwelcome.

Occupation
Female Police Officers

As with women in other professions, female police officers respond in a variety of ways to the sexually harassing behaviors that they experience. As Martin and Jurik (1996) describe it, some suffer in silence while others laugh at the jokes in an effort to "fit in." Many women try to "give it back" by responding with humor or witty comebacks. Also like women in other professions, female officers frequently respond informally by confronting the harasser, threatening to call the harasser's spouse or partner, discussing the situation with friends, seeking transfers, or resigning. More formal methods are quite rare, although some victims do, of course, file complaints and lawsuits; these typically result in swift and severe retaliation (Martin & Jurik, 1996).

Female Firefighters

In firefighting, the limited evidence suggests that victims of sexual harassment may be more likely than those in other professions to take active measures to change the situation; however, most still do not file a formal complaint, as discussed previously. For example, the African-American women in the interview study previously described used a variety of strategies, including confronting the harasser, filing an external complaint, seeking a transfer, and even physically retaliating. Some of these women even described pushing, hitting, and physically restraining the harasser. In one situation, for example, the woman described grabbing the harasser's penis after he failed to heed her warnings not to touch her breast (Yoder & Aniakudo, 1995). Another woman stated that she "had to put the guy up against the wall with my forearm under his neck" (Yoder & Aniakudo, 1995, p. 131). Although these responses may not be typical of those of other women in firefighting who are sexually harassed, these responses were seen as successful in the eyes of the women in this particular interview study.

Work Culture

As discussed above, anyone trying to address the problem of sexual harassment must understand that most victims do not file a grievance or otherwise formally complain. A great deal of research documents this fact in a wide range of occupations and organizations, including law enforcement and firefighting. However, it is reasonable to assume that a number of characteristics of the culture in police and fire departments make reporting of sexual harassment especially unlikely. Women in law enforcement and firefighting may be especially reluctant to see themselves—or to be seen by others—as "victims;" they typically see themselves as problem-solvers who can manage the situation informally, without filing a formal complaint; they are often unaware of either their right to a workplace environment free of sexual harassment or the policies for reporting and investigating such problems; and they often view sexual harassment as "part of the job" and not a reason to complain.

Of course, the brotherhood that exists in police culture means that many police officers view themselves as a "family" in a world of "us against them." Because of the potential for physical danger and even life-and-death situations, police officers often see their brotherhood as their only defense in a hostile world and believe that they must be able to count on each other.

As a result, those within law enforcement often adhere strongly to the code of silence: Officers do not report the misconduct of their peers and do not contribute any information to those investigating such misconduct. All these factors combine to create a situation in which victims of sexual harassment within law enforcement are extremely unlikely to report their experiences, and coworkers are equally unlikely to take the complaint seriously, report it to their supervisors, or cooperate with any investigation or effort to resolve the situation. Similar factors operate in firefighting and other fields that are nontraditional for women.

Instead, victims within law enforcement or firefighting may simply request a shift change or a new supervisor without explaining that the request is a result of sexual harassment. Victimized employees may call in sick to avoid their harasser or may eventually quit their job when the harassment becomes unbearable. Yet all employees have the right to work in a harassment-free environment, and they are not obligated to modify their own work conditions simply because they are being sexually harassed.

Agency Reporting Policy

Fortunately, one of the most important factors for victims who decide to report the sexual harassment that they experience is their belief that reporting will be an effective strategy (Cochran, Frazier, & Olson, 1997). Victims are therefore more likely to report sexual harassment when the following is true:

- Their employer has a clear policy and procedure for responding.
- This policy has been communicated to all employees.
- Managers convey the message that sexual harassment will be taken seriously.
- Previous reports of sexual harassment have been handled fairly.
- Other victims who reported harassment did not experience retaliation.
- Harassers in other situations were held accountable for their misconduct.
- There is a general climate of respect for employees and for women in general.
- There are staff with training and resources dedicated to the investigation.
- At least one of the contact people for reporting sexual harassment is a woman.
- The organization values the emotional well-being of employees.

These are the factors that are discussed throughout the book, with extensive recommendations for agencies to design effective policies, training programs, and complaint and investigative procedures. Our understanding of the problem is therefore clear. Now let's move on to the solutions.

ENDNOTES

1. For a review of this research, see Fitzgerald, Drasgow, & Magley, 1999; Hesson-McInnis & Fitzgerald, 1997; Sbraga & O'Donohue, 2000.
2. For a review of this research, see Bartol et al., 1992; Haar, 1997; Martin, 1994; Nichols, 1995.
3. These statistics are published by the Equal Employment Opportunity Commission (EEOC), and they are available at www.eeoc.gov/stats/harass.html.
4. For a review of this research, see Dansky & Kilpatrick, 1997; Hesson-McInnis & Fitzgerald, 1997; Sbraga & O'Donohue, 2000.
5. For a review of this research, see Cochran, Frazier, & Olson, 1997; Dansky & Kilpatrick, 1997; Fitzgerald, Gold, & Brock, 1990; Reese & Lindenberg, 1999; Reilly, Lott, & Gallogly, 1986; Sbraga & O'Donohue, 2000; Tangri, Burt, & Johnson, 1982; U.S. Merit Systems Protection Board, 1987.

Chapter 3

The Law and Sexual Harassment

Investigators must be familiar with the laws pertaining to sexual harassment and other forms of discrimination and have a sense of how they have evolved over time as a result of legislation and court decisions.

FEDERAL AND STATE LAWS

Federal Prohibitions Against Sex Discrimination

Sex discrimination is a violation of Title VII of the 1964 Civil Rights Act. The law was principally written to stop racial discrimination, but it also states that it is unlawful to discriminate on the basis of gender. The 1964 Civil Rights Act defines several federally protected classes and prohibits discrimination on their basis. Subsequent legislation then expanded the list of protected classes with the 1967 Americans with Disabilities Act (ADA) and the Family and Medical Leave Act (FMLA), so the following list currently represents federally protected classes, and any discrimination on the basis of the following categories is illegal according to federal law: race, sex (including pregnancy), religion, color, age, national origin, and disability. Federal prohibitions against discrimination generally apply to employers with 15 or more employees. They protect both employees and applicants for employment.

Sexual Harassment Is Form of Sex Discrimination. Unlike other forms of discrimination prohibited by the 1964 Civil Rights Act, however, sexual harassment was not explicitly defined by federal legislative mandate. Rather, sexual harassment was defined by the courts as a form of sex discrimination as cases moved their way through the adjudication process. Of course, the process of defining a concept through case law is slow and cumulative and often results in inconsistencies, ambiguities, and even outright reversals. As a result, it is not surprising that confusion and debate continue to surround the exact legal definition of the term "sexual harassment."

After a few initial court cases, the Equal Employment Opportunity Commission (EEOC) issued federal guidelines regarding the definition of the term "sexual harassment." The Supreme Court, however, did not explicitly recognize sexual harassment as a form of sex discrimination until 1986 in the case of *Meritor Savings Bank* v. *Vinson*. (This case is discussed in detail later in the chapter.) Since that time, court rulings and subsequent EEOC guidance have clarified many of the issues of confusion. At this point, it is relatively straightforward to outline the types of sexual harassment that are federally prohibited, the legal responsibilities of employers, and the standards for appropriately investigating and resolving complaints; however, investigators must keep in mind that sexual harassment and discrimination law are constantly evolving. Legal advisors should therefore be consulted on a regular basis. It is also important to note that federal circuit courts have the power to make rulings for their district that may be different from those of other federal districts.

State and Local Prohibitions Against Sex Discrimination

In addition to the federal prohibitions outlined above, some state and local laws protect individuals from discrimination on the basis of other categories: marital status, sexual orientation, medical conditions, and physical appearance.

Investigators should thus check with legal advisors to determine if their county or city has passed laws that add additional protections. State and local prohibitions may also apply to all employers, not just those with 15 or more employees. Yet regardless of what protections are offered by federal, state, and local laws, we advise that organizations design a comprehensive policy that prohibits workplace harassment more generally because of the serious negative consequences for employees.

Federal Protection Against Retaliation

Federal law also provides protection against retaliation under Title VII, Section 704(a). The law states:

> It shall be unlawful employment practice for an employer to discriminate against any of his employees ... because he has opposed any practice made an unlawful employment practice by this subchapter, or because he has made a charge, testified, assisted or participated in any manner in an investigation, proceeding, or hearing under this subchapter.

Such retaliation is a separate violation, as described in detail in a later chapter.

GENERAL DEFINITION OF SEXUAL HARASSMENT

Although sex discrimination was first prohibited in 1964 with the federal Civil Rights Act, claims of sexual harassment were not awarded until 1976. In those early decisions, the courts reasoned that sexual advances constituted illegal sex discrimination because they were made on the basis of the victim's gender. The legal definition of sexual harassment evolved in those early cases to include unwelcome sexual advances, requests for sexual favors, and other verbal, physical, or visual conduct of a sexual nature. These behaviors constitute sexual harassment when any of the three following factors are present:

1. Submission to such conduct is made either explicitly or implicitly a term or condition of an individual's employment.

2. Submission to or rejection of such conduct by an individual is used as the basis for employment decisions affecting the individual.

3. Such conduct has the purpose or effect of unreasonably interfering with an individual's work performance or creating an intimidating, hostile, or offensive working environment.

As previously mentioned, the Supreme Court then clarified the definition of sexual harassment in the case of *Meritor Savings Bank* v. *Vinson* (1986). In that decision, the Supreme Court distinguished two forms of sexual harassment: *quid pro quo* and a hostile work environment. Each of these is discussed in turn.

Quid Pro Quo Sexual Harassment

"*Quid pro quo*" literally translates to "this for that," and it is used to describe situations in which an employee is forced to submit to unwanted sexual advances as a condition of employment. This type of harassment is typically the easiest to identify and define. In such a situation, the employee is subjected to unwanted sexual advances, with a corresponding promise or threat of tangible job actions. To constitute *quid pro quo* sexual harassment, the promise or threat must be realized by having the employee either gain some tangible job benefit for cooperating with the unwanted sexual advance or suffer some tangible job loss for not cooperating.

To illustrate, the employee may be required, either explicitly or implicitly, to perform some type of sexual activity in order to get or keep a job or benefit. This benefit could be a job, raise, promotion, or other tangible benefit. The person may be forced to submit to the sexual demand, even if it is "just understood" and not explicitly stated. On the other hand, the harasser may threaten to fire, demote, or otherwise retaliate against the employee for not complying with the sexual demand.

Examples of Quid Pro Quo *Harassment*

Some common examples of this type of harassment might include the following:

- A supervisor who states or implies that successful completion of a probationary period will depend on sexual activity by the probationer with the supervisor

- A supervisor who states or implies that a good performance evaluation report is dependent on sexual activity with the supervisor

- A supervisor who states or implies that a promotion, a raise, or some other job benefit is dependent on sexual activity with the supervisor

- A supervisor who states or implies that the employee's failure to engage in sexual activity with the supervisor will result in taking away a benefit (e.g., a demotion, a transfer to a less desirable assignment, the loss of overtime pay, or other similar situations in which the employee loses a benefit)

Elements to Establish

To determine that complainants have experienced *quid pro quo* sexual harassment, it is therefore necessary to establish three elements:

1. They were subjected to unwelcome sexual advances by a supervisor, manager, or other agent of their employer. These advances could be either explicit or implicit (i.e., just "understood"), and they could be made either on- or off-duty.

2. The conduct was based on their gender. The complainant could be male or female, and the supervisor could be of the same or opposite sex. Complainants must simply establish that the behavior was based on their gender in some way.

3. They suffered a tangible job action.

Based on the law, *quid pro quo* sexual harassment can only be committed by a supervisor, manager, or other agent of the employer (see item 1 above). Yet the EEOC has clearly noted that the definition of a supervisor may include employees who are not formally considered to be supervisors within the organization. According to the EEOC, a supervisor is someone who has the authority to undertake or recommend tangible job actions and/or direct the employer's daily work activities.

This means that persons may be designated as supervisor if they direct the daily work activities of another employee, even if they are not formally held accountable for the actions of that employee. In other words, a shift leader may give daily assignments and clear requests for time off before forwarding them to a manager. While this shift leader does not have formal supervisory authority (and cannot, for example, officially approve the requests for time off), the person is still likely to be considered a supervisor for the purposes of sexual harassment litigation.

Another factor is tangible job action (see item 3 above). Tangible job actions can be positive: Complainants are hired, promoted, or given a desirable reassignment for cooperating with the sexual demands. However, tangible job actions are more typically negative: Complainants are fired, demoted, or given an undesirable reassignment. According to the EEOC, tangible job actions include hiring/firing, promotion/failure to promote, demotion, reassignment with significantly different responsibilities, significant change in compensation or benefits, and significant change in work assignment.

In cases of *quid pro quo* sexual harassment, the complainant does not need to prove that the agency knew of the supervisor's actions if the situation resulted in a tangible job action. Rather, organizations are automatically liable for the actions of their supervisors and managers when a tangible job action is taken because they are acting as an agent of the employer. This is referred to as "strict liability" for the tangible job actions of supervisors or managers. Therefore, if the complainant has established the elements described above, the claim of sex discrimination would be substantiated.

If the promise of positive job action or threat of negative job action is not fulfilled, however, the case is one of hostile work environment and not *quid pro quo* sexual harassment. In other words, to constitute *quid pro quo* sexual harassment, the courts have determined that a tangible job action must have resulted from the complainant's response (i.e., cooperation or refusal) to the unwanted sexual advances.

Hostile Work Environment

In the *Meritor* decision, the Supreme Court recognized that some situations constitute sexual harassment even though no sexual activity is actually required of the employee. In these situations, the environment in which the employee is required to work is so oppressive that it becomes hostile or intimidating to the employee. As the Supreme Court noted in *Meritor,* no one should have to "run a gauntlet of sexual abuse in return for the privilege of being allowed to work and make a living." The courts have thus recognized that being forced to work in a hostile or intimidating work environment can be sufficiently damaging to constitute illegal discrimination. As the Supreme Court noted in *Robinson* v. *Jacksonville Shipyards* (1991):

> Sexual harassment has a cumulative, eroding effect on the victim's well-being.... When women feel a need to maintain vigilance against the next incident of harassment, the stress is increased tremendously.... When women feel that their individual complaints will not change the work environment materially, the ensuing sense of despair further compounds the stress.

To constitute a hostile work environment, the conduct does not need to include any promise of a tangible job benefit for cooperation or threat of adverse job action for noncompliance. Alternatively, the situation might include threats or promises of job action as long as they are not actually fulfilled. (If the threats or promises are realized, the situation is one of *quid pro quo* sexual harassment.) The term "hostile work environment" is therefore used to describe unwelcome sexual or gender-based conduct that creates a hostile, offensive, and intimidating workplace when it is severe or pervasive enough to interfere with an employee's ability to work.

Examples of Hostile Work Environments

Typical behaviors involved in a hostile work environment might include the following elements (Conte, 1997).

Visual Materials. Displaying posters or other visual depictions that are sexually related or demeaning is one element. This could include pictures of nude or scantily clad bodies, depictions of sexual acts, or written sayings that are posted in the work-place. It could also include sexually explicit or sexist cartoons, calendars, literature, films, magazines, or photographs.

Verbal Behavior.   Regularly using sexually explicit or otherwise offensive language and sexually explicit or otherwise offensive jokes is another example. This could also include language or jokes based on gender, such as comments that are demeaning to women or men. Remarks to or about a coworker's body parts could also be included. It could even encompass language or jokes that are racially motivated if they are directed primarily at women of color while white women and minority men are not targeted.

Nicknames.   Regularly using terms such as "dear," "honey," "sweetie," "baby," or "stud" or other nicknames based on gender or sexual connotations could also contribute to a hostile work environment.

Physical Contact.   Exposing employees to physical contact (e.g., touching, rubbing, fondling, giving a "shoulder massage," blocking someone's passage, or any similar act) is another type of behavior that could be cited. This could also include lingering touches, such as holding the hand after a handshake. Similarly, employees who request a coworker to touch them or reach in their pocket could contribute to a hostile working environment. At its most extreme form, physical contact could include threatened or actual assault.

Compliments.   Regularly giving seemingly innocuous compliments such as "You smell good" or "That dress fits you so well" could qualify. Such "compliments" are particularly likely to be seen as inappropriate if they are frequent, sexualized, gender-based, and/or accompanied by leers or other inappropriate eye contact.

Sexual Behavior.   Repeatedly requesting dates and engaging in sexual conduct or sexual conversation would also be examples. This category could include asking questions about the employee's sex life or engaging in other conversations about sex. It could also involve spreading rumors about the employee's sex life or other information that is personal and/or demeaning. In police and fire departments, sexual behavior sometimes includes having a nude dancer or other sexually oriented activity at a work party or other work-related social function.

Stereotypes.   Making comments that perpetuate myths or stereotypes can also contribute to a hostile work environment. This could include making jokes about "dumb blondes" or using sentences that begin with the phrase "Women can't …." In law enforcement and firefighting, these remarks are often about a woman being unable to perform the job as well as a man.

Hazing.   Singling out a coworker for ridicule or pranks can also contribute to a hostile environment. Such hazing is particularly common in fire departments because personnel must live and work together. It could also include constantly picking on an employee or repeatedly putting that employee down in front of others.

Shunning.   Ostracizing or excluding an employee from activities in the workplace is another example. This could consist of not including female employees in conversations that pertain to work or not inviting women employees to social activities such as golf tournaments where the men will be able to interact with the command staff.

Job Actions.   Monitoring the employee's work performance more closely than that of others or otherwise threatening the employee's job security or situation also would qualify. This could include giving the employee different kinds of work assignments, holding the employee to a different standard of performance, or providing less desirable physical facilities for working.

Even from these brief descriptions, it is clear that many of the behaviors that constitute a hostile work environment are not an attempt to gain sexual favors or get a date; rather, most are behaviors designed to create a sexualized workplace and to communicate that the workplace is not one where women are welcome.

Determination of "Hostile"

In determining a hostile work environment, the central inquiry is whether the conduct unreasonably interferes with an individual's work performance or creates an intimidating, hostile, or offensive working environment. That determination will likely take into account whether the behavior is severe and/or pervasive. For example, these six factors are to be considered:

1.   Whether the conduct was verbal or physical or both
2.   How frequently the conduct was repeated
3.   Whether the conduct was hostile and patently offensive
4.   Whether the harasser was a coworker or a supervisor
5.   Whether others joined in perpetrating the harassment
6.   Whether the harassment was directed at more than one individual

To make the determination that a work environment is sufficiently hostile, it is therefore necessary to look at the totality of the circumstances, including the pattern and context of the behavior. For example, in the case of *Faragher* v. *City of Boca Raton,* the Supreme Court noted that a single incident of offensive behavior is unlikely to be considered sufficient to constitute a hostile working environment, unless the incident is particularly severe or threatening. Establishing that a work environment is hostile typically requires showing that there is a *pattern* of offensive conduct. Consider the following:

> A rookie police officer was continually subjected to "pranks" by her coworkers. There were pornographic pictures of women hanging in the roll-call room; she was made the subject of sexual comments at roll call. The officers continually pressured her to go out with them even after she made it clear that she was not interested, and when she objected to any of the conduct, she was told that she did not belong in police work and that she should leave.

While any one of these behaviors may not be sufficient to constitute a hostile work environment, the determination is likely to take into account the frequency of the conduct, its sexual and demeaning nature, the involvement of many coworkers, the tacit approval of supervisors, and the fact that the behavior persisted after the female officer asked her coworkers to stop.

Typically, a single incident or a few isolated minor incidents will not suffice to create a hostile work environment. However, the EEOC did note in its guidelines that a single unwelcome *physical* advance can seriously poison the victim's working environment. The EEOC would therefore likely find a violation of federal law if a supervisor touches an employee or the situation involves both physical and verbal conduct. In some situations, it may even be necessary to investigate off-duty behavior if it creates or contributes to the hostile environment of the workplace.

Elements to Establish

In sum, a hostile work environment exists when these four elements are present:

1. Employees create and/or supervisors condone a hostile work atmosphere with the type of behaviors described above when the conduct is not directly linked to a tangible job reward or punishment.

2. The conduct is based on gender. The complainant could be male or female, and the supervisor could be of the same or opposite sex. Complainants must simply establish that the behavior was based on their gender in some way.

3. The conduct is unwelcome by the person experiencing it.

4. The conduct unreasonably interferes with the terms, conditions, or privileges of employment.

Employer Liability for Hostile Work Environment: Coworker Behaviors

When the behavior creating a hostile work environment is limited to coworkers (i.e., non-supervisory personnel), an employer will be held liable if it *knew* or *should have known* of the conduct yet failed to take prompt corrective action. For example, if the victim files a formal complaint or complains informally to a supervisor, the organization will be considered "on notice" about the behavior. Of course, any behavior that is personally observed by a supervisor will also be considered to be known by the employer. Even if the behaviors were not personally observed by a supervisor, the employer can be liable if supervisors would have known if they had demonstrated reasonable care to prevent sexual harassment. For example, sexually harassing behaviors are often the subject of workplace rumors or gossip, and these must be considered a source of information that requires investigation to determine their legitimacy; in other words, rumors of sexual harassment cannot be ignored by supervisors and managers because they serve to put the agency "on notice" that misconduct may potentially be occurring in the workplace.

It is therefore important that employers monitor the workplace for signs of a hostile work environment because the longer the environment exists, the greater the opportunity for serious consequences to the employee and the organization. Within law enforcement agencies, potential liability exists not only for the treatment of employees but also for the treatment of inmates, persons in custody or under supervision, and others having reason to interact with criminal justice personnel (e.g., complainants, victims of crime, Explorer Scouts, or other volunteers).

Employer Liability for Hostile Work Environment: Supervisor Behaviors

On the other hand, when supervisors engage in behaviors that are sufficiently severe or pervasive to create a hostile work environment, the employer is typically liable for the misconduct. This liability can be avoided only if the employer can prove the two elements of an affirmative defense outlined by the Supreme Court in the cases of *Faragher* v. *City of Boca Raton* and *Burlington Industries* v. *Ellerth*. This is often referred to as the "*Faragher/Ellerth* affirmative defense."

Faragher/Ellerth *Affirmative Defense*

In cases in which a hostile work environment is created by supervisors or managers, an employer can avoid liability for sexual harassment in federal court only if it can establish that (1) the organization took reasonable care both to prevent sexual harassment and to promptly correct any such behavior that was reported and (2) the victim unreasonably failed to take advantage of the employer's mechanisms for preventing or correcting the situation.

To prove the first element, it is not sufficient for an employer to simply note that it has a policy on the books. Rather, the policy and complaint process must actually work. For example, employers can even avoid liability in cases of severe sexual harassment if they can demonstrate that they do the following:

- Have a comprehensive policy against harassment and discrimination.
- Communicate that policy effectively to employees.
- Respond promptly and appropriately to complaints.
- Investigate complaints thoroughly and fairly.
- Take appropriate corrective actions.
- Engage in actions designed to prevent both breaches of confidentiality and retaliation.

The second element requires that the victim unreasonably failed to take advantage of these mechanisms by filing a formal complaint. This would be proven if the complaint process was shown to be effective and safe for employees to use, yet the victim still told no one about the harassment. For example, the courts have ruled that it is not unreasonable for victims to delay reporting sexual harassment for weeks or even months, especially in situations in which either the individual behaviors are relatively minor or the victims take alternative approaches to correct the situation, such as reporting to a union steward. The courts also do not consider it unreasonable for victims to not report any behaviors that are personally observed by a supervisor or manager who took no action to stop the situation or report it. In such a situation, the employer would be directly liable because of the negligence exhibited by the supervisor or manager who observed the behavior yet failed to respond appropriately.

Elsewhere in this book, we have discussed how many victims of sexual harassment decide not to file a formal complaint because they fear retaliation or other negative consequences. Therefore, victims do not unreasonably fail to report if the complaint process is ineffective or is widely seen as risky. If there are obstacles that keep victims from reporting or if their fears of retaliation are well founded given the history and behavior of the organization, the employer will remain liable even if the victims did not report the situation. In such situations, the victims are not considered to have been unreasonable in failing to participate in the agency's formal complaint process. Thus, employers cannot avoid liability for sexual harassment by implementing a complaint procedure that victims cannot actually use without overcoming barriers or experiencing retaliation.

Also, there are some states in which no such affirmative defense is available for claims of sexual harassment. These include California, Illinois, Michigan, and Missouri. In these states, employers are strictly liable for all harassment that is perpetrated by a supervisor, regardless of any actions taken by the employer.

Constructive Discharge

The Supreme Court recently ruled in a case involving the Pennsylvania State Police that people can also sue their employer for constructive discharge, as a form of tangible job action, if they are forced off the job due to a hostile work environment (*Pennsylvania State Police* v. *Suders*, 2004). In these cases, employees claim that they resign only because their working conditions have became so intolerable they have no alternative but to quit. In other words, if an employee quits because of a tangible job action (e.g., demotion, pay cut, or negative job transfer or reassignment), the liability of the employer is absolute, as previously discussed. However, if there is no such tangible job action and the employee quits because of a hostile work environment, the employer will still typically be liable unless it can prove both elements of the *Faragher/Ellerth* affirmative defense as described above.

Determination of Unwelcome Behavior

The Supreme Court also noted in *Meritor* v. *Vinson* (1986) that the critical factor in evaluating a hostile work environment is whether or not the behavior is considered unwelcome by the person experiencing it. Of course, the most obvious indication that a behavior is unwelcome is if the person experiencing it files a formal complaint, using either the formal mechanism or more informal avenues. Given that most victims of sexual harassment do not file a formal complaint, however, evidence that the behavior is unwelcome will typically include the complainant's efforts to prevent or avoid the situation as well as their observed reactions; for example, a complainant may react with obvious disgust to the behavior, appear to be upset by it, or discuss the situation with coworkers. Any of these responses would suggest that the behavior was unwelcome by the complainant.

Even when employees engage in sexual conduct themselves, this does not necessarily prove that they welcomed the behavior described in their complaint. In some cases, employees may simply feel that they have no choice but to comply or possibly lose their job. In other cases, an employee may have previously had a consensual sexual relationship with another employee, but this does not mean that all subsequent sexual behavior is welcome. In that situation, one employee must inform the other that he or she wants to end the sexual relationship, and this action establishes that any subsequent sexual conduct is unwelcome. In such a situation, employees may confront the person themselves, write a letter, or ask a coworker or supervisor to inform the person that the sexual relationship is ended and that any sexual behavior will now be considered unwelcome.

When determining whether a particular behavior was unwelcome, many courts have decided that the focus should be on the perceptions of the particular person who suffered the harassment. Assuming the person is a woman, the law thus asks: Did this woman find the conduct unwelcome or offensive? The law is designed in this way to make certain that courts do not decide that behavior that is unacceptable to the person experiencing it is somehow considered okay because it was seen as acceptable by others. For example, it does not matter if the behavior is seen as acceptable by the harasser or others in the workplace as long as the person experiencing it found the behavior to be unwelcome and offensive and this perception was reasonable for a person in that situation.

*Reasonable Woman Standard (*Ellison *v.* Brady*, 1991)*

After the landmark decision in *Meritor Savings Bank* v. *Vinson,* the next major development in sexual harassment law and a hostile work environment was the 1991 decision by the Ninth Circuit Court of Appeals in *Ellison* v. *Brady.* In that case, the court held that a hostile work environment must be judged from the perspective of a "reasonable woman" rather than a "reasonable man." As previously stated, behavior constitutes illegal sex discrimination only if it unreasonably interferes with an individual's work performance or creates an intimidating or offensive work environment. However, in considering the severity of sexual conduct, the decision in *Ellison* v. *Brady* states that the courts must take into consideration the different perspectives between men and women.

To illustrate, if the courts were to rely on a standard of the reasonable man, they would run the risk of allowing sexual harassment and discrimination of women to persist simply because the practices are common and men in the workplace do not see a problem with it. In contrast, a reasonable woman standard takes into account the different perspective of women, which is affected in large part by women's fear that behavior may escalate into violence and/or sexual assault. In the *Ellison* decision, the court observed that women are disproportionately the victims of sexual assault, and because of this fact, women typically have a stronger incentive to be concerned about sexual behavior. This type of reasoning is seen in more recent decisions such as *Petrosino* v. *Bell Atlantic* (2004), in which the Second Circuit noted that even when men and women are exposed to the same offensive conduct, the impact will be different.

Thus, employers in the Ninth Circuit or other federal circuit courts in which this standard has been adopted must take into account the perspective of the reasonable woman when determining whether sexual or gender-based conduct is sufficiently objectionable to constitute a hostile working environment. In other federal circuits, the standard that is commonly used is that of a reasonable person in a similar type of situation. Therefore, while the standard in these federal circuits is not explicitly described as being a reasonable woman, the perceptions of women must still be considered whenever the complainant is a female because a reasonable person in a similar situation is in fact a woman. (If the complainant is a male, he is in a quite different situation, at least on this dimension.)

Psychological Injury Not a Requirement (Harris v. Forklift Systems, 1993)

Another evolution in sexual harassment law took place in 1993 when the Supreme Court ruled in the case of *Harris* v. *Forklift Systems* that plaintiffs in a hostile work environment case do not need to prove tangible psychological injury. Specifically, the Supreme Court stated: "So long as the environment would reasonably be perceived, and is perceived, as hostile or abusive, there is no need for it also to be psychologically injurious."

In this case, the lower court had stated that although the plaintiff was subject to numerous behaviors that were inappropriate and unacceptable, they were not severe enough to have a meaningful impact on the plaintiff because she did not seek psychological counseling. The high court disagreed, ruling that just because the victim has the psychological strength to withstand a hostile work environment does not mean that the behavior is acceptable. Because individuals have different thresholds of psychological strength, courts look at the nature of the behavior in determining whether it constituted a hostile work environment, not whether or not the behavior incapacitated the victim.

Same-Sex Sexual Harassment (Oncale v. Sundowner Offshore Services, Inc., 1998)

In 1998, the U.S. Supreme Court extended the federal prohibition on sexual harassment and a hostile work environment to incidents involving members of the same sex in *Oncale* v. *Sundowner Offshore Services, Inc.* In that case, the Court held that the harassing behavior need not be motivated by sexual desire as long as it is based on sex (i.e., gender). The plaintiff alleged that his male coworkers forcibly subjected him to sex-related humiliating actions; he was physically assaulted in a sexual manner and threatened with rape. Thus, employers must examine whether conduct is based on sex—whether it is targeted toward women or men—and not just if it is overtly sexual in nature.

Third-Party Harassment

In other cases regarding a hostile work environment, the courts have also ruled that employers may be held liable for complaints by male or female employees who experience third-party harassment if another employee receives benefits that they do not based on *quid pro quo* sexual harassment or other sexual cooperation. Third-party employees can also complain of a hostile work environment due to sexual harassment—even if it is not directed at them personally—because it poisons the work atmosphere. For example, third-party harassment can take place when two people engage in talk or behavior that offends a third person. Such behaviors are not typically seen as equally severe as actions that are targeted at a particular individual, but they can nonetheless contribute to a hostile work environment and should be taken seriously. This is particularly true if the third-party harassment takes place in conjunction with more direct actions targeting an individual and creating a hostile work environment.

In these situations, the same standard for liability will be used as with other forms of hostile work environments by coworkers: The question is whether the employer knew about the situation or should have known had it demonstrated reasonable care. For example, an employer would be liable for failing to stop harassing behavior after a complaint was filed or if a supervisor was otherwise aware of the situation.

Lessons of Weeks v. Baker & Mackenzie (1994)

Perhaps the most famous sexual harassment/hostile work environment case in the legal community is *Weeks* v. *Baker & Mackenzie*, in which the plaintiff worked as a secretary for a period of less than three months in 1991. During that short time, she was subjected to a sexually hostile work environment by one of the firm's partners. When Weeks complained, she was quickly separated from the harassing partner and assigned to work for another attorney. The firm also required the harassing partner to attend sensitivity training. Nonetheless, several other women came forward during the litigation and testified that the same partner had engaged in other sexually offensive conduct and that the firm had failed to take any appropriate remedial action.

The jury found the firm liable on the basis that the measures taken in response to the plaintiff's complaint were inadequate. While the jury members awarded Weeks only $50,000 for emotional distress, they ordered the firm to pay $6.9 million in punitive damages in order to "send a wake-up call." This figure represents 10 percent of the firm's net worth. On appeal, the judge allowed a $3.5 million award of punitive damages plus attorney fees of up to $2.7 million.

The lessons for police and fire departments are clear. First, the case illustrates how behavior that takes place over a short period of time can nonetheless result in a substantial award. Second, the award demonstrates the outrage that juries can feel against those in authority. In this case, the reasons the jury members gave for the size of the award were that they expected the attorneys to follow the law because they are officers of the court. The jury members were therefore upset that nothing was done to the harassing partner until after the lawsuit was filed; in addition, they felt that the firm had been arrogant in its handling of the entire situation. This is a lesson that police and fire departments disregard only at their own peril.

SUMMARY OF EMPLOYEE RIGHTS UNDER THE LAW

As outlined in this chapter, federal and state laws assert that employees have a right to be free from sexual harassment, whether it is a situation of *quid pro quo* or a hostile work environment. However, employees have additional rights that provide valuable protection if sexual harassment has already occurred:

- Employees have a right to be free from sexual harassment by nonemployees in their workplace. Examples would include people who come into the workplace to repair equipment, provide training, or conduct business (e.g., vendors and suppliers).

- Employees have a right to complain about the sexual harassment of coworkers, even if they themselves are not being sexually harassed. This is sometimes referred to as "bystander" sexual harassment.

- Any employee who is fired for refusing sexual demands has the right to sue his or her employer for sexual harassment and/or to file a complaint with the appropriate state or federal administrative agency.

- Employees who quit their job because sexual harassment has made it too difficult to work can sue their employer and/or file a complaint with the appropriate state or federal agency. If they did not report the behavior within their employer's complaint procedure, however, they will prevail only if the agency fails to prove that it took reasonable actions to prevent and correct sexual harassment.

- An employee who has been sexually harassed has the right to be free from retaliation. It is illegal for an employer to punish an employee for making a complaint of sexual harassment. Such retaliation is a separate violation of the law against sexual harassment, as discussed in detail in a later chapter.

- Employees also have the right to be free of retaliation even if they are not the one who experienced the harassment or filed the complaint. For example, an employee cannot be punished for reporting sexual harassment of a fellow coworker or for testifying on behalf of a coworker who has been sexually harassed.

SUMMARY OF EMPLOYER RESPONSIBILITIES UNDER THE LAW

Employers governed by Title VII (i.e., those with 15 or more employees) are currently encouraged but not required to take preventive action against sexual harassment. However, if they do not take such actions, they are likely to be unable to defend against any lawsuits claiming illegal sex discrimination. At a minimum, federal law states that an employer should do the following: (1) fully inform employees of their rights both under the law and under the employer's written sexual harassment policy (e.g., the employer is required to post the EEOC guidelines in a conspicuous place), (2) investigate the complaint fully and effectively to determine the extent of the sexual harassment, and (3) take prompt and appropriate corrective action.

Beyond this minimum standard, organizations that are sued for a hostile work environment will be protected from liability only if they can demonstrate that they took actions that were reasonably calculated to prevent sexual harassment and that they responded appropriately when incidents were brought to their attention. Such actions include developing an effective policy and complaint procedure, providing the policy to employees, following the policy and procedure when complaints are made, and disciplining those who are found to have violated the policy and engaged in sexual harassment or other forms of discrimination.

Employer Liability

To illustrate, in *Faragher* v. *City of Boca Raton* (1998), the U.S. Supreme Court found that the employer was liable for sexual harassment experienced by a female employee because it failed to disseminate its policy regarding sexual harassment. In that case, the Supreme Court articulated that an employer has to demonstrate "reasonable care" to provide a work environment that is free of sexual harassment. At a minimum, this must include writing an effective policy, developing an effective procedure, disseminating the policy and procedure, and providing training on sexual harassment.

Liability is thus determined by an organization's proactive actions taken to prevent sexual harassment as well as the response to actual complaints. For example, did the organization take measures that were reasonably likely to prevent sexual harassment and retaliation for those who report it? Did the organization stop any sexual harassment that was known? Was there any delay in responding to a complaint? Did the organization investigate the harassment even if it stopped? Clearly, an organization cannot sit back and wait for complaints; instead, meaningful actions must be taken both to prevent sexual harassment and retaliation and to respond appropriately when complaints are made.

Employers' Common Mistakes

In their review of recent Supreme Court Cases, Stokes, Stewart-Belle, and Barnes (2000) summarized some of the most common mistakes made by employers in the area of sexual harassment:

- Failing to write formal policies regarding sexual harassment
- Ignoring formal written policies that do exist
- Disregarding employee complaints of problems
- Failing to follow the spirit of the law when addressing harassment
- Treating sexual harassment as a personal problem that does not require intervention by the organization
- Acting as if sexual harassment is a difficult problem to identify
- Believing that the organization is not liable for sexual harassment that is not reported

To avoid these mistakes, this chapter concludes with specific guidelines for police and fire departments to protect themselves against liability by meaningfully addressing the problem of sexual harassment and other forms of discrimination.

Dissemination of Policy

Clearly, the courts have found that organizations must do more than simply have a policy on the books to protect them from liability for sexual harassment. The Supreme Court held in the landmark case of *Meritor Savings Bank* v. *Vinson* (1986) that policies and procedures are relevant in determining liability for sexual harassment, but at least equally important is the question of whether these policies and procedures are communicated to employees and whether the employer responds adequately to problems when they do arise (Lindemann & Kadue, 1992; see also *Robinson* v. *Jacksonville Shipyards,* 1991).

Timely Response

The courts have also examined the question of timely response and determined that organizations should typically initiate an investigation within one to two days of receiving a sexual harassment complaint; depending on the complexity of the circumstances, the whole investigative process should then typically be completed in a matter of weeks rather than months. If there are any delays in this process, the reasons must be carefully documented. In general, a good-faith effort must be demonstrated to complete the investigative process as quickly as possible while balancing quick action with the need for a thorough examination of the issues.

Quality of Investigation

The adequacy of the investigation could be reviewed in a variety of situations. For example, if there is a sexual harassment lawsuit against the organization, it is inevitable that the adequacy of the investigation will be at issue when determining whether or not the agency should be held liable; however, the investigation will also be evaluated if the harasser countersues for defamation, violation of privacy rights, or wrongful termination. In addition, the investigation will be reviewed if a harasser who is terminated applies for unemployment benefits. The best way to defend against such lawsuits is to conduct investigations in a reasonable manner and in good faith.

To illustrate, in *Fuller* v. *City of Oakland* (1995), the investigation was seen as *inadequate* because (1) the individual accused of harassment was not interviewed promptly, (2) the allegations were not corroborated when they easily could have been, (3) important witnesses were not interviewed, and (4) evidence in favor of the complainant was not given sufficient weight.

It is therefore not sufficient to simply document the fact that the respondent denied the incident or that the employer discussed the incident with the respondent. On the other hand, the court in *Silva* v. *Lucky Stores, Inc.* (1998) described six factors in determining that the investigation was adequate, even if it wasn't perfect (Oppenheimer & Pratt, 2003):

1. The investigator was neutral and trained on the issues.
2. The investigator interviewed the complainant, the respondent, and all the relevant witnesses.
3. The investigator reviewed pertinent documents.
4. The findings of the investigation were documented.
5. The investigator prepared a written report with the findings.
6. The findings were communicated confidentially to the interested parties.

Of course, no investigation is perfect, but it must be thorough, fair, and conducted in good faith.

Appropriate Discipline

With respect to discipline, review of case law suggests that the courts consider progressive sanctions to be appropriate for repeated complaints, although the specific penalty will vary depending on the circumstances of the situation. Termination is not necessarily required for a first-time offense if it is relatively minor, although this is probably the most appropriate response to repeated infractions. Rather, the courts want to see meaningful action that can include a written reprimand, suspension, demotion, or transfer, with progressive discipline for subsequent violations.

The courts have thus made it clear that agencies cannot respond to problems of sexual harassment by simply telling the harasser to stop the behavior; instead, organizations are held responsible by the courts for developing, enacting, and actually using more formal disciplinary procedures to respond to sexual harassment complaints. After the harasser has been disciplined, the courts also expect the organization to monitor the workplace to ensure that the harassment or discrimination does not continue and that the victim does not suffer retaliation for reporting.

Tips for the Investigator

For investigators to be effective, it is absolutely crucial for them to check with legal advisors to determine current law on sexual harassment and discrimination. In order to stay current, therefore, investigators should do the following:

- Ask legal counsel to review the agency's policies and procedures and to evaluate whether they meet current legal standards.

- Ask to be updated by legal advisors regarding any major case decisions that will affect the way investigations are conducted.

- Attend training seminars conducted by law firms or human resources experts to learn about the latest court decisions on and advances in the relevant policy, training, or investigation.

- Subscribe to publications that regularly review court decisions. These may be issued by a chamber of commerce, a firm that specializes in employment discrimination law, or other professional organizations.

Some websites that may be helpful to investigators include the following:

Americans for Effective Law Enforcement (www.aele.org)

Equal Employment Opportunity Commission (www.eeoc.gov)

National Employment Lawyers Association (www.nela.org)

U.S. Department of Labor, Women's Bureau (www.dol.gov/wb)

Chapter 4

Gender Harassment and Discrimination

The scope of sexual harassment investigations includes gender harassment and discrimination. Sometimes investigators concentrate on the actions, remarks, and behaviors that are explicitly sexual—but completely ignore those that are not overtly sexual but are nonetheless based on gender. Gender-based harassment and discrimination often co-occur with sexual harassment and other forms of workplace abuse, and they are prohibited as a form of sex discrimination.

HARASSMENT: NOT ALWAYS SEXUAL

While the prior chapter reviewed the laws pertaining to sexual harassment, one of the biggest problems we see when reviewing investigations is that they often do not address gender harassment and discrimination. We differentiate gender harassment from sexual harassment in this way: Sexual harassment has sexual overtones, while gender harassment is not overtly sexual but is nonetheless based on gender. Most commonly, gender harassment is based on the fact that the victim is a woman, and it often takes place in environments where sexual harassment (as well as other forms of workplace incivility and abuse) is also occurring.

It is perhaps unfortunate that years of training classes on sexual harassment have focused on behavior that is sexualized while ignoring remarks, actions, and other behaviors that degrade women as a class. Yet the law is clear that any such harassment is illegal if it is based on gender, regardless of whether the behavior is overtly sexual; in other words, most laws prohibit discrimination based on "sex," but they actually mean "gender."

GENDER HARASSMENT/DISCRIMINATION IN POLICING AND FIREFIGHTING

Law Enforcement

In policing and firefighting, gender harassment and discrimination are both commonplace. In fact, research consistently shows that one of the most significant problems faced by female police officers is the negative attitude of their male colleagues (Adams, 2001; Christopher, 1991; Timmins & Hainsworth, 1989; Wexler & Logan, 1983). Not surprisingly, this negative attitude can be a considerable source of stress for female officers (Bartol, Bergen, Volckens, Knoras, 1992; Morash & Haar, 1995; Seagram & Stark-Adamec, 1992). Even if they often attribute it to other aspects of the job that are unrelated to gender, it still is a source of stress (Brown, Campbell, & Fife-Schaw, 1995). For example, one study revealed that 80 percent of the women officers from several large police departments described negative attitudes of male officers that were expressed in a variety of ways including making blatantly sexist comments, asking questions about their sexual orientation, making threats of not backing them up, pushing women out of fights, refusing to work with or talk to women, refusing to let women drive, and engaging in other "gross behavior and comments" (Wexlar & Logan, 1983, p. 48).

In general, women join policing and stay in the field for many of the same reasons that men do, including good pay and benefits, challenges associated with the job, desire to be promoted, and opportunity to help others (Belknap & Shelley, 1992; Campbell, Christman, & Feigelson, 2000; Felkenes & Schroedel, 1993; Poole & Pogrebin, 1988; Timmins & Hainsworth, 1989). Nonetheless, women often leave policing for reasons that are very different from those of men. These reasons include unique stresses that female officers face, but male officers do not; for example, many female officers describe problems with coworker gossip, poor training, lack of promotional opportunity, inflexible work schedules, and administrative policies that disadvantage female officers (Adams, 2001; Belknap & Shelley, 1992; Martin, 1989; Morash & Haar, 1995; Wexler & Logan, 1983).

Women officers also say that they have to "prove themselves" at a level that is far beyond what the men officers have to do. In fact, both women and minority officers often feel required to constantly prove their worth because of the perception that they got the job due to affirmative action rather than merit. Some researchers have explained that this type of environment creates "overperformance demands" that cause women and minorities to experience psychological distress. For example, one study revealed that 48 percent of female police officers believed that they had to work twice as hard as their male colleagues some, most, or all of the time; only 9 percent of the men said they experienced such a demand. Overperformance demands are particularly pronounced among women in the higher ranks of an organization, resulting from the hostile attitudes of some of their male coworkers (Parker & Griffin, 2002).

To make the problem even worse, women officers also often feel isolated from the networks that provide male officers with information, support, mentoring, and protection. Not surprisingly, research demonstrates that women of color within law enforcement often face additional difficulties based on the combination of their gender and race (Belknap & Shelley, 1992; Felkenes & Schroedel, 1993; Haar, 1997;

Morash & Haar, 1995). For example, research has documented that both female and minority officers experience more negative social interactions on the job than their white male counterparts (Morris, 1996).

Such factors probably explain why women leave policing at much higher rates than men do, both at the academy and on the job (Boni, Adams, & Circelli, 2001; Dantzker & Kubin, 1998; Felkenes & Schroedel, 1993; Fry, 1983; Horne, 1980). In one Canadian study, for example, women left policing at three times the rate of men (Seagram & Stark-Adamec, 1992).

Firefighting

Similar issues are seen in the field of firefighting. As described in a prior chapter, one study of African-American women firefighters revealed numerous forms of gender harassment; these included being the object of pranks, being ignored or excluded, not having their accomplishments recognized, coworkers focusing on their mistakes, supervisors holding them to a different standard for discipline and performance, others viewing them as affirmative action hires, and having their physical needs neglected in ways such as ill-fitting gear and insufficient sleeping and restroom facilities (Yoder & Aniakudo, 1996). The authors of the study noted that the consequences of such behaviors could be serious in a firefighting situation because lacking critically important gear or being the object of pranks could lead to injuries. Not surprisingly, the more often these harassing behaviors were experienced by the women firefighters, the less accepted they felt in their work environment and the less they valued their own contribution to the organization (Yoder & Aniakudo, 1996).

Examples

Clearly, gender harassment can occur in both law enforcement and firefighting, as well as other fields that are nontraditional for women, and investigators must seriously examine any such allegations made by a complainant. Fortunately, many expressions of gender harassment are easy to recognize. For example, the following remarks are commonly heard in policing and firefighting:

"I don't want to work with a woman as a partner."

"Women are not strong enough to be firefighters; they should be paramedics."

"Women can't work SWAT (Special Weapons & Tactics)."

"I don't want a woman backing me up in a dangerous situation."

"I won't work for a woman supervisor."

These comments are not difficult to recognize as gender harassment because of their blatantly gendered nature. These are the types of comments that are prohibited by law if they are pervasive enough to create a hostile work environment or if they are used as excuses to prevent women from being treated as equals in the workplace.

ROLE OF STEREOTYPES IN GENDER HARASSMENT/DISCRIMINATION

In general, gender harassment is typically based on cultural stereotypes about women: Women are physically weak; women are overly emotional, especially when they are premenstrual, menstrual, or menopausal; women are just looking for a man to marry; and women should stay home and take care of the children.

While it is not illegal to believe these stereotypes, they do breed problems in the workplace, especially in occupations that have been traditionally seen as "male" occupations (e.g., policing and firefighting). Therefore, investigators need to be aware of these stereotypes in order to recognize their expression as a form of gender harassment because it can be against the law to express these beliefs through discriminatory behaviors. In general, investigators can identify gender harassment by hearing statements that begin "Women can't...," "Women shouldn't...," and "Women don't...."

Unfortunately, other expressions of gender bias are a little more subtle. For example, the following statements may also be considered expressions of bias against women:

"Domestic violence is not a real crime; it is a family problem."

"If she hangs around in bars like that, she is asking to be raped."

"Women should be protected; that's why they shouldn't be police officers."

"I won't work with her because she does not have good survival skills."

"She won't be able to hold her own in a fight."

"I would rather work with lesbians; at least they can fight."

In addition to being offensive and degrading to women in the workplace, such expressions of sexist stereotypes demonstrate a person's attitude toward women and can therefore be used to help investigators make determinations of credibility.

INVESTIGATION OF GENDER HARASSMENT/DISCRIMINATION

Often when a woman files a complaint about sexual harassment, she reports a variety of behaviors that she has found offensive. Some of them may be sexualized behaviors, and others may not be sexual but are nonetheless aimed at women as a group. When interviewing complainants, supervisors or investigators must therefore listen closely to every issue that they raise. The entire context of the situation cannot be clearly understood until all of the offensive behaviors have been documented and investigated. When a female employee accuses a coworker of sexual harassment and the event was not witnessed by anyone else, it is often difficult to determine who is more credible—the complainant or respondent. However, a good investigator who understands the issues of gender harassment can talk to coworkers to determine if the respondent has shown any other expressions of hostility toward women in the workplace. By asking questions such as the following, the investigator will often uncover issues of gender bias:

> "Have you ever heard Officer Doe express any opinion about women officers?"

> "Have you ever heard Officer Doe make any negative statements about women?"

> "How does Officer Doe deal with women who are victims of sexual assault?"

> "How does Officer Doe handle domestic violence calls?"

> "Does Officer Doe socialize with any of the women employees?"

> "Have you ever heard Officer Doe express an opinion about [the complainant's] abilities as a police officer?"

The response to such inquiries may reveal a great deal about the attitudes, the behaviors, and, ultimately, the credibility of the respondent.

Common Excuses for Gender Harassment/Discrimination

When investigating allegations of harassment, investigators will invariably be told that the real reason the complainant is having problems in the workplace is either because of the complainant's own personality or work performance. These allegations must be carefully examined, because they are often just bogus excuses for harassment.

Personality Clash

Sometimes respondents will claim that there is no discrimination or harassment occurring; it is just that they have a "personality clash" with the complainant. Investigators must never simply accept this as an explanation for improper behavior; probing into the evidence for the personality clash will often bring hidden issues to the surface. The following are some examples of instances in which the respondent explains the problem as a personality clash, but further questioning reveals underlying problems with gender bias.

"She Is Too Aggressive."   Often, the personality clash will be explained by the fact that the female complainant is simply "too aggressive." Yet this characterization must be carefully scrutinized because some men come from families and backgrounds in which women are expected to be submissive and to not question men in the family. When these men are confronted with a female officer or firefighter who has been trained to be in charge, they may not know how to react. This is especially true if the woman is older than the man or if she is of higher rank. In some situations, the statement that the woman is too aggressive is based on an incident in which she confronted the male officer, especially if it happened in front of other employees.

"She Thinks She Knows Everything."   Similarly, many respondents will explain that the personality clash is based on the fact that the woman "thinks she knows everything."

Again, because of their families and backgrounds, some men may be threatened by women who are smarter or more educated than they are. These men may then resent the fact that a woman is successful within their shared profession or that she corrected them on a question of policy or procedure.

"She Likes to Get All the Attention; She Is a Show-off." The personality clash may also be explained as due to the fact that the woman is a show-off or that she craves the attention of her peers. This type of comment is likely to be based on recognition that the woman recently earned for superior performance. For example, it could be that the woman recently solved a major case or made an arrest of a dangerous suspect. This may not sit well with those men who do not want women in their profession or do not expect women to be as successful as their male colleagues.

These are some common explanations for a personality clash; others may be given. The goal of the investigator, therefore, is to examine the behavior of the complainant, respondent, and others and to determine whether the underlying factor is actually bias against women. One of the best ways to do this is to ask the respondent to give examples of the complainant's behavior that demonstrate the problems of the personality clash. When these examples are given, it may become evident that the complainant's behavior is actually typical for a police officer or firefighter. The most important question for the investigator to consider is whether the respondent would react the same way to the same behavior if the complainant were a man. If the behavior would be seen as typical or even admirable if exhibited by a man but is condemned for a woman in the same position, the underlying problem is actually one of gender bias.

Investigators must also talk to the coworkers of the respondent and complainant to determine whether there are any ongoing clashes between the two and to determine how the respondent typically deals with women. All these inquiries will contribute to an understanding of the attitudes and credibility of both the respondent and the complainant.

Performance Issue

Although problems with gender harassment are often explained as an issue of conflicting personalities, the most common excuse given for treating women differently in policing and firefighting is that they are not performing acceptably. Yet negative performance evaluations and disciplinary sanctions are all too often examples of gender harassment and/or retaliation. Two examples (Example 4-1 and Example 4-2) will illustrate this problem.

As Example 4-2 illustrates, it can be extremely detrimental for those in policing and firefighting to be accused of endangering someone or improperly handling an emergency situation, but such accusations are commonly seen in situations of gender harassment. Typically, the accusations are not made formally but are a topic of gossip in the workplace. For example, rumors are often started by a male officer who accuses a woman of panicking, almost getting him shot, or engaging in other risky behaviors. These rumors are then circulated within the agency, and the woman is labeled as unfit, untrustworthy, and dangerous. If the woman complains that her coworkers are shunning her or trying to overtly push her out of the workgroup, coworkers then respond with allegations of poor performance or poor officer safety skills.

EXAMPLE 4-1

"She Didn't Clean the Refrigerator"

In one example, a female firefighter filed a complaint of sexual harassment by one of her coworkers. Then when her next performance evaluation came due, she was severely downgraded on the maintenance of the workplace. She filed a complaint of retaliation. When questioned about the evaluation, her commanding officer defended the unacceptable rating he had given her. He stated that it was her turn to clean the refrigerator at the station. The commander reminded her of her duty. She did not do it, and after three days he gave her a rating of unacceptable for station maintenance.

Yet the investigation revealed that the day the commander told her to clean the refrigerator, the female firefighter and her partner were extremely busy running from call to call. They never even had time for lunch. At the end of the shift, she was off-duty for 48 hours. When she returned to work, she and her partner again had an extremely busy shift. As a result, the woman simply never had time to clean the refrigerator. The investigation also uncovered that on her days off other firefighters who had tours of duty that were quite slow did not complete their station maintenance chores. None of these other firefighters received an unacceptable rating. When confronted with the findings of the investigation, the commanding officer changed the evaluation and was counseled about retaliation.

EXAMPLE 4-2

"She Almost Got Me Killed!"

In another example, a male officer called a female commanding officer at home at 3 A.M. to tell her that he had been ordered to work with a new woman trainee that night and that she nearly got him killed. When asked to describe the situation, he said that they were called to an assault. When they arrived at the scene, he told the trainee to get the shotgun out of the trunk of the car. He then leaped into the middle of the fight. According to the male officer, the female trainee came running up with the shotgun, got rattled, threw the shotgun on the ground, and tried to take one of the combatants into custody. When the fight was over, the male officer took her back to the precinct and told her to go home. He then wrote up a report about her throwing the shotgun on the ground, and he told everyone that she should be fired because she nearly got him killed.

An investigation was started immediately; it revealed a very different version of events. At the time of the incident, shotguns were not routinely carried in the squad cars, so officers who wanted to carry them were required to go through a special certification process. Trainees were not routinely certified. Therefore, when the officer told the female trainee to get the shotgun out of the trunk of the car, she did; however, she put the ammunition in her pocket because she had not been taught how to load the shotgun and realized that she had no legal authority to shoot under the circumstances. She saw that her partner was losing the fight and needed her help. But before she ran to assist her partner, she called for backup and threw the shotgun underneath the patrol car where she felt no one could get it. She then jumped into the fight and pulled two men off her partner, who was getting the worst of the fight. The two officers eventually managed to arrest and handcuff two of the combatants.

Obviously, the investigation revealed quite a different story from the initial report. It also revealed that this officer had frequently expressed his opinion that women should not be in police work and that he did not want to work with them.

Obviously, an investigator faced with issues such as these must try to find the truth of the matter. In our experience, questioning everyone in the workplace will often reveal that the rumors of the terrible things the woman did (or failed to do) can all be traced back to a single source—the one officer who initially "spread the word." When that officer is confronted and asked to describe what actually happened, the result is often that a situation has been blown totally out of proportion and that the work climate has been poisoned with exaggerated statements. As a result, investigators must always carefully examine such rumors of inferior or unsafe job performance, especially when they are made in the context of other expressions of gender harassment or discrimination.

Other Forms of Gender Harassment/Discrimination

In addition to these forms of gender harassment/discrimination, women in law enforcement and firefighting may also experience other forms based on their gender. Again, many of these are not overtly sexual or gender-based.

Adverse Treatment

For example, investigators must always be on the lookout for signs of gender harassment/discrimination if complainants state that women are more likely than men to be

- Denied promotions.
- Given undesirable assignments, work schedules, or transfers.
- Denied vacation time or other leave.
- Given negative performance evaluations.
- Held to a higher standard of performance.
- Denied opportunities for overtime or specialized training.
- Denied backup in emergency situations.
- Investigated for minor policy violations.
- Disciplined more severely for comparable infractions.

Under the law, when members of a protected class experience negative job actions that their colleagues do not, this type of gender discrimination is referred to as adverse treatment. Proof that such a negative job action is discriminatory might be found in direct evidence such as a document or a statement that the action was based on the woman's gender. However, more commonly the courts will infer that the action was discriminatory if there is circumstantial evidence supporting the notion. For example, when a women gets a top score on a promotional test and the position is left vacant until a man scores high enough to be promoted. This would suggest that the denial of promotion was in fact based on gender.

If a complainant makes an allegation that women within the organization are experiencing such adverse treatment, investigators must look into the claim by examining organizational records, statistics, and other evidence. Evidence for adverse treatment is particularly likely to be found when examining records and statistics for women and men in comparable positions. For example, an investigator could review all the disciplinary sanctions for men and women committing comparable violations of policy. If women receive more severe sanctions for the same type of infractions as were committed by men, this would suggest that the women are in fact experiencing discriminatory adverse treatment.

Adverse Impact

Somewhat more subtle is the form of harassment/discrimination referred to as "adverse impact." This means any policy or practice that does not appear on the surface to be discriminatory but in fact serves to disadvantage members of a protected class. For example, physical agility tests frequently serve to weed out female applicants because men pass the test at a significantly higher rate than women do. To establish evidence of adverse impact, it is irrelevant whether the organization intended to discriminate; the question is simply whether the policy or practice has a negative impact on members of a protected class, regardless of discriminatory intent.

To determine whether adverse impact exists, federal civil rights enforcement agencies have developed a formula referred to as the 4/5 or 80 percent rule. When examining statistical data, adverse impact will be found if the success rate for members of a protected class is less than 4/5 (80 percent) of the success rate for other individuals. For example, if 5 percent of the women applying for promotion are in fact promoted in comparison with 20 percent of the men, a problem may exist. In this example, the women's success rate of 5 percent is only one-quarter (or 25 percent) of the success rate for men (20 percent). This one-quarter (25 percent) proportion is considerably lower than the 80 percent set forth in the rule of 4/5, and it suggests that adverse impact does exist. With such a conclusion, investigators must ensure that management and legal counsel are notified and that they respond appropriately.

FOR MORE INFORMATION

It is not our intent in this book to go into all the areas of gender harassment and discrimination that may occur in the workplace; instead, we are trying to focus our discussion on the issues of sexual harassment. However, it is critically important to note that investigators must *not* limit their investigations to just looking at sexual harassment when they receive complaints of unfair treatment in the workplace. Investigators must always consider whether there are other forms of gender harassment or discrimination being committed.

The courts have ruled that the existence of gender harassment and discrimination may help to interpret the hostile and discriminatory nature of behaviors that might otherwise be ambiguous. For example, a small number of comments or behaviors are not typically considered to be severe or pervasive enough to constitute a hostile work environment under Title VII sex discrimination law, but when these comments or behaviors take place in a work environment where other discrimination or harassment exists, the courts are more likely to determine that it constitutes a hostile work environment based on the totality of the circumstances.

An example of this type of situation occurred in a case in Santa Barbara, California. In that case, two women officers filed a lawsuit alleging that they were exposed to sex discrimination in a variety of ways:

No woman had ever been promoted.

The manual of procedures was not written in gender-neutral language; it usually referred to officers as "he" and used other exclusive language.

The women were subjected to explicit sexual language in the workplace.

The women suffered retaliation after making internal complaints about these issues.

As in many other similar cases, these two women did everything in their power to bring these issues to the attention of the top command in their police department and the Human Resources Department for the city, yet they were repeatedly rebuffed. The city is now paying for those mistakes, as the jury again awarded more than $3 million to the plaintiffs.

For more information and concrete guidance in handling these issues, we therefore recommend that investigators obtain a copy of *Recruiting and Retaining Women: A Self-Assessment Guide for Law Enforcement.* This book includes a thorough discussion of how gender discrimination occurs in law enforcement organizations. It also includes several checklists to use when determining whether gender discrimination is occurring and whether proper policies and procedures are in place to prevent this discrimination. The book will likely be invaluable for investigators who are responsible for conducting investigations of gender discrimination within law enforcement organizations. Fortunately, it is available for free at a number of websites, including the National Criminal Justice Reference Service (www.ncjrs.org), the National Center for Women & Policing (www.womenandpolicing.org), and Penny Harrington & Associates (www.pennyharrington.com). Similar information is provided for the field of firefighting by the Women in the Fire Service, Inc. (www.wfsi.org).

MENTORS FOR INVESTIGATORS

In addition to obtaining such resource materials, we strongly recommend that investigators seek a mentor to help them deal with allegations of gender harassment or discrimination—especially for their first such investigation. A mentor can help to identify problems of sexual and gender harassment. Typically, the best type of mentor will be a woman who has been in law enforcement or firefighting for at least 10 years. These women have seen a lot during their careers and can help investigators to sift through the issues and relevant evidence. However, we recommend that this mentor be someone from a different organization; women within the same agency as the investigator may be understandably reluctant to talk about these issues, especially if they have future career plans in the agency.

To find a trusted mentor outside the organization, investigators can contact professional associations such as the National Center for Women & Policing, Women in Federal Law Enforcement, the International Association of Women Police, and Women in the Fire Service, Inc. Professional human resources associations also typically have local chapters and may be a good source of mentors. Finally, investigators can locate a mentor through one of the many online expert witness directories in which professionals can identify experts in the area of employment discrimination with a particular focus on law enforcement or firefighting. Although there may be a fee for the services of such experts, it is often worth the expense to make sure that an investigation is thorough, complete, and fair.

Chapter 5

Retaliation

Investigators must understand the legal prohibitions and common dynamics of retaliation in order to successfully prevent, identify, investigate, and correct it. One of the primary reasons that sexual harassment victims do not report their experience is because they fear retaliation, and research documents that these fears are well founded. Complainants do typically experience a range of work and social retaliation, which can have negative effects on their personal and professional well-being.

LEGAL PROTECTION AGAINST RETALIATION

As discussed in the chapter on legal issues, federal law provides protection against retaliation under Title VII, Section 704(a). Specifically, the law prohibits any adverse action from being taken against an employee that is linked with the person's participation in any legally protected activity, which generally includes challenging an illegal employment practice and participating in any investigation, proceeding, or hearing related to the practice. In the context of sexual harassment, this may include such behaviors as resisting sexual advances, filing a formal complaint and participating in the complaint process, supporting other employees who have filed a complaint, and testifying on behalf of other employees who have filed a complaint.

Any negative employment action that occurs at least partly due to participation in these legally protected activities will constitute retaliation that is actionable under Title VII. Retaliation is thus a separate violation of the law against sexual harassment, and it is increasingly common. To illustrate, retaliation currently constitutes approximately 25 percent of the charges filed by the Equal Employment Opportunity Commission (EEOC),

and that figure is increasing. In fact, lawyers often say that retaliation claims are generally easier to prove than discrimination and that they can result in bigger verdicts against
employers. Plaintiffs may prevail in retaliation claims even if the underlying complaint of
harassment or discrimination is not substantiated because the act of filing such a complaint
is a legally protected activity. Clearly, investigators must be aware of the laws prohibiting retaliation and the means of effectively investigating and resolving such issues.

Elements to Establish

To determine that retaliation has taken place, it is therefore necessary to establish the
following four elements:

1. The complainant engaged in a legally protected activity, such as reporting or
   opposing an employment practice that was seen as illegal or discriminatory.

2. The employer was aware of the complainant's legally protected activity.

3. The complainant suffered an adverse employment action, which does not
   necessarily have to be tangible but could be primarily social in nature.

4. There is a causal connection between the two events, often based simply on
   the timing of the complaint and the adverse employment action.

Note that the complainant does not have to be a member of a protected class to
establish a claim of retaliation; rather, the negative employment action must be based
on the person's participation in a legally protected activity, such as opposing a workplace practice that the person viewed as illegal or discriminatory. In fact, it doesn't matter whether or not the practice actually turns out to be illegal. As long as the report or
opposition of the workplace practice was made in good faith, it will be legally protected
under Title VII.

The report or opposition must also be made in a reasonable way, but the courts
have given wide latitude to employees seeking to report or oppose a practice they view
as illegal. For example, the courts have determined that it is reasonable for employees
to disclose the workplace practice that they see as illegal by picketing or going to the
press. It would not be reasonable, however, for an employee to copy and disseminate
confidential documents or to coerce coworkers to participate in the complaint process.

To determine whether an action constitutes retaliation, investigators must examine
the causal connection between the legally protected activity and the adverse employment
action being reported. Often, investigators can do so by simply establishing the timing
of the two events: If the adverse employment action immediately followed the legally
protected activity on the part of the complainant, it suggests that the action might have
indeed been retaliatory. However, the causal connection between the two events can also
be established with other types of evidence; for example, there is sometimes direct evidence that a supervisor or other employee has stated verbally or in writing that the complainant was being punished for reporting the behavior in question.

More typically, the evidence for retaliation is seen in the fact that the complainant
was treated differently from other employees in a similar situation. For example, the complainant may have been disciplined severely for a violation that is typically overlooked

when committed by other employees. Complainants are often subjected to heightened scrutiny following their report, which can generate negative performance evaluations or reports of suspected policy violations. In such situations, it would be necessary to establish whether the supervisor who was responsible for the negative job action was aware that the complainant had reported sexual harassment in order to determine the causal connection between the two events and establish that it was retaliation.

TYPES OF RETALIATION

The fear of retaliation is perhaps the most important reason why employees do not report sexual harassment or discrimination that they experience in the workplace. Victims are often afraid to file a formal complaint because they fear retaliation from coworkers, supervisors, and the administration. Sadly, these fears are often well founded. Research documents that retaliation is frequently experienced both in tangible job actions and in less tangible social relations. These are often referred to as *work retaliation* and *social retaliation* (Cortina & Magley, 2003).

Work Retaliation

By Supervisors

For example, employees who experience work retaliation from supervisors may be

- Denied promotions.
- Transferred involuntarily.
- Given different assignments, duties, or work schedules.
- Denied vacation time or other leave.
- Denied transfer to specialty jobs or other desirable positions.
- Hindered in their ability to perform their job.
- Demoted.
- Denied training opportunities.
- Given negative performance evaluations.
- Denied benefits or given decreased or delayed benefits.
- Assigned inadequate equipment or physical facilities.
- Denied opportunities for overtime.
- Given unwarranted or unfair disciplinary sanctions.
- Terminated.

Work retaliation can even be experienced after the complainant has left the organization. For example, employers sometimes retaliate against complainants by providing a negative reference to a future or potential employer or by refusing to provide any reference at all. It would also be considered retaliation for the organization to provide information about the charge or investigation to the future or potential employer.

In law enforcement, one of the most common types of work retaliation by a supervisor is that the complainant is held to a higher standard of performance as compared with coworkers. As a result, performance evaluations become more negative after the employee filed a complaint or otherwise cooperated with an internal investigation.

By Coworkers

Other forms of work retaliation can be perpetrated by coworkers without supervisory authority. For example, complainants are often targeted with administrative investigations as a form of retaliation. Within policing, these investigations typically result from complaints made to Internal Affairs by other members of the agency or by citizens who have been enlisted to help the respondent and are based on violations by the complainant that are either minor or nonexistent.

The most dangerous form of work retaliation in both law enforcement and firefighting is the failure to provide immediate backup or other assistance in emergency situations. In firefighting, it also includes stealing or tampering with necessary safety equipment. Such acts represent the ultimate form of retaliation unique to the kind of workplace where emergency situations can easily become life-threatening. For many complainants, this is the point at which they begin to fear for their lives and consequently leave the organization.

Social Retaliation

In contrast with work retaliation, social retaliation can come from anyone within the organization including peers, supervisors, and even subordinates. It includes both verbal and nonverbal behaviors, such as "name-calling, ostracism, blame, threats, or the 'silent treatment'" (Cortina & Magley, 2003, p. 248). Social retaliation is much more common than work retaliation, although it is often unclear exactly when it crosses the line from an issue of negative workplace relations to illegal retaliation (Cortina & Magley, 2003). Some of the most common forms of social retaliation within law enforcement and firefighting are described below.

Shunning or Ostracizing the Complainant

This situation exists when no one in the workplace will talk with or provide the complainant with information needed to perform a job safely or effectively.

Stalking or Harassing the Complainant

Obscene telephone calls received at home, telephone calls when the caller says nothing, hang-up calls at all hours of the day and night, threatening or harassing letters or notes, damage to the complainant's automobile, articles left in the complainant's desk, mailbox, or work area that are intended to intimidate or harass—all these are examples.

Spreading Rumors or Jokes about the Complainant

Complainants are often made the subject of jokes that are told or repeated in the workplace, particularly jokes with respect to sexual activity or other demeaning information.

TRIGGERS FOR RETALIATION

Clearly, the fears of employees who experience sexual harassment or discrimination are well founded—many do in fact experience retaliation not only when they file a formal complaint but also when they use more informal strategies such as confronting the harasser or talking with coworkers. For example, research documents that retaliation is more severe when the victim has lower rank or status than the harasser. Particularly when the harasser is someone who has high ranking within an organization, those with power may retaliate against the victim "to correct this challenge to authority" (Cortina & Magley, 2003, p. 249). Retaliation is also more severe when the victim confronts the harasser directly. On the other hand, victims may experience retaliation simply because they discuss the issue with colleagues informally. Often coworkers may try to distance themselves from the victim to avoid experiencing negative consequences themselves (Cortina & Magley, 2003).

IMPACT ON VICTIMS

Retaliation is upsetting to victims for a number of reasons, due to both the distress of the experience and the perceived unfairness of being punished for blowing the whistle. Not surprisingly, victims who experience retaliation often have a range of negative effects on their psychological, professional, and even physical well-being. These negative effects are especially pronounced if the victim experienced both work and social retaliation (Cortina & Magley, 2003). However, those victims who voice their concern in some form and do not experience retaliation do better than those who remain silent. The worst effects are seen on those victims who experience a great deal of harassment yet tell no one about it (Cortina & Magley, 2003).

PREVENTING AND RESPONDING TO RETALIATION

Ways to Prevent Retaliation

In our experience with sexual harassment lawsuits, juries frequently side with complainants who experience retaliation that the employer did nothing to prevent or stop. Fortunately, there are many things that employers can do to prevent retaliation.

Develop Clear Policy.   First and foremost, agencies must clearly state in the policies governing sexual harassment and discrimination that any act of retaliation will be treated as a separate offense and will be severely disciplined if substantiated.

Follow Policy. However, having a policy and distributing it are not enough. Organizations must actually follow the policy in order to prevent, identify, investigate, and correct retaliatory actions. For example, anyone who complains of sexual harassment should receive follow-up from the investigator or other person responsible for handling the complaint to determine if retaliation has occurred and to take action in response. (These measures are described in greater detail in the chapters on the complaint process and the investigation.) If retaliatory actions are reported, they should then be investigated thoroughly, and any substantiated charges should result in progressive discipline against those responsible.

Separate Parties. Because of the high risk of retaliation when sexual harassment complaints are made, it is often desirable to separate the parties during the time an investigation is being conducted. Yet the questions of who to reassign and how to do so are extremely complicated. These issues are discussed in detail in the chapter on the complaint process; for the present purposes, it is enough to note that measures must be taken to protect the complainant in order to prevent allegations of retaliation.

Monitor Workplace. Regardless of any reassignment decisions, supervisors must always monitor the workplace for retaliation while a complaint is being investigated as well as after it has been resolved and any discipline is being imposed. (This issue is highlighted in the chapter on the responsibilities of supervisors and managers.) The good news is that such efforts can have a positive effect both by decreasing the likelihood that employees will actually experience retaliation and by reducing the fear of retaliation that inhibits so many employees from reporting problems.

Assign Discipline Appropriately. As discussed above, employers should always investigate allegations of retaliation and assign progressive discipline for any retaliatory actions that are substantiated. Some of the most common problems in this area are summarized in the following four examples:

1. The harasser is found to have violated policy and given either an oral warning or a letter of reprimand. While this may be appropriate for a very minor violation, it is clearly *not* appropriate for behavior that has been repeated and has had a serious negative impact on the complainant. For example, this would not be an appropriate sanction for an employee who subjected a coworker to years of gender discrimination or sexual harassment.

2. Harassers are promoted or given a desirable assignment soon after the investigation is completed. All too often, we have seen harassers almost immediately promoted after the investigation of very serious instances of sexual harassment. Even if some disciplinary action is taken, the act of promoting a known offender sends a very strong message throughout the organization that sexual harassment will be tolerated and that harassers will not be held truly accountable for their actions.

3. Harassers are often recognized with an award for Officer of the Year or some other recognition after being found to have violated the policy. As with the promotion issue above, this undermines the message that agencies need to communicate regarding the seriousness of sexual harassment and the true accountability for those found to have committed such acts.

4. The harasser is assigned as an Equal Employment Opportunity (EEO) or Internal Affairs investigator after the investigation is completed. We hope we don't even need to elaborate on the problems with this, but it is surprising how often we have seen law enforcement agencies assign someone with prior complaints of sexual harassment against them to the investigation of future complaints. Needless to say, this can discourage victims of sexual harassment from reporting the problem and undermine employee confidence that the investigative process is truly fair and unbiased.

A Detailed guidelines for assigning appropriate discipline and other remedial measures are discussed in a later chapter; however, it is important to note in this context that the failure to discipline appropriately can contribute to an environment of retaliation.

Ways to Discipline Complainant

In addition to the complexities surrounding ways to prevent retaliation, a difficult issue sometimes arises for employers when a *complainant* engages in activity that violates policy and merits discipline. Most commonly, this happens when the complainant violates the confidentiality policy by discussing the case with coworkers. Perhaps not surprisingly, complainants often discuss the case as they look for moral support during the difficult process of the investigation. It is common for officers to form close personal relationships with coworkers, so it is not surprising that complainants often feel a need to turn to these coworkers in difficult times such as these. We therefore caution employers about disciplining complainants who have violated the confidentiality policy by talking to someone in the workplace who is their close personal friend. While violations of the confidentiality policy do need to be addressed, this must be done extremely carefully.

Complainants may also be accused or suspected of committing some other policy violation. In these situations, it is understandable that managers are reluctant to assign disciplinary sanctions in case the action is perceived to be retaliation for filing the complaint of sexual harassment. On the one hand, employers must treat the potential infraction like any other—by thoroughly and fairly investigating the allegation, carefully documenting the investigative process and findings, and assigning disciplinary sanctions for any charges that are substantiated. On the other hand, complainants are often targeted with administrative investigations for minor or nonexistent infractions as a form of retaliation. Thus, repeated or questionable reports of misconduct on the part of the complainant must be examined to determine whether they are actually retaliatory in nature. However, if the investigation does substantiate any charges against the complainant, investigators must ensure that the discipline assigned is consistent with that given to other employees who committed a comparable offense. It is always a good idea to consult legal counsel in such a situation.

Tips for the Investigator

To effectively address the issues of retaliation in a sexual harassment investigation, it is important for investigators to take the following measures:

- Be sure to caution all persons interviewed that they are not to discuss the case with any other employee or to take any action against the complainant.

- Review the sexual harassment policy to make sure that it contains a prohibition against retaliation.

- Review the information in the chapter on the complaint process regarding the reassignment of the complainant, the respondent, or both. Make sure that steps are taken to protect the complainant against retaliation for filing a complaint.

- Periodically check with complainants to update them on the progress of the case and to ask if they are experiencing any retaliation. Document these conversations, and inform the complainant that retaliation should be reported directly to the investigator and not through the usual complaint process.

- Keep in mind that complainants will often be extremely reluctant to report retaliatory actions because they are already concerned about being seen as a troublemaker.

- Remember that the severity of the retaliation is not necessarily related to the severity of the underlying complaint. In our experience, many lawsuits arise from relatively minor situations of sexual harassment or discrimination that nonetheless result in severe retaliation when the victim files a complaint. Retaliation is therefore a serious offense even when the underlying complaint is trivial or even unfounded.

- Continue to periodically check with the complainant to make sure that no retaliation is occurring after the investigation is concluded.

- Immediately initiate an investigation into any allegations by the complainant that retaliation is occurring, and discipline those responsible for any actions that are substantiated.

Chapter 6

Preventing Sexual Harassment

To prevent sexual harassment, it is important to understand the characteristics and motivations of those who engage in such behavior. Employers must also appreciate the benefits of preventing sexual harassment and the most effective means to do so. This chapter provides detailed information on how to successfully prevent sexual harassment within law enforcement agencies, fire departments, and other workplaces that are nontraditional for women.

MEN WHO SEXUALLY HARASS

The evidence is clear that men who sexually harass have a variety of other personality characteristics. Research documents that they tend to

- Be more authoritarian and less able to empathize with others.
- Hold more negative and/or traditional attitudes toward women.
- Believe that the relationship between the sexes is adversarial (men versus women).
- Believe in hypermasculine (macho) stereotypes.
- Pay more sexual attention to coworkers.
- Want to control their sexual partner.
- Believe in various myths about rape and are actually more likely to rape.
- Have a strong link between concepts of sex and power.
- Accept sexualized behavior and sexual harassment in the workplace.[1]

Men Harass Only in Certain Situations.   The evidence is equally clear that even men who sexually harass will do so only in certain situations—in workplaces that tolerate sexual harassment, in places where sexual harassment is actually taking place, and in places where others who sexually harass are not held accountable for their behavior (Pryor & Whalen, 1997). For example, researchers have demonstrated that men are much more likely to touch a woman sexually in a situation in which they are asked to teach a woman to putt a golf ball than when they are asked to teach a woman to play poker at a table (Pryor, 1987). Furthermore, these men are particularly likely to sexually harass a woman in a research situation in which there is a "harassing role model," such as an experimenter who makes sexual innuendoes about the woman (Pryor, LaVite, & Stoller, 1993). These examples point out the importance of having clearly defined policies and expectations of workplace behavior. Such efforts will likely prevent sexual harassment, even among those men whose personality characteristics predispose them toward sexually harassing.

Harassers Have Different Motivations.   Not all harassers are created equal. Men who sexually harass might have a range of different motivations for their behavior, some of which are based more in sexual awkwardness and others are clearly driven by hostility and/or sexual exploitation. However, most sexual harassment is based on negative attitudes toward women and have no sexual component whatsoever. This type of sexual harassment is particularly likely to be seen in male-dominated workplaces such as law enforcement and firefighting. There is even some evidence to suggest that it is this underlying attitude of hostility (as opposed to the sexual component) that is most distressing to victims of sexual harassment.

Harassment Has a Specific Purpose.   In traditionally masculine workplaces such as law enforcement and firefighting, sexual harassment often has the explicit purpose of reminding women that they are not welcome. By communicating their hostility with behaviors such as name-calling and patronizing, some men strive to keep women "in their place" and protect the "good old boy" culture of these workplaces. At the same time, these men work to reduce or eliminate the threat of competition posed by women. Sexualized behavior such as jokes, innuendoes, and pornography can maintain the image of women as sex objects and outsiders in these workplace cultures.

There is even some evidence that men who are likely to sexually harass are also likely to evaluate women more negatively in a professional situation (Driscoll, Kelly, & Henderson, 1998). This suggests that a woman whose supervisor is predisposed to sexually harass may experience negative job actions such as lowered performance evaluations, smaller raises, and denial of promotions even if he doesn't actually sexually harass her.

PERILS OF NOT PREVENTING SEXUAL HARASSMENT

We hope that it is clear by now that those organizations that tolerate sexual harassment will pay a heavy price. These organizations communicate—through a variety of means—that problems with sexual harassment will not be taken seriously, that victims who report harassment will experience negative consequences, and that harassers will not be held accountable with meaningful sanctions. Some of these consequences can be summarized as follows.

Problems Are More Frequent.   A great deal of research documents that organizations with a climate that is tolerant of sexual harassment have more frequent incidents of sexually harassing behavior (Fitzgerald, Swan, & Magley, 1997; Hesson-McInnis & Fitzgerald, 1997; Hulin, Fitzgerald, & Drasgow, 1996; Mueller, De Coster, & Estes, 2001; O'Hare & O'Donohue, 1998; Pryor, Geidd, & Williams, 1995; Timmerman & Bajema, 2000).

Problems Are Not Reported.   Furthermore, when sexually harassing behaviors are pervasive in an organization, victims are less likely to identify them as sexual harassment and report them (DuBois et al., 1999; Fitzgerald, Drasgow, & Magley, 1999). In some situations, this may happen only when the behaviors involve physical threats or violence or when they extend beyond the workplace, as in stalking (Williams, Giuffre, & Dellinger, 1999).

The Climate Itself Hurts Employees.   Research has also documented that the organizational climate itself can have negative effects on employees, even on those who do not personally experience sexual harassment (Culbertson & Rodgers, 1997; Fitzgerald, Drasgow, & Magley, 1999; Fitzgerald, Swan, & Magley, 1997; Hulin, Fitzgerald, & Drasgow, 1996). In other words, there are negative effects on employees in organizations or workgroups where others are being harassed (Glomb et al., 1997; Schneider, 1996; Sorenson, Luzio, & Mangione-Lambie, 1994).

Employees Are More Likely to Quit and Are Harder to Replace.   Finally, when employees believe that their workplace has a problem with sexual harassment, they indicate that they are both less satisfied with their work and more likely to quit. These employees are also less likely to recommend their employer to others, which can make it more difficult for an agency to recruit women (Culbertson & Rodgers, 1997). This is particularly true in police and fire departments where personal referrals are one of the primary sources for identifying new employees.

Clearly, organizations that communicate a tolerant attitude toward sexual harassment do so at their peril, at the risk of both increasing the incidence of sexual harassment and decreasing the likelihood that it will be identified as a problem and reported; in addition, the workplace climate that is tolerant of sexual harassment hurts employees, both men and women. These employees, often referred to as bystanders, can experience negative outcomes similar to those of the victims themselves. These negative outcomes include decreased satisfaction with supervisors, coworkers, and life in general as well as negative effects on mental health and psychological well-being.

SEXUAL HARASSMENT PREVENTION

Benefits of Prevention

The good news is that agencies making a real effort to integrate their workforce and convey a philosophy of zero tolerance for sexual harassment will reap a variety of rewards. Research documents that such proactive agencies experience the following[2]:

- Decreased frequency of sexually harassing behaviors
- Increased sense among employees that reports of sexual harassment are acceptable
- Decreased fear of retaliation for reporting sexual harassment
- More favorable views among employees of the organization's complaint process
- Greater commitment among employees toward the organization
- More favorable perceptions of sexual harassment victims within the organization

Research even documents that employees do better professionally in organizations that make a meaningful effort to address sexual harassment *whether or not the employees themselves are harassed* (DuBois et al., 1999; Hunter-Williams, Fitzgerald, & Drasgow, 1999).

Methods of Prevention

There are obviously many important benefits for agencies making real efforts both to prevent sexual harassment and to respond appropriately through enforcement, education, and training. Of these, the most powerful effect seems to result from prevention and enforcement efforts; less impact is seen with resources such as hotlines and counseling services. These are some meaningful methods to prevent harassment:

- Design an effective sexual harassment policy and complaint procedure.
- Screen new applicants and supervisors for prior problems with sexual harassment and for appropriate attitudes and responses to the problem.
- Inform employees about the problem of sexual harassment and the organizational policy through general means such as posters and memos.
- Train employees through special programs on the topic of sexual harassment.
- Enforce the sexual harassment policy with thorough investigations, appropriate disciplinary sanctions, and other corrective actions.
- Rate the performance of supervisors in implementing the policies and procedures with respect to sexual harassment.
- Provide resources for employees to handle problems with sexual harassment through ombudsperson programs, contact people, hotlines, and counseling services.
- Evaluate the effectiveness of all sexual harassment programs, particularly training programs for employees and supervisors.

Agencies can also demonstrate leadership by allocating sufficient resources to conduct a thorough investigation when problems do arise. This would include dedicating the time of the investigator (which may be considerable) and the people being interviewed as well as providing access to documents and records within the agency. An agency also has other options in dealing with sexual harassment.

Promote a Professional Work Environment.   As previously reviewed, it is absolutely clear that sexually harassing behaviors are more common in organizations with a work environment that is generally unprofessional, sexualized, or sexist and in organizations in which employees do not know about relevant policies and procedures regarding harassment. Thus, police and fire departments seeking to prevent sexual harassment must also work to promote a professional work environment by addressing more general problems such as alcohol or drug use; general mistreatment of employees; misuse of the organization's time, resources, and equipment; and a sexualized work atmosphere based on appearance, comments, and nonverbal behaviors. In police and fire departments, for example, these efforts could include notifying employees that there will be surprise inspections for pinups, cartoons, and other sexually offensive materials.

Recruit and Retain More Women.   In contrast, sexual harassment is less common in workplaces with a more balanced number of men and women. In fact, research conducted in the military has documented that the relationship is linear, so the number of women in a particular assignment or position directly predicts the level of sexual harassment there (Fitzgerald, Drasgow, & Magley, 1999). To put it simply, the more women an agency has, the fewer incidents of sexual harassment. Therefore, one of the most important things a police or fire department can do to prevent sexual harassment is to increase the number of women throughout the agency and to integrate them in all departments, units, and ranks. Of course, increasing the number of women and changing the culture of an organization are complex, difficult, and time-consuming tasks that may require overhauling both recruitment efforts and organizational support for retention. For example, agencies might consider setting up formal or informal structured networks for women so that they can receive support, information, and mentoring. Such networks also provide a forum for challenging policies or practices that disadvantage women or that are seen as discriminatory or even harassing. All of these can contribute to the improved recruitment and retention of female personnel.

For guidance in this area, law enforcement administrators can consult a recent publication by the Bureau of Justice Assistance titled *Recruiting and Retaining Women: A Self-Assessment Guide for Law Enforcement*. Developed by the National Center for Women & Policing, this guide highlights numerous ways for agencies to successfully recruit and retain female personnel; more importantly, it provides step-by-step guidance for agencies seeking to conduct a self-assessment of their own recruitment policies and procedures.

To illustrate the potential for success with this approach, a demonstration project was implemented with the Albuquerque Police Department to increase the recruitment and retention of women (Polisar & Milgram, 1998). Within two years, the percentage of female recruits increased from 10 percent to 25 percent. Using a similar approach, the Tucson Police Department was able to increase its percentage of female recruits from 10 percent to 29 percent. The strategies described as successful by both departments included the following (Polisar & Milgram, 1998):

- Hosting a career fair specifically for women
- Getting media coverage for the event
- Designing posters and brochures that feature female officers
- Creating a targeted recruitment list

Best of all, these women were retained at the same level as their male colleagues, perhaps because the recruitment drive was supported by efforts to improve the work environment for female officers. One critically important component of this effort was a survey conducted with male and female officers (Polisar & Milgram, 1998).

Administer Climate Surveys.   The advantages of surveying employees are highlighted throughout this book, and surveys can be used for a variety of purposes. One of their most important uses is evaluating an employer's efforts to prevent sexual harassment and other forms of workplace discrimination. For example, agencies can evaluate the effectiveness of their training program by asking whether employees feel free to discuss or report problems with sexual harassment and whether they believe that these complaints will be taken seriously. These are important assessment measures that can be used to determine whether an agency's policies, procedures, and training programs are having the desired effect. In addition, surveys can be used to collect information on a variety of topics:

- Recruitment
- Selection
- Academy training
- Sexual harassment
- Workplace climate
- Employee relations
- Pregnancy issues
- Child care
- Equipment
- Uniforms
- Promotions

The results of such surveys also can guide other prevention efforts by helping to recruit, retain, and integrate women within the agency and otherwise promoting a professional work environment. They are also a particularly good way to elicit information from members of minority groups who might not feel comfortable voicing their opinions in a more public forum. Based on the findings, administrators can therefore evaluate their current policies and practices and make changes to improve the work environment for everyone.

Conduct Exit Interviews.   Because of the tremendous peer pressure placed on women not to report sexual harassment, some choose to resign rather than go through the stress of an investigation and any possible retaliation. One way to determine if this is occurring is to conduct exit interviews with all sworn and civilian employees who leave the organization. These interviews should be conducted by personnel in the Human Resources Department at the time the person resigns and should be followed up with a mail survey at least six to nine months after the person has left. Of course, it is important to keep in mind that employees will often be reluctant to talk about their real reasons for leaving because they need a positive employment reference from their current employer; nonetheless, exit interviews can provide a wealth of information for employers seeking to address problems with sexual harassment and other forms of workplace discrimination. As with employee surveys, exit surveys may be a particularly good way to elicit information from members of minority groups who do not feel comfortable voicing their opinions while still employed by the agency.

Accountability for Prevention

Perhaps the single most important step administrators can take to prevent problems with sexual harassment and other forms of workplace discrimination is to hold supervisors and managers strictly accountable for activities occurring in their work units. First-line supervisors are especially important to the success of any efforts to eliminate harassment and discrimination because they personally observe workplace behaviors taking place on a daily basis. Toward this end, administrators may want to consider taking the following actions:

- Imposing immediate, meaningful, and appropriate discipline on any supervisor or manager who fails to take reasonable care to identify and stop harassment

- Publicly announcing rewards for supervisors and managers who take proactive measures to prevent harassment

- Implementing policies requiring supervisors and managers to forward any information about complaints of harassment or discrimination and any steps they took to respond

- Documenting any violation of the policy on harassment and discrimination in the performance evaluations of supervisors (and these evaluations should then be used as a basis for denying promotions and pay raises when appropriate)

- Holding command staff responsible for inspecting the workplace on a regular basis to make certain that it is not hostile

In general, leaders with the greatest impact on employees are those closest to them in the institutional hierarchy. Thus, police and fire departments need to make sure that first-line supervisors receive training in sexual harassment prevention and response because they play the most important role in setting the tone for what kinds of behaviors will and will not be tolerated among employees. They are also likely to be the first people to whom a victim reports problems of sexual harassment, so they need to have the knowledge and tools to respond appropriately.

Monitoring of Prevention

Of course, prevention efforts can actually make the situation worse if they fail to meaningfully address the problem while creating a sense of false security within the organization that the problem is being handled (Grundmann, O'Donohue, & Peterson, 1997). Thus, prevention efforts must be monitored in an ongoing way. This can be accomplished by taking the following steps:

1. *Create standing committee to monitor prevention efforts.* This standing committee should consist of high-level managers responsible for monitoring the workplace to ensure that harassment is effectively prevented and should be responsible for recommending directly to the agency head the policies, training initiatives, and other steps needed to ensure effective prevention of sexual harassment. This standing committee should also have a large representation of women and minority members.

2. *Collect and evaluate data.* Whoever is responsible for investigating complaints of sexual harassment and discrimination should be directed to collect, compile, and evaluate data about all incidents. This data would include names of harassers, specific behaviors, locations of incidents, timeliness of the investigation, results of the investigation, discipline or remedy imposed, and timeliness of the corrective actions.

3. *Collect other forms of data.* Agencies should also consider using a variety of other means to collect data on harassment and discrimination such as employee surveys, focus groups, and exit interviews. This data can be used to assess the effectiveness of the prevention efforts.

4. *Remind supervisors and managers of their responsibilities.* Supervisors and managers must be regularly reminded of their duty to continuously monitor the workplace to ensure that a hostile work environment does not exist. Any posted pornography, sexually explicit materials, cartoons, jokes, or other items that demean or ridicule persons should be immediately removed and investigated.

5. *Hire outside experts.* Agencies may even want to hire outside experts to conduct formal written assessments of the organization and to make recommendations for eradicating harassment.

E N D N O T E S

1. For a review of the research, see Bargh, Raymond, Pryor, & Strack, 1993; Bartling & Eisenman, 1993; Begany & Milburn, 2002; Dekker & Barling, 1998; Driscoll, Kelly, & Henderson, 1998; Pryor, 1987; Pryor & Stoller, 1994; Pryor, Giedd, & Williams, 1995.
2. For a review of the research, see DuBois, Faley, Kustis, & Knapp, 1999; Fitzgerald, Drasgow, & Magley, 1999; Miceli & Near, 1985; Offermann & Malamuth, 2002; Timmerman & Bajema, 2000.

Chapter 7

Designing a Comprehensive Sexual Harassment Policy

Investigators must examine the sexual harassment policies of their agency to determine if they are adequate and/or to recommend that they be redesigned to comprehensively address the issues of sexual harassment and discrimination. When a complaint is made, investigators must then determine, through the course of a fair and thorough investigation, whether any of these policies were violated.

Most large private companies in the United States have a written sexual harassment policy, but this is not necessarily true for public employers such as governmental agencies. To illustrate, a 1993 survey of 300 companies with 500 to over 50,000 employees found that 95 percent had a written sexual harassment policy, but a 1999 survey of small government units revealed that only 56 percent had such a policy (both cited in Eberhardt, Moser, & McFadden, 1999). The researchers also found the following (Eberhardt, Moser, & McFadden, 1999):

- Only 63 percent of the policies outlined procedures for conducting an investigation.

- Only 24 percent of the employers had posted their policy in the workplace.

- Only 18 percent of the employers provided sexual harassment training to supervisors.

- Only 13 percent of the employers provided sexual harassment training to new employees.

Not surprisingly, the authors concluded that small government units had a long way to go to meaningfully address the problem of sexual harassment. In general, there is evidence to suggest that the public sector has lagged behind the private sector in developing and implementing effective sexual harassment policies. However, there is at least some evidence to suggest that police and fire departments are doing better than other agencies within the public sector. For example, in one statewide survey of female police officers in Florida, Captain Robinson found that 82 percent believed their agency had a written policy on sexual harassment and 62 percent of them felt that their agency was enforcing the policy as written (Robinson, 1993). In a survey of women firefighters, 84 percent said their agency had an official policy against sexual harassment or discrimination (Rosell, Miller, & Barber, 1995).

Regardless of percentages, it is likely that many of these written policies do not address the issues of sexual harassment and prevention comprehensively. Of course, to address any issue comprehensively is much easier said than done, but it is especially difficult in the complex and sensitive arena of sexual harassment. As one city's affirmative action officer asked researchers, "What is it about this policy that makes it so hard to get right?" (Reese & Lindenberg, 1999, p. 36). The current chapter is designed to help managers in law enforcement agencies and fire departments "get it right" by offering specific guidance in writing an effective policy and/or redesigning the policies currently in place.

GOALS OF A SEXUAL HARASSMENT POLICY

While we don't often think explicitly about the goals for a policy that is being developed, it is helpful to articulate exactly what it is we are trying to achieve. There are several goals of a sexual harassment policy:

- To clearly communicate that the organization has a zero-tolerance policy for sexual harassment or discrimination
- To communicate the zero-tolerance policy throughout the organization
- To educate employees about the types of behaviors that are not allowed in the workplace
- To encourage victims of sexual harassment to come forward with complaints
- To educate employees about the dynamics of sexual harassment and ways to respond effectively
- To outline procedures for responding to sexual harassment complaints
- To put supervisors and managers on notice regarding their responsibilities to monitor the workplace and to intervene in unacceptable behaviors
- To defend the organization against sexual harassment lawsuits

By articulating these goals, it becomes clear that many existing policies on sexual harassment are not sufficiently comprehensive to achieve the goals. For example, we know from experience that many police and fire departments simply adopt the Equal Employment Opportunity Commission (EEOC) guidelines as their policy both because it is easy and because the policy is likely to be seen as legally adequate in the event of litigation. On the one hand, the EEOC guidelines are reasonably clear and well written, and they are certainly better than having no policy at all. However, by simply adopting the EEOC guidelines rather than developing a more tailored policy, an agency risks jeopardizing the very goals for which a policy is adopted (Gutek, 1997).

ELEMENTS OF INADEQUATE SEXUAL HARASSMENT POLICIES

In fact, by simply adopting the EEOC guidelines as their agency's official policy, managers may actually communicate to personnel that they *do not* take the issue of sexual harassment seriously. Indeed, this practice may communicate the exact opposite to employees—that the agency doesn't actually care enough to spend time developing a policy that will work in its unique context. Some have also argued that the EEOC guidelines are actually not as clear as they could be; although the guidelines may be legally sufficient, they are not comprehensive enough to give employees meaningful guidance on the kind of behaviors that are expected in the workplace. For example, many policies based on EEOC guidelines fail to recognize that sexual harassment is frequently very subtle, so explicit behaviors such as sexual jokes may be prohibited while more general demeaning comments about women are not.

Along a similar line, there are also problems with briefly worded policies that focus primarily on communicating an ideological stance such as zero tolerance without any detailed information on what sexual harassment is and how it will be handled within the organization. Such policies are ineffective, mainly because employees do not understand them and therefore ignore them. Sadly, sexual harassment and other forms of discrimination often persist in police and fire departments despite official policies prohibiting them because the written policies are inadequate, unpublicized, and unenforced.

In response to this problem of inadequate sexual harassment policies, the Commission on Accreditation for Law Enforcement Agencies (CALEA) states:

> Agencies need to have strong policies and directives that prohibit such conduct; immediate and thorough investigation of any allegation of unlawful harassment; effective and appropriate disciplinary action in any case where allegations of harassment can be substantiated; and efforts to make agency employees aware of their responsibilities and the legal issues involved. (Committee on Accreditation for Law Enforcement Agencies, 1991, p. 26.1)

To do this, managers in police and fire departments are therefore advised to work to tailor the EEOC guidelines for their agencies and to craft a comprehensive policy based on the recommendations in this book. The remainder of this chapter is dedicated to providing concrete guidance for police and fire departments seeking to develop and disseminate a comprehensive sexual harassment policy.

ELEMENTS OF A COMPREHENSIVE
SEXUAL HARASSMENT POLICY

When designing a comprehensive sexual harassment policy, it should contain all the following information:

- Statement that the organization supports the right of every employee to be free of sexual harassment in the workplace as well as discrimination based on gender, race, sexual orientation, age, disability, or other difference

- Statement that offenders will be held accountable for acts of sexual harassment and discrimination and disciplined appropriately

- Statement that supervisors and managers are responsible for maintaining a harassment-free workplace; that they will be held accountable for monitoring behaviors, stopping any harassment, and appropriately reporting any harassment; and that appropriate disciplinary action will be taken against those who fail to enforce the policy

- Statement that acts of retaliation against employees who complain about sexual harassment or discrimination are separate violations of antidiscrimination law that will be considered as additional acts of misconduct and will be investigated and disciplined accordingly

- Explanation of the laws prohibiting sexual harassment

- Definitions and examples of harassing behaviors (including same-sex harassment and sexual harassment by nonemployees) that can be easily understood (including the fact that the behaviors do not have to take place during work hours but could occur at any work-related social function or off-site work event such as travel or training)

- Description of the informal process designed to encourage early intervention and resolution of hostile work environment complaints, such as a program with ombudspeople or other contact people

- Description of the formal procedures used to resolve complaints of harassment

- Process for reporting complaints (with emphasis on multiple access points) so that employees can file a complaint with any of the following:

    Supervisor

    Command officer

    Ombudsperson or contact person

    Designated women's coordinator

    Person in Human Resources Department

    Commission overseeing the agency

    Human Resources Department of the political entity involved

    State labor division responsible for enforcing discrimination laws

    U.S. Equal Employment Opportunities Commission

- Description of an investigation procedure that is prompt, thorough, and fair
- Assurance that complaints will be kept confidential to the extent possible (including a list of individuals routinely notified of complaints and examples of realistic limitations on confidentiality)
- Assurance that the employer will take immediate and appropriate steps to correct the situation if it is substantiated
- Description of the level of discipline that will be imposed for violations of the policy, for sexual harassment and other forms of discrimination, and for acts of retaliation and violations of the confidentiality provisions
- Timeline for investigating and resolving complaints of sexual harassment promptly
- Statement that complainants will be notified of their rights, statutes of limitation for filing civil complaints, and referrals to administrative agencies
- Names and telephone numbers of persons to contact if employees have questions about the policy or to gather more information about sexual harassment
- Statement that the complainant and respondent will be notified of the results of the investigation

Obviously, a comprehensive sexual harassment policy must contain a number of very detailed provisions, and it would certainly be helpful if we could provide a sample policy that police and fire departments could simply adopt for use in their own agencies. Unfortunately, developing such a "one size fits all" policy is impossible because of the variations across agencies, labor contracts, cities, counties, states, and federal court circuits. We recommend that investigators use this chapter as a guideline for the elements of a comprehensive sexual harassment policy that must be tailored to the unique complexities of their own agencies and locations, and consulting with legal counsel is always a good idea.

Broadened Prohibitions

To be truly comprehensive, a policy can be designed to prohibit all forms of discrimination and harassment based on federally protected classes and other groups of people who are not protected under federal law but who can be included based on state, local, or even organizational regulations. For example, the policy could explicitly state that discrimination and harassment are prohibited against employees based on their sexual orientation, a category not protected under federal law or most state laws. The policy could even address forms of abuse or mistreatment that are not based on class status in order to set a higher standard for professional conduct in the workplace than that outlined in the legal prohibitions. This will allow the employer to investigate and address behaviors that are not covered by laws but that are nonetheless damaging and disruptive to the workplace.

Sexual Harassment of Citizens

For police and fire departments, a comprehensive sexual harassment policy should also address sexual harassment that might be experienced by citizens and others outside the agency. In fact, several agencies have been sued because on-duty law enforcement officers sexually harassed women in the community. Some of these cases involved officers who stopped women for traffic violations and then subjected them to sexual misconduct. Others involved sexual misconduct between officers and Explorer Scouts or other volunteers. As a result, the policy must clearly spell out a standard of conduct for interaction with members of the public.

Complaint Procedures for State and Federal Agencies

In some states, employers are required to provide information about the complaint procedure and legal remedies provided by the EEOC as well as the state's fair employment agency. Even if this is not legally required, however, it is still a good idea to include this information in a comprehensive sexual harassment policy.

ELEMENTS *NOT* TO INCLUDE IN A SEXUAL HARASSMENT POLICY

When designing a comprehensive policy on sexual harassment, there are a number of provisions that should *not* be included (even though some agencies do).

Statement about False Complaints

For example, policies should *not* include a statement that complainants must be able to prove their allegation or that they will be disciplined or even terminated for filing a false complaint. Some police and fire departments have included such a provision in their policy in the interest of appearing balanced and impartial; however, this type of provision will actually deter victims from coming forward and will fail to provide accountability for those who sexually harass.

Although the cultural stereotype suggests that false accusations of sexual harassment are rampant, there is no evidence to support this. In fact, given the sizable body of research documenting that only a small minority of victims report their experiences of sexual harassment, organizations are advised to avoid any policy statements or complaint procedures that will further discourage victims from coming forward.

The reality is that most police and fire departments already have a policy on the books to address false complaints that can be enforced in the rare instance of a false allegation of sexual harassment. Furthermore, by conducting a fair and impartial investigation in accordance with the guidelines offered in this book, agencies will go a long way toward preventing the damage incurred by a false accusation, particularly if the confidentiality provisions are clearly communicated and strictly enforced.

Guarantee of Confidentiality

Policies also should *not* contain any statement guaranteeing the anonymity of complainants or the confidentiality of the information revealed during the course of the investigation. While the guarantee of confidentiality and anonymity may sound good to victims, it is not realistic and in fact is not always desirable. Rather, policies should include a statement that the agency will seek to protect the confidentiality of the complainant's identity and the information revealed during the investigation *to the extent possible*. To achieve that goal, everyone involved in the investigation should be required to sign a written statement acknowledging that they have been informed of the agency guidelines for confidentiality and the potential consequences for violating them.

Despite these protections of confidentiality, any complaints of sexual harassment must be referred to the appropriate individuals (as outlined in the policy), and this may require notification even in cases in which this is against the wishes of the complainant. Moreover, serious problems such as stalking and threats of violence may require coordinated effort within and even outside the agency (including possible contact with appropriate law enforcement officials). Therefore, while every effort should be made to protect the confidentiality of all the parties involved in an investigation, complainants should always be informed of the realistic limits on that protection and the process for reporting any violation of the confidentiality agreement by another employee.

Ultimately, one of the best protections of confidentiality is a fair and impartial procedure for accepting and investigating complaints because people tend to talk most when they feel that they have been treated unfairly and that their employer has betrayed them (Reese & Lindenberg, 1999). Supervisors must therefore repeatedly assure the complainant, the accused, and others of the protections of confidentiality, and the potential sanctions should be visibly imposed for any breaches. This will increase confidence in the process and may potentially decrease fear of reporting among those who experience sexual harassment.

Requirement to Report

Another element that should *not* be included in a policy is the requirement for victims to report problems with sexual harassment or discrimination. Some agencies have developed policies with such a requirement to immediately report harassment or discrimination that they experience, with disciplinary consequences for failing to do so; however, such a provision can be extremely harmful because it does more to discourage reporting than to encourage victims to actually come forward. As discussed in the chapter on victim responses, most people who are sexually harassed take a range of more indirect approaches to address the problem, such as avoiding the harasser and talking with colleagues. Very few victims of sexual harassment file a formal complaint for a variety of reasons:

- They do not recognize the incident as sexual harassment, or they do not perceive it as serious enough or frequent enough to file a formal complaint.

- They are not aware of the policy or procedure for reporting sexual harassment.

- They do not understand the policy or procedure for reporting sexual harassment.

- They prefer to handle the situation informally, avoiding more formal mechanisms.

- They fear negative reactions or repercussions for reporting.

- They know of others who had negative experiences after reporting, or they share a general perception that the policy and procedures are unfair.

Obviously, managers in police and fire departments want their employees to report this type of misconduct. However, rather than including a requirement to report in the sexual harassment policy, a better approach is to proactively encourage victims to report, make it easy for them to report, and provide support to them throughout the investigative process. When victims are reassured that the behavior will be stopped and that they will not be subjected to retaliation for reporting, such a provision is likely to be unnecessary.

DISSEMINATION OF A SEXUAL HARASSMENT POLICY

As discussed in the chapter on legal issues, the courts have clearly stated that organizations must do more than simply have a policy on the books to protect them from liability for sexual harassment. Once a policy is developed, management has the responsibility to disseminate it as widely as possible throughout the agency. To accomplish this, police or fire departments must at a minimum post the policy permanently and prominently in a location such as the employee bulletin board, so it can be seen by all employees, applicants, and other people who come in direct contact with the agency (e.g., members of the public, contractors, and vendors). Such public posting will go a long way toward ensuring that employees and others are aware of the prohibition on sexual harassment and other forms of discrimination and that they are familiar with the procedures for filing a complaint. In addition, a statement of zero tolerance for harassment from the head of the organization should accompany the policy.

All employees should also be given a copy of the policy and be asked to sign a statement that they have been given the policy, that they have read it, and that they are familiar with its contents. This statement can be used later if an employee accused of violating the policy claims to not have known that his or her behavior was illegal. In addition, the policy should be mailed to the homes of all employees on at least an annual basis. There are several other means of publicizing the policy:

- Having the employee read and sign the policy every year during the performance evaluation process
- Providing the policy in the employment package for new employees
- Periodically distributing the policy along with paychecks
- Describing the policy in a newsletter or other publication within the agency
- Mentioning the policy in an annual statement from the sheriff or fire chief
- Distributing the policy to contractors, vendors, and trainers who come in contact with employees
- Rating employees on their compliance with the policy during their annual performance evaluation

In particular, the performance evaluation of supervisors should include their effectiveness in responding to instances of sexual harassment, their protection of confidentiality, and their sanctions for any breaches of confidentiality by the parties, the witnesses, or others involved in the process (Reese & Lindenberg, 1999).

As discussed in the chapter on legal issues, the Supreme Court has found employers liable for failing to disseminate their policy regarding sexual harassment; however, the Supreme Court has also ruled that employers will *not* be held liable for sexual harassment if they have adequate policies and procedures in place and the victim unreasonably failed to use these policies and procedures. Police and fire departments would therefore be well advised to design a comprehensive policy against sexual harassment and other forms of discrimination and to disseminate it widely throughout the organization using the means described above.

SEXUAL HARASSMENT POLICY AND DATING

When crafting a policy on sexual harassment, some police and fire departments may seek to include a provision in their policy manual regarding consensual sexual relationships such as dating. On the one hand, some organizations ban *all* sexual relations between employees and require them to disclose any such relationship, with termination as the penalty for noncompliance (Williams, Giuffre, & Dellinger, 1999). The courts have typically upheld this practice in cases in which an employer fires or transfers employees who engage in a sexual relationship—even if the practice negatively influences more women than men—as long as the rule is clearly stated and is consistently enforced (Williams, Giuffre, & Dellinger, 1999). Yet many people believe that such prohibitions cannot realistically be enforced and can even encourage dishonesty (Rowe, 1996). Such a policy may also exacerbate the fear of reporting sexual harassment if the potential complainant was in a relationship that was prohibited by the policy. In many instances, workplace relationships begin voluntarily but then deteriorate into sexual harassment.

On the other hand, some organizations have taken the opposite approach by either explicitly or tacitly condoning intimate relationships between employees (Williams, Giuffre, & Dellinger, 1999). Most organizations, however, take the middle road and make some effort to regulate intimate relationships between employees without banning them across the board. For example, some organizations have policies against dating between a supervisor and subordinate but nothing against employees of the same rank dating (Williams, Giuffre, & Dellinger, 1999). Others have asked that employees involved in an intimate relationship sign a contract with terms for handling the dissolution, such as relocation of one or both people (Pierce & Aguinis, 1997). Still others deal with dating issues in a policy governing potential conflicts of interest. Such a policy would not be punitive but would be designed to make alternative working arrangements to eliminate any negative effects of the conflict of interest, particularly when a supervisor and a subordinate are involved (Rowe, 1996). Whatever the policy, it must be enforced consistently or the employer will be vulnerable to charges of disparate treatment.

Supervisors and Subordinates

It should hopefully go without saying that there are a variety of potential problems that arise when a supervisor dates a subordinate. Dating between supervisors and subordinates may not be completely voluntary, may become unwanted, may result in favoritism and subsequent complaints from coworkers, and may degenerate into sexual harassment or even stalking. As a result, it is often recommended that employers prohibit all sexual relationships between supervisors and subordinates who are in a direct reporting relationship.

When such a situation does arise, the supervisor and the subordinate should not be allowed to remain in their current positions while engaging in a sexual relationship.

One or both employees may be transferred, in accordance with the agency's policy and with the assistance of legal counsel. Both employees should first be consulted separately in order to determine whether the relationship is indeed voluntary and does not constitute an instance of *quid pro quo* sexual harassment. At this point, the meetings do not constitute a formal investigation; rather, they are conducted privately by a designated supervisor or a Human Resources Department professional.

In other situations, a supervisor or manager may be in a sexual relationship with an employee who is subordinate in rank but who is not in a direct reporting relationship. In such a situation, there is still a power differential between the two employees, so they should be consulted separately to ensure that the relationship is voluntary. The employees can also be advised (separately) of the provisions of the agency's sexual harassment policy and the standards for professional behavior in the workplace. In addition, the supervisor or manager must be cautioned against interfering with the work environment of the subordinate employee. It must be clear that engaging in such a relationship entails risk to their careers because the higher-ranking employee will typically bear the brunt of any subsequent problems. As with the other examples, this meeting should be documented.

Regardless of the exact circumstances, it is clear that there is a narrow line between trying to prevent possible sexual harassment charges and interfering in an employee's personal life. Therefore, whatever actions are taken must be done in consultation with legal advisors and/or personnel from the Human Resources Department and must be applied uniformly to all employees.

Dating Between Coworkers

Dating between coworkers of equal rank is less problematic. A consensual dating relationship should not generally be investigated unless it violates agency policy.

Sexual Favoritism

Sometimes an investigator is informed of sexual favoritism within the workplace. Because such a situation can contribute to a hostile work environment, allegations of sexual favoritism should be investigated even when the underlying relationships are consensual. This would include situations where employees are seen as receiving special treatment because they are involved in a sexual relationship with a supervisor or coworker.

CONCLUSION

The present chapter is designed to give managers in law enforcement agencies and fire departments concrete guidance in developing or redesigning their policies to comprehensively address the issues of sexual harassment and other forms of discrimination. However, we all know that the "proof" of any policy is not in its words but in its implementation and enforcement:

> Even if model policies are in place, if employees don't use them, if employees don't like them, if employees perceive that policy implementation is flawed in some way, or if,

Tips for the Investigator

Although investigators are not typically the ones responsible for developing a policy on sexual harassment, a number of steps can be taken to increase its effectiveness:

- Obtain a copy of the most current sexual harassment policy and examine it for these issues:

    When was it issued/last updated?

    Does it correctly reflect the law?

    Does it clearly spell out unacceptable behavior?

    Does it clearly assign responsibility to supervisors or managers for monitoring and correcting behavior?

    Does it specify a reporting procedure?

    Does it prohibit retaliation?

- Determine when the policy was last reviewed by a legal advisor. If it has been more than a year, recommend that such a review be undertaken.

When investigating a specific complaint of sexual harassment, do the following:

- Determine whether the behavior complained about falls under the policy.
- Find out whether and how the agency disseminated the policy:

    Did the respondent receive a copy of the policy? When?

    Did the complainant receive a copy of the policy? When?

    Was the policy posted in the workplace? Where and when?

    Was the policy issued in other ways (e.g., mailed to the homes of employees)?

indeed, it is flawed, then the quality of the overall policy becomes a moot point (Reese & Lindenberg, 1999, p. 5).

Our best advice, therefore, is that law enforcement agencies should develop a clear and comprehensive policy that prohibits harassment and discrimination. This policy will need to be reviewed by legal experts and Human Resources Department personnel to make certain that it is adequate. Once this review is complete, the policy must then be implemented and disseminated. After that, the policy should be reviewed—and then redistributed—at least annually. If there is a major change in any laws, the policy should obviously be revised immediately and then again redistributed.

Developing an effective sexual harassment policy is only the first step. The rest of this book is dedicated to the implementation and enforcement of the policy by conducting thorough and impartial investigations and fairly resolving complaints of sexual harassment and other forms of workplace discrimination.

Chapter 8

Developing an Effective Training Program Regarding Sexual Harassment

Investigators must examine the training provided to employees in order to determine what information they are given regarding sexual harassment. This can be especially important when looking at the actions of supervisors and deciding whether they were in compliance with the agency's policies and procedures.

In his survey of women police officers in Florida, Captain Robinson found that almost half (49 percent) did not know when training on sexual harassment was last offered within their agency (Robinson, 1993). In a similar study of fire departments, only 49 percent had a training program in place to address the problem of sexual harassment, and more than one-third reported that this training program was met with resistance by male personnel (Rosell, Miller, & Barber, 1995). Obviously, this is a serious problem if half of all police and fire departments are not offering sexual harassment training on a regular basis.

CHALLENGES IN SEXUAL HARASSMENT TRAINING

Human Resources Department professionals say that the biggest training problem in this area is that employees are uncertain regarding what constitutes sexual harassment.

There are also other problems with training programs designed to prevent and respond to sexual harassment:

- Employees typically don't know the policy on sexual harassment, even when it is repeatedly publicized.

- Even those employees who can correctly identify sexual harassment in hypothetical scenarios are often unable to apply that same assessment to their actual workplace and to real behaviors by their supervisors and coworkers.

- The information provided in training is often inconsistent with the agency's actual policies and procedures and may even be inconsistent with current legal rulings.

- Supervisors often cannot correctly identify sexual harassment, especially in workplaces that are nontraditional for women. This may be either because the culture in the organization is so strong that supervisors are desensitized to such harassing behavior or because they do not recognize the seriousness of complaints about such behavior. Regardless, research demonstrates that front-line supervisors are less likely to correctly identify sexually harassing behaviors than are upper-level managers (Wilkerson, 1999).

- Supervisors are often reluctant to forward complaints of sexual harassment to the Human Resources Department, as required by most agency policies (Reese & Lindenberg, 1999). Some believe that the complaints are petty or that the person making the complaint is overly sensitive; others simply do not want to have to deal with the issue.

- Supervisors often do not know how to respond to complaints even when they do recognize that there is a problem (Reese & Lindenberg, 1999).

Fortunately, training can remedy these problems by helping supervisors to correctly identify sexual harassment and to respond appropriately when it does occur. For example, there is some evidence that training can make supervisors feel more positive about resolving sexual harassment through formal complaint mechanisms (Wilkerson, 1999). Two other types of problems are created when training is done poorly and when there is a gender difference in perceptions.

Poorly Done Training

Obviously, problems can arise when training is done poorly. For example, training programs sometimes feed the unrealistic fear that a single comment or some other trivial behavior will result in a lawsuit. Such misinformation is counterproductive because it doesn't reflect the reality of the situation; instead, it serves to polarize men and women in the workplace. This creates the perception among some employees that the training is "male-bashing" or that it takes "all the fun out of work" by forbidding all personal and/or sexual behaviors.

All too often, these training programs are conducted by someone with a legal background who emphasizes only the prohibitions and penalties against engaging in sexual harassment. This type of training frequently results in officers becoming angry with their female coworkers instead of increasing their understanding of the dynamics of sexual harassment and making a commitment to exhibit proper behavior in the workplace. Therefore, blame-based training programs that concentrate on legal issues and penalties are often counterproductive to increasing the understanding of sexual harassment dynamics.

Gender Difference in Perceptions

Yet another challenge facing anyone seeking to design an effective training program is the substantial difference between how men and women perceive sexual harassment. This is especially true for more minor and/or ambiguous behaviors. For example, men and women are equally likely to identify a situation involving *quid pro quo* behavior with a supervisor as sexual harassment. However, women are more likely than men to correctly identify less blatant behaviors, including sexual comments, derogatory jokes, and displays of pornographic materials, as sexual harassment This is especially true when the women have been sexually harassed themselves. (For a review of this research please see Rotundo, Nguyen, & Sackett, 2001; also Reese & Lindenberg, 1999.)

One of the goals of any effective training program must be to ensure that men and women can accurately identify workplace behaviors that constitute sexual harassment or other forms of gender discrimination. Of course, the same issues arise with differing perceptions between members of other social groups such as age, class, race, religion, color, and sexual orientation. It is therefore critically important to collect information from trusted members of each of these groups to incorporate into a training program if it is to be effective with employees with diverse perspectives.

CONTENT OF A COMPREHENSIVE SEXUAL HARASSMENT TRAINING PROGRAM

Sexual harassment takes place in a workplace culture where abuse of power based on difference is tolerated. In these environments, other forms of discrimination may also be condoned, based on sexual orientation, race or ethnicity, and other forms of difference. Thus, sexual harassment training has to address some of the most fundamental attitudes, perceptions, and misperceptions that people hold. This means that adequate time and resources must be allocated to training on these issues or the agency will waste its resources and fail to adequately address the problem.

In our experience, the best training programs educate people about the dynamics of sexual harassment: why it happens, what effect it has on the victims, and how employees can successfully handle problems that do occur in the workplace. Good training also addresses the perceptions, attitudes, and behaviors about gender differences and the issue of sexual orientation. To be truly comprehensive, sexual harassment training programs should address each of the following areas:

- Elements included in sexual harassment (discussing ways sexual harassment affects employees and emphasizing the message that it will not be tolerated in this workplace)

- Elements not included in sexual harassment (discussing common misconceptions regarding sexual harassment and stating that it is not about mutually desired relationships)
- Legal definition of sexual harassment:

  Quid pro quo sexual harassment

  Hostile work environment

  Reasonable woman standard
- Kinds of behaviors constituting sexual harassment (discussing specific examples that are easily understood in the context of policing or firefighting)
- Sexual harassment laws:

  State laws

  Federal laws

  Relevant court decisions
- Reasons sexual harassment occurs (discussing issues of power and control in the workplace)
- Organizational policies and procedures and the complaint process
- Ways to recognize sexual harassment when it occurs in the workplace
- Measures employees can take to stop sexual harassment:

  Formal measures

  Informal measures
- Other available resources for victims
- Issues of retaliation
- Disciplinary consequences for harassers
- Supervisors' responsibilities (discussing case law)

Additional Sexual Harassment Training for Supervisors

In addition to the mandatory training provided to all employees, additional training must be provided to supervisors to outline their responsibilities for preventing, detecting, and responding to problems of sexual harassment. Training for supervisors must provide both information and opportunities to practice doing the following:

- Monitoring the workplace for signs of sexual harassment, such as offensive materials and comments, sexual jokes, and conversations degrading women
- Employing effective techniques for investigating sexual harassment
- Actively listening to employee complaints to identify workplace problems (often the employee does not use the words "sexual harassment," but the supervisor should nonetheless be able to identify the root of the problem)

- Applying provisions of the policy and the formal complaint procedure, especially when the supervisor must document and forward complaints to the Human Resources Department

- Differentiating legal issues and employer responsibilities

- Applying protections of confidentiality and other legal rights for everyone involved in the investigative process

One of the most important messages for supervisors is that they need to avoid even the appearance of blaming the complainant for any reported sexual harassment. Previous research has documented that complainants who felt blamed by the person to whom they reported their experience of sexual harassment were the most dissatisfied with the process. This element was more important than any other in determining their perceptions of the fairness and effectiveness of the complaint procedure (Reese & Lindenberg, 1999).

DESIGN OF AN EFFECTIVE SEXUAL HARASSMENT TRAINING PROGRAM

Fortunately, experts have offered a number of recommendations regarding the ideal format for sexual harassment training. These are summarized in the sections that follow.

Regularly Scheduled Training Sessions

Most importantly, there is general consensus among the experts that training in sexual harassment must be systematic and ongoing. Specifically, training must be mandatory for all employees within an organization, including members of the command staff and civilian employees. Employees should be asked to sign a form to acknowledge that they were involved in the training program, and this form should be placed in their personnel file. When training programs are regularly conducted, they can reach all the employees within an organization and provide documentation of the organization's efforts to train their employees, thereby reducing organizational liability in future lawsuits. Ongoing training opportunities for employees can therefore include all the following:

- Training sessions for new employees on the sexual harassment policy

- Roll-call sessions (or their equivalent), offered on a quarterly basis, to discuss different aspects of the sexual harassment policy and the complaint procedure

- In-service training sessions, offered on a regular (preferably annual) basis, to provide detailed information about the problem of sexual harassment, including recent legal updates, the agency's policy and complaint procedure, and strategies for preventing sexual harassment and responding effectively.

In fact, we recommend that agencies develop a variety of training sessions that can be used with different audiences, settings, and time constraints.

Sufficient Time for Learning

It should go without saying that a single isolated training session will not be sufficient to change attitudes and behaviors regarding such a difficult problem as sexual harassment. Therefore, training must be provided regularly to all employees, and sufficient time must be allocated for real learning. Additional training must also be given to supervisors on how to maintain a harassment-free workplace and how to respond if harassment occurs. We recommend that this training for supervisors be conducted separately from that provided for nonsupervisory employees both to address the responsibilities of supervisors and to provide an environment amenable to free and open discussions. In addition to this initial training, there should be time set aside for an annual refresher course to give supervisors an update on recent cases and to reemphasize their responsibility to maintain a harassment-free workplace. During the training programs, all employees and supervisors should receive resource materials, such as the agency's sexual harassment policy, its complaint procedures, and appropriate referrals.

Strong Agency Leadership

For a training program to be truly successful, it is important that the chief administrater (e.g., Chief, Sheriff, or Director) of the agency exhibit leadership in the strongest possible terms. For example, the chief administrater should open all sexual harassment training classes, emphasizing his or her commitment to a harassment-free workplace. This message must make it clear that harassment is unprofessional and unacceptable behavior that will not be tolerated and that the agency will enforce sanctions against such behavior. If the chief administrater cannot personally appear at all classes, a videotape of this message should be made and played at the beginning of every class. A high-ranking member of the organization should also be present at every training class to reinforce the department's commitment to a zero-tolerance policy on discrimination or harassment and to ensure that there is no improper behavior during the training session.

Experiential Learning

Of course, training programs are effective only if learning actually takes place, so training is not likely to be effective if it simply consists of reading the policy and listing the penalties for committing sexual harassment. Rather, employees and supervisors must learn what sexual harassment is and how incidents can be prevented, reported, and resolved. Better yet, they should be given the opportunity to *practice* these new skills—with constructive feedback—before transferring them to the workplace. This is especially true when training supervisors about how to respond to sexual harassment complaints.

Strong Facilitators

Effective training in sexual harassment also requires strong facilitators to maintain the focus of discussion on how behaviors are experienced and how they make people feel. It is particularly important that the training session does not deteriorate into one in which victims tell their stories and others vent their anger and frustration over the issues. For this reason, it is usually best to have training teams consisting of men and women from different ethnic groups and including at least one white male command officer. Within law enforcement agencies and fire departments, it is desirable to have command staff involved in presenting the training.

It is also important to have trainers who are highly skilled in both the concepts of sexual harassment and the techniques of teaching adults. Sometimes this requires bringing in a trainer from outside the agency, which can have a number of advantages. Most important, employees often feel more free to discuss the topics openly with someone from outside the agency who is not part of the organizational hierarchy.

Use of Victim's Perspective

Research has further suggested that training may be most effective when it is focused on the victim's perspective and experiences of sexual harassment. This is consistent with the reasonable woman standard discussed in the chapter on legal issues, because the courts view behavior from the perspective of the person experiencing it, not from that of the person engaging in the behavior. This also incorporates the idea that the same behavior will have different meanings for individuals, based not only on their gender but also on their age, class, ethnic background, religion, national origin, sexual orientation, etc.

In other words, it doesn't matter what an employee's motivations or intentions are when they are engaging in sexual harassment or other forms of discrimination. It is the behavior that counts, especially how that behavior is perceived by the person experiencing it. Employees should therefore be advised that the most effective way of preventing sexual harassment is to err on the side of caution by refraining from any questionable behaviors and by checking with coworkers to see if their behavior is in fact unwelcome.

Small Workshops for Different Groups

Effective training programs can employ both small mixed-gender workshops and same-sex discussions. It is our opinion that sworn staff should be trained only in mixed-gender workshops because attempts to train women separately from men have proved to be divisive. However, we believe that it is appropriate to train nonsworn civilian employees separately from sworn personnel because the former often have serious issues that they are reluctant to discuss when sworn personnel are present. It is our experience that women working in nonsworn positions in law enforcement, in particular, often suffer much more sexual harassment and gender discrimination because of their "inferior status" in the organization.

Some have also recommended that training programs should break up peer groups and structured workgroups to facilitate a wider range of discussion. In addition, it is best if the groups can be structured so that there is more than one member of each gender and ethnic group. It can be extremely intimidating to be the single (token) female or minority group member in a sexual harassment training program, and this situation should be avoided whenever possible.

Response to Anonymous Complaints

One of the advantages of ongoing training programs is that they can be used to reach specific workgroups or units in which there have been problems, rumors, or anonymous complaints of sexual harassment. Training can be provided to a workgroup or unit, sometimes even without members realizing that the real motivation was a problem or complaint (Reese & Lindenberg, 1999).

Remedial Training

It is sometimes desirable to provide remedial training to employees who have been found to have violated the policy on sexual harassment. One method is to schedule a private training session with the offender and an attorney experienced in employment discrimination law. The purpose is to have the attorney explain the personal ramifications of further violations of the policy and to discuss what types of behaviors are prohibited. Based on our experience, this makes a serious impression on the offender and provides excellent documentation of the agency's efforts to correct the problem.

OTHER EDUCATIONAL EFFORTS

In addition to the formal training program, police and fire departments must also pursue other avenues for educating employees on the topic of sexual harassment and the agency's policy and complaint procedure. As with the formal training program, these other educational efforts must demonstrate a strong commitment by upper management and highlight the critical importance of eliminating sexual harassment within the organization. This message of zero tolerance must be communicated regularly in a variety of ways. For example, education on the problem of sexual harassment and the agency's policy and complaint procedure can be provided in annual training bulletins, published every year to provide legal updates and reinforce messages from the formal training program. Videotapes, made by the agency head and addressing the problems of discrimination and harassment, can be played at roll-call training sessions or staff meetings; when not in use, the videotapes should be stored somewhere and be easily accessible to all agency employees.

Dissemination of Agency Policy

As discussed in the chapter on policies, other educational efforts can also include repeatedly disseminating the policy on sexual harassment and discrimination in the following ways:

- Having employees read and sign the policy every year during the performance evaluation process
- Providing the policy in the employment package for new employees
- Periodically distributing the policy along with paychecks

- Describing the policy in a newsletter or other publication within the agency
- Mentioning the policy in an annual statement from the sheriff or fire chief
- Rating employees on their compliance with the policy during their annual performance evaluation

Such efforts remind employees that sexual harassment will not be tolerated and that the agency has a commitment to taking the issue seriously. Sexual harassment issues can also be addressed in more general training programs targeting team building, employee wellness, ethics issues, and other programs focused on inappropriate workplace behaviors; however, such training should never be used to *replace* specific training in sexual harassment.

Importance of Employee Surveys

Within the context of training and other educational efforts, managers within police and fire departments should consider regularly conducting surveys with their employees. Such surveys can be extremely useful in uncovering sexual harassment or other problems that may not be evident to those in upper-level management. The data from these surveys can be used for a number of purposes, such as providing data for improving policies and procedures, evaluating the impact of the training program, designing problem-solving efforts, and sparking discussion in training programs.

Of course, these surveys must be confidential and be conducted by someone with expertise in social sciences methodology; there are often individuals in the community or in institutions of higher education who can assist. Surveys can be particularly helpful in gathering information from various social groups within the organization based on their gender, age, ethnic background, class, religion, national origin, and sexual orientation. Often an anonymous survey is the best way to uncover issues and problems that are being experienced by members of minority groups.

EVALUATION OF SEXUAL HARASSMENT TRAINING

The primary goal of sexual harassment training is prevention, and research documents that individuals with greater awareness and less tolerance of sexual harassment are less likely to engage in problematic behaviors. However, other training goals include improving the organizational response to problems so that employees are better able to report harassing situations, supervisors are better able to respond effectively, and the agency can protect its employees from workplace stress and avoid costly litigation. Other results of a sexual harassment training program are somewhat more intangible; for example, training in sexual harassment might have the goals of improving employee morale and productivity, increasing sensitivity, and improving negative attitudes and behaviors directed toward women. However, keep in mind that it is not uncommon for an effective training program to actually *increase* reporting of sexual harassment, as people become more aware of their rights and the complaint process. If this happens, managers in police and fire departments can take heart—this is actually a positive result of the training.

To determine whether training is achieving the desired goals, evaluation research is critical. The effectiveness of the training program can be evaluated in a number of ways, including the number of reported instances of sexual harassment, results of employee surveys, performance appraisals of supervisors, and interviews with employees to determine if targeted behaviors have changed as a result of the training. On the other hand, measures of participant satisfaction are often inadequate because the perception that employees like the program may not tell us anything about whether it is effective. For assistance with designing such evaluation research, police and fire departments can consult with an expert drawn from the community or a local university.

RESULTS OF EXISTING EVALUATION RESEARCH

While police and fire departments are encouraged to conduct evaluation research to determine whether their training programs are meeting their desired goals, it is possible to learn from existing research about what is and is not likely to be effective. In sum, the research tells us that training programs, even when they are relatively brief (approximately two hours), can be effective at improving the knowledge and perceptions of participants (Barak, 1994; Beauvais, 1986; Blakeley, Blakeley, & Moorman, 1998; Bonate & Jessell, 1996; Jacobs, Bergen, & Korn, 2000; Lillich, Webster, Marshall, Smith, Seaver, & Szeluga, 2000; Moyer & Nath, 1998; Roscoe, Strouse, Goodwin, Taracks, & Henderson, 1994; Thomann, Strickland, & Gibbons, 1989; York, Barclay, & Zajack, 1997) however, common sense suggests that programs are much more likely to be effective if they are longer, more frequent, and supported with strong messages from upper management.

Most employers use videotapes as part of their training program, but the videotapes' effectiveness is limited, especially if they are shown without any subsequent discussion or additional training (Perry, Kulik, & Schmidtke, 1998; Robb & Doverspike, 2001). In fact, the evidence seems to suggest that written materials may be more effective than video presentations, although this would obviously depend on the content and quality of each method. Written materials are particularly effective when participants are asked to make a series of judgments after reading the information, as in a case study analysis (Bonate & Jessell, 1996; Moyer & Nath, 1998; York, Barclay, & Zajack, 1997).

On the one hand, research has documented that videos can be effective in improving the identification of behaviors as sexually harassing, perhaps because they can show more subtle forms of human interaction than a written scenario. On the other hand, these improvements may actually be due more to the discussion afterward than to the video presentation itself (Blakeley, Blakeley, & Moorman, 1998). Based on the principles of adult education, videos may not be sufficiently engaging to produce real learning unless they are accompanied by discussion, role-play exercises, case analyses, or other interactive activities.

Regardless of the format used (written information or videotape), it is critically important for training programs to require participants to actively process the information by making detailed judgments or engaging in structured discussions. Employees are not likely to learn as effectively if they are simply exposed to the information by passively reading it or by viewing a videotape presentation by itself.

Tips for the Investigator

As was the case with issues of policy, investigators are not typically responsible for designing, implementing, or evaluating the agency's training program for sexual harassment prevention. Nonetheless, investigators can take a number of steps to improve the agency's response to this problem. They will also need to review training records when investigating a complaint of sexual harassment to determine what information was provided to the respondent and when this information was last updated. When evaluating the quality of the training program, it is important for investigators to do the following:

- Review the training program provided to employees for the following issues:

  Was the training program ever reviewed for legal accuracy? When?

  Is the program based on principles of adult education, and does it include opportunities to practice new skills (such as case studies or scenarios)?

  Does the program emphasize harm to the victim?

  Are the training participants given handout materials?

  Does the program cover the agency policy?

  What are the qualifications of the individuals providing the training?

  Are men and women both utilized as trainers?

  Do the facilitators represent different racial, ethnic, and social groups within the organization?

  Are command staff involved in monitoring the classes?

  Are command staff involved in conducting the training?

  Was the program ever evaluated to determine whether training objectives are actually being met? (This could be accomplished using employee surveys or other types of evaluation research.)

  Was the head of the agency present at the training to issue a message on policy? If not, was a video message from the agency head included?

When investigating a specific complaint of sexual harassment, it is important to do the following:

- Review the training records of the respondent for these issues:

  What dates did the respondent attend training?

  How many hours of training were provided on each date?

  Did the respondent successfully pass any tests conducted in class?

  Were there dates that the respondent was scheduled to attend sexual harassment training but failed to do so? If so, was that training rescheduled?

(continued)

Tips for the Investigator (*continued*)

What other types of training were documented as being provided to the respondent?

Is there a record of roll-call training at which the respondent was present?

Do the training records reflect that the respondent attended outside training programs in which sexual harassment was discussed?

What other types of related training (e.g., ethics, team building) did the respondent receive?

Did the respondent receive a copy of the sexual harassment policy?

Was a copy of the policy mailed to the respondent's home?

Was a copy of the policy included in the respondent's paycheck?

Were training bulletins issued that were presented to the respondent?

- Determine whether the respondents who are supervisors should have been aware of their responsibilities for monitoring the workplace, intervening in situations of unacceptable behavior, and appropriately dealing with employee complaints by finding out the following:

What efforts were made by the agency to make sure that supervisors were aware of these responsibilities?

Is there documentation that supervisors disseminated the policy statement, participated in training programs, received a supervisor's manual, and attended special classes for supervisors?

Chapter 9

Responsibilities of Supervisors and Managers Regarding Sexual Harassment

Investigators must understand what the law requires of supervisors and managers when they know or should know about problems in the workplace. This chapter also addresses the situation in which a supervisor or a manager is accused of committing sexual harassment or failing to respond appropriately to a complaint.

DEFINITION OF SUPERVISOR OR MANAGER

When the courts attempt to determine who is a supervisor or manager, these are some questions they consider: Does the person have the authority to hire and fire or to give meaningful input for those decisions? Does the person evaluate performance? Does the person assign work? Does the person have the authority to impose discipline? Within law enforcement and firefighting, the first-line supervisor often has many of these powers, as do others not formally considered to be a supervisor or a manager by the organization (e.g., shift leader, team leader).

SUPERVISORS' AND MANAGERS' LEGAL RESPONSIBILITIES

According to the law, supervisors and managers have a special responsibility for preventing or stopping any problems with sexual harassment, discrimination, and retaliation in the workplace. In fact, supervisors and managers may even be held personally liable in some states based on either their involvement in discrimination and retaliation or their failure to properly handle these issues. Agencies are therefore responsible for providing the training that supervisors and managers need to fulfill their responsibilities.

In fact, some states have even begun to enact legislation mandating that employers provide training in sexual harassment prevention for those employees in supervisory or management positions. Supervisors and managers must do the following:

- Learn the policies and procedures for responding to sexual harassment, and be able to explain them to subordinates.

- Monitor their unit for problems with sexual harassment and respond proactively, even in situations in which no one comes forward with a complaint.

- Respond in accordance with agency policy when problems occur, which typically requires referring the situation to the appropriate contact person.

- Monitor the workplace for breaches of confidentiality and retaliatory actions while an investigation is underway. (This responsibility extends even after the investigation has been completed and any discipline imposed.)

To ensure that supervisors and managers are fulfilling these responsibilities, their performance evaluations must include ratings of these activities, which are taken into account when they are being considered for promotion or specialized assignments. Similarly, they should include ratings of their subordinates on the degree to which the subordinates comply with the agency's sexual harassment policy and generally treat others with respect.

SUPERVISORS' AND MANAGERS' SEXUAL HARASSMENT PREVENTION STRATEGIES

As we have previously stated, the single best way for a supervisor or manager to prevent any problems with sexual harassment is to set a standard for professional conduct in the workplace and to hold subordinates responsible for abiding by that standard. For example, the workplace should be free of any favoritism, jokes, and ridicule. By treating all employees in a professional manner and with respect, supervisors and managers will help to establish a productive workplace. There are also other ways that supervisors and managers can deal with the issue of sexual harassment.

Model Appropriate Behavior

This modeling will include exhibiting workplace behaviors that are professional and respectful. It also requires addressing issues of harassment regularly to communicate expectations and give information on how to report problems that do arise.

Pay Attention to the Way Women Are Treated in Workplace.   By observing the behavior of subordinates and how they interact with each other, supervisors can determine whether women are being singled out or subjected to hazing, jokes, or other inappropriate behaviors.

Establish Good Communication With Female Employees. If supervisors and managers establish open lines of communication with the women working for them, female subordinates will be more likely to raise any issues or problems they experience.

Immediately Put a Stop to Inappropriate Behaviors. When supervisors and managers observe any inappropriate behavior occurring in the workplace, they must immediately stop it. In some cases, this may require taking the offender aside to discuss the inappropriate behaviors and make sure they will stop. For a supervisor or manager who is uncertain whether a particular behavior was considered offensive by another employee, it may sometimes be a good idea to check with the employee privately to determine whether the behavior was in fact unwelcome. However, in most situations, the supervisor or manager should not rely on other employees to indicate that the behavior is offensive or unwelcome but should take measures immediately to stop any behavior that is obviously unprofessional or in violation of the agency's policy.

Intervene in Problem Situations.   In some situations, it is necessary for supervisors and managers to intervene to stop the inappropriate behavior, even if other employees are present. For example, at a staff briefing, one employee might make a sexual comment to another. The supervisor or manager must then take immediate action. One way to handle this would be to say, "That is inappropriate language for this workplace." This action sends a message to that employee and all others present; it also lets the victim know that such behavior will not be tolerated.

Respond Appropriately to Complaints. When supervisors and managers are informed of sexual harassment or discrimination taking place—even if it is through anonymous channels or workplace gossip—they must take immediate steps to stop it, protect the victim, and make sure that the appropriate people are contacted. They are also responsible for preventing retaliation against the complainant or other employees who cooperate with the investigation. In some situations, supervisors and managers may be assigned to investigate the incident themselves, although we recommend that the investigation be referred to someone within the Human Resources Department. Either way, supervisors and managers should always document complaints and the actions they took to resolve the situation, including appropriate referrals.

SUPERVISORS' AND MANAGERS' INAPPROPRIATE ACTIONS

In contrast, there are a number of things that supervisors and managers should *not* do if they want to avoid problems with sexual harassment, discrimination, and retaliation.

Use or Condone Use of Inappropriate Language.   Words that have sexual meanings or that degrade women are not appropriate in the workplace.

Tell or Allow Jokes.   When humor is analyzed, most jokes either make fun of someone or have a sexual meaning, and neither is appropriate in the workplace. Therefore, supervisors and managers must avoid telling jokes and see to it that other employees do not tell jokes in the workplace. It is not part of the supervisor's or manager's job to see that employees are entertained. Jokes are particularly inappropriate if they refer to women or other social groups such as those defined by race, religion, ethnic background, national origin, age, or sexual orientation.

Touch Employees.   There are a few exceptions when a training situation might necessitate touching an employee. However, in general, supervisors and managers should not develop the habit of touching subordinates, even though their intentions might be good. For example, a hug that is intended to reassure an employee can be perceived as a sexual overture; in addition, it may send the wrong message to other employees that touching is acceptable.

Hold Employees to Different Standards of Performance.   As much as possible, supervisors and managers should strive to establish levels of performance that are consistent for all the employees in a particular job classification. Requiring more work from some employees in comparison with others can certainly be the basis for a legitimate complaint.

Fail to Listen to and Act on Complaints of Discrimination or Harassment.   If an employee complains about inappropriate behavior in the workplace, supervisors and managers must always follow the agency's rules for investigating and resolving the complaint. Many lawsuits are based on their failure to act when they are advised of a problem.

Try to Talk Complainant Out of Filing Complaint.   Supervisors and managers must never try to talk the complainant out of filing a complaint. Given the sensitivity of the issue, even simple comments—such as "Are you sure you want to file a complaint?" or "Do you realize that this could affect the respondent's chances for promotion?" or "Filing a complaint could be upsetting to the morale of the unit"—may be interpreted by the complainant as pressure to not file a complaint. Such comments should be avoided; in fact, they may result in additional charges in a lawsuit for failing to respond appropriately.

Retaliate Against Complainant or Others.   If an employee makes a complaint about discrimination or harassment, supervisors and managers must never retaliate against that person or anyone else for cooperating with the investigation. The courts view retaliation as a very serious act, and employees must be able to come forward with complaints without fear of retaliation from their supervisors and managers.

Fail to Stop Retaliation on Part of Coworkers.   During and after a sexual harassment investigation, it is extremely important for supervisors and managers to be alert for signs of retaliation. If they fail to stop retaliation, it can increase their personal liability as well as the liability of the organization. This is one of the areas in which an agency's liability can increase substantially—when an employee experiences retaliation after filling a complaint, testifying for the complainant, or otherwise cooperating with an investigation.

These issues are discussed in greater detail in the chapter on retaliation.

SUPERVISORS' AND MANAGERS' RESPONSES TO SEXUAL HARASSMENT

As we have discussed previously, supervisors and managers can become aware of problems with sexual harassment, either because an employee has complained or because they have observed the situation personally. In either case, they must immediately meet with the complainant to take a complete statement of the facts. During that preliminary interview, supervisors and managers must also take the following actions.

Explain Investigative Procedures and Rights of Complainant.　Usually this will mean that the complaint will be sent to a person who is trained to handle discrimination investigations. The complainant should therefore be told where the complaint will be sent and when he or she can expect to be contacted. The supervisor or manager should also call personnel in the investigative unit to alert them that a complaint is coming and to explain that the complainant is expecting to be contacted.

Ask Complainant What He or She Would Like to See Happen in Situation. Oftentimes, the complainant just wants the behavior stopped. As a result, the supervisor or manager may be able to take some immediate steps to resolve the situation, such as removing offensive pictures or intervening to preventing joking in the workplace. Nevertheless, the complaint must still be forwarded for investigation.

Ask Complainant if He or She Is Comfortable Remaining in Current Assignment. If so, the supervisor or manager must monitor the workplace to ensure that retaliation does not occur. If not, the supervisor or manager should ask the complainant what assignment would make him or her feel more comfortable; then command staff will determine what actions will be taken. This issue is discussed in greater detail in the chapter regarding the complaint process.

Explain Steps to Be Taken to Prevent Retaliation.　The steps may include moving the complainant at his or her request, reassigning the respondent, monitoring the workplace, and keeping in touch with the complainant.

Document Meeting.　A complete report of the interview and any actions taken by the supervisor or manager must be immediately prepared and forwarded to the investigative unit.

Notify Supervisor, Manager, or Other Employee Responsible for Receiving Complaints. This notification process is usually laid out in the policy on harassment and discrimination.

For supervisors and managers who are assigned to investigate the issue themselves, they must notify the respondent of the allegations and clearly state that retaliation is prohibited and that it will be punished if substantiated. They must then proceed by following the guidelines outlined in the previous chapters. They must also review the documents and other evidence and make a determination before writing the final investigative report and forwarding it for administrative review. At the end of the investigation, all parties must be notified of the results of the investigation and actions to be taken. Investigators must be sure to review labor agreements, personnel policies, and state laws to determine what information can be given to each party.

SUPERVISORS' AND MANAGERS' PREVENTION OF RETALIATION

For supervisors and managers who become aware of retaliation experienced by the complainant or anyone else who is cooperating with an investigation, it is critically important to meet with that person as soon as possible. Whether it is the complainant or another witness, the employee must be reassured that the agency does not allow retaliation and that it will be thoroughly investigated and will be punished severely if substantiated. The supervisor or manager must also notify other management staff of the situation and ask for their assistance in monitoring for any retaliation. All these efforts should be carefully documented and forwarded for administrative review.

ACCUSATIONS OF HARASSMENT OR DISCRIMINATION AGAINST SUPERVISORS AND MANAGERS

When a supervisor or a manager is the person accused of sexual harassment or discrimination, the challenges of a successful investigation only increase. In these situations, it is especially important to have the respondent read and sign the policy regarding confidentiality and retaliation. The accused supervisor or manager must then be directly ordered to not discuss the case with anyone other than the investigative staff, to not conduct a personal investigation, and to not retaliate against the complainant or anyone else involved in the investigation. The respondent should also be reminded that breaches of policy regarding confidentiality and retaliation both constitute separate violations that will be investigated and will be punished severely if substantiated.

In such a situation, it is also critically important to make immediate changes to the work environment to ensure that the accused supervisor or manager is no longer in the complainant's direct chain of command. While this can be accomplished by removing the complainant, the supervisor or manager, or both from the workplace, each option has a number of serious concerns that must be addressed. Legal counsel is always recommended. For further discussion of this issue, please see the chapter on the complaint process.

As we have discussed in other chapters, it may be possible in situations in which the supervisor or manager is accused of harassment or discrimination to "disguise" the identity of the complainant by asking questions about others who are not involved in the investigation. This can be accomplished by asking questions about everyone in the work unit or everyone in a position comparable to that of the complainant. Such a strategy is likely to be particularly helpful when investigating complaints of a hostile work environment that is created or condoned by the accused supervisor or manager because the same work environment would be shared by all employees in the unit and anyone—at least theoretically—could have filed the complaint.

When supervisors and managers are interviewed as respondents, it is also particularly important to ask whether they have received a copy of the sexual harassment policy and whether they have read it and understand it. They must also be asked whether they have attended a training class in sexual harassment and whether they understood the information provided. For more information on exactly what to ask supervisors and managers and how to document their responses, please refer to the chapter on interviewing the respondent.

Tips for the Investigator

Supervisors and managers have responsibilities regarding sexual harassment in the workplace. Investigators should do the following:

- Review the sexual harassment policy to determine what responsibilities are placed on supervisors and managers with respect to this issue. Make sure this policy is updated in accordance with new laws, court decisions, and agency regulations.

- Review the training provided to supervisors and managers regarding their responsibility to monitor the workplace and prevent discrimination, harassment, and retaliation. Encourage members of the management staff to systematically evaluate the quality and impact of this training.

- Encourage members of the management staff to implement a tracking system to identify when supervisors and managers last received training on the subject of sexual harassment prevention.

- Review the situation carefully when a complainant makes allegations against a coworker for sexual harassment *and* against a supervisor for failing to take action. It may be in the best interest of the complainant to be reassigned to avoid being in the direct chain of command with that supervisor. Be sure to discuss options with the complainant to determine how this situation should be handled, and consult with legal counsel.

- Open a second and separate investigation if allegations are made that sexual harassment was reported to a supervisor or a manager who failed to take action. The interview with the supervisor or manager can then follow the guidelines in the chapter on interviewing the respondent, as the same issues apply. Such an approach is necessary to truly hold supervisors and managers accountable for fulfilling their responsibilities with respect to monitoring the workplace and responding to complainants appropriately.

Chapter 10

Complaint Procedures

Many police and fire departments offer only a single formal complaint procedure, but victims of sexual harassment should be given a number of options for reporting their complaint. This chapter outlines a number of informal and formal complaint procedures that can be successfully implemented in police and fire departments.

FORMAL VERSUS INFORMAL COMPLAINT PROCEDURES

Advantages and Disadvantages of Formal Complaint Procedures

Effective complaint procedures can take a variety of forms, both formal and informal. Formal complaint procedures have the advantages of accountability, closure for the complainant, and written records. Many police and fire departments offer only a single formal complaint process, and this is unfortunate for a number of reasons. First, the formal process is not always the best in terms of time and cost as well as the emotional toll it takes on everyone involved. Second, a formal process may not be the most effective means for addressing more subtle or covert behaviors that are not easily documented, proven, or corrected, such as the silent treatment.

Third, formal complaint procedures often require employees to report complaints through the rank structure. Of course, someone in the complainant's rank structure may actually be the harasser, so this will obviously discourage many victims of sexual harassment from coming forward. For all of these reasons, formal complaint procedures should constitute only one avenue for responding to sexual harassment; victims of sexual harassment should also be given a number of other options for reporting their complaint informally.

Advantages and Disadvantages of Informal Complaint Procedures

Informal complaint procedures have a number of advantages for victims of sexual harassment because they can often provide more immediate relief while preserving confidentiality. They can even serve a function that is communicative and educative rather than punitive, which some victims of sexual harassment find empowering. Informal complaint procedures may be particularly effective in situations that are based on misunderstanding or ignorance on the part of the harasser. For example, outcomes of an informal complaint procedure could include a verbal or written apology from the harasser, which is unlikely in a more formal complaint process.

Given that a formal investigation can often permanently damage work relationships, polarize the work environment, and fuel the potential for retaliatory actions, it is understandable why many victims choose a more informal procedure for responding to sexual harassment if given the option.

On the other hand, there are also a number of important disadvantages to an informal complaint process:

- Because discipline is not included as part of the informal process, it obviously lacks the accountability of a formal process. It may therefore send the wrong message (especially to the respondent) that sexual harassment is not taken seriously.

- It may also fail to provide the kind of closure that some employees want because an informal complaint process does not typically reach a definitive conclusion or finding of fault.

- Informal complaint procedures can also be quite arbitrary if they depend entirely on the skill of the persons responsible. This can be particularly problematic when there are no records kept because it is then impossible to evaluate the competence of the persons handling complaints or assess the consistency of the process from one complainant to the next.

- Informal procedures may even create a situation in which some victims are discouraged from filing a formal complaint and pushed toward more informal mechanisms. This can later result in liability for the organization.

- The informal nature of the process can make it difficult to keep accurate records, but it is critically important to track the behaviors and individuals involved in complaints to ensure that the organization is responding consistently to sexual harassment problems. Records must be kept for tracking even if they are not included in an employee's personnel file.

Of course, none of these flaws are fatal because anyone who is not satisfied with the outcome of these informal procedures can then turn to the formal complaint process. Employees can also choose to skip the informal options altogether and proceed directly to the formal complaint process. By having both a formal and informal process, an organization provides victims with a wider range of options and increases the likelihood that they will come forward to seek some form of assistance.

INFORMAL COMPLAINT PROCEDURES

An informal complaint procedure can include an ombudsperson, contact people, general training, mediation, and other procedures; these models are described below. However, we want to add a strong word of caution about establishing an informal procedure. Regardless of the specific form of informal complaint process that is implemented, it is critically important that all the people involved are highly trained and keep careful records. There should be frequent audits of the programs to make sure that complaints are being appropriately handled and that complainants are not being discouraged from pursuing more formal options.

Ombudsperson Programs

Organizations across the country are increasingly using an ombudsperson as an alternative confidential means to encourage the resolution of workplace issues informally and at an early stage. In some situations, an ombudsperson may serve as a mediator to address workplace conflicts; in other cases, the ombudsperson might provide assistance to complainants so they are better equipped to address the issues on their own by telling the respondent to stop the offensive behavior and documenting the situation.

Because there is no investigation conducted by the ombudsperson, discipline is not one of the possible outcomes, but the informal nature of the ombudsperson program means that confidentiality can typically be protected to a greater extent than in the formal complaint system. This is an important advantage of the program for many victims seeking to come forward for referral and assistance in a situation of sexual harassment. Ombudsperson programs may even include a hotline number to provide information anonymously. In her description of the ombudsperson model, Spratlen (1997) described a five-stage process:

1. A complaint is received by the ombudsperson, who educates the complainant about the process and helps him or her to select among the available options, depending on the specifics of the situation and the stated needs.

2. The ombudsperson counsels the complainant to help him or her understand the situation and to practice skills in responding effectively.

3. An intervention is designed that is unique to the situation and the people involved. For example, interventions can involve confronting the respondent, engaging in mediation, and making specific changes to the work environment to improve the situation.

4. The ombudsperson might next meet with the respondent to explain the situation and to assist in resolving the problem. This discussion must include a clear message that the harassing behavior will stop and that the complainant will not be targeted with retaliation.

5. All cases require follow-up to ensure that the harassment has stopped and that no retaliation has occurred. This is typically most effective when it includes follow-up with the supervisor in the unit in which the harassment occurred in order to implement more systemic changes to prevent similar future occurrences. Referral information may also be provided to the complainant, respondent, or both; this can include referrals for mental health counseling, education or training, and other services.

To be effective, the ombudsperson must keep records on the cases handled in order to track the kinds of situations and outcomes that are achieved. Reports can then be submitted periodically to describe workplace issues that have been brought to their attention and to offer suggestions for improving the policies and procedures of the organization. While an ombudsperson program is likely to be most effective with individuals who are formally assigned that role within the organization, smaller organizations may consider utilizing volunteers—as long as they receive sufficient training, resources, and support to fulfill their responsibilities as ombudspersons.

Experience has shown that significant workplace issues can be identified and successfully resolved through ombudspersons, even when the problems do not surface through more formal reporting mechanisms. As a result, the U.S. Department of Justice, the Federal Bureau of Investigation, and the Federal Bureau of Prisons have all used ombudsperson programs. In addition to their documented success, the savings of these programs are obvious, in terms of both money and personal turmoil, by avoiding more formal mechanisms for resolving disputes. For example, one university ombudsperson program reported that only 4 of 600 sexual harassment complaints were referred to the formal process for resolution. (Spratlen, 1997)

Contact Person Programs

A variant on the ombudsperson model is the use a cadre of volunteers throughout the organization to serve as contact people. Because they are volunteers, contact people typically play a more limited role than an ombudsperson, primarily serving as an access point to the formal complaint process; however, they offer additional avenues for employees to report situations and provide information, advocacy, referrals, and other forms of assistance.

The primary job of a contact person is to take preliminary information on an incident and refer it to either informal mediators or the more formal complaint process. Their role is not to investigate, judge, counsel, or intervene; instead, contact people are trained to listen to the complainant describe the problem, inform the person of the options for responding, follow up with the complainant regarding his or her welfare, and notify the coordinator that a case was received (Blaxall, Parsonson, & Robertson, 1993). This program could therefore easily be incorporated into the peer counseling programs that already exist in many agencies.

When this type of contact person program was implemented in one organization, initial training included not only written information but also a series of video simulations to practice the required skills. All contact persons received a total of 11 hours of training time, and they were required to master the role-play simulations by exhibiting 90 percent of the required behaviors. The research documented that contact people did in fact master the desired behaviors, suggesting that such a program can be successful for supplementing an agency's response to problems of sexual harassment (Blaxall, Parsonson, & Robertson, 1993).

One of the advantages of the contact person model is that numerous individuals can be trained to play this role and act as access points throughout the organization. Their presence can therefore serve to encourage victims of sexual harassment to come forward and discuss their situation with someone who can help them evaluate their options for responding. The contact people are most likely to be effective if they represent varying social groups within the organization, based on their rank, assignment, gender, age, ethnic identification, class, religion, national origin, and sexual orientation. They should also meet regularly to share experiences, learn from each other, and participate in ongoing training opportunities.

General Training

Victims of sexual harassment can also be given the option of requesting training for their workgroup or unit to improve their work situation. If this option is selected by the complainant, the ombudsperson or another person who is responsible for handling the training request must follow up to determine whether the harassment has stopped and whether the complainant has experienced any retaliation as a result.

General training may be particularly effective with more subtle or covert behaviors that do not lend themselves well to investigation and formal adjudication. The training program can also be accompanied by other changes in the workplace, such as recruiting more women and minorities or improving supervision in the unit. Although there is no investigation conducted, records still must be kept to track the situation and outcome.

Mediation

Mediation is also sometimes recommended as an option for resolving complaints of sexual harassment and other forms of workplace discrimination, so a settlement agreement can be negotiated and signed by the parties. Such a process may be seen as fair by employees and therefore increase compliance with the settlement provisions. However, it requires considerable premediation discussion with each party and an advocate present for each party at every proceeding. The mediation process must obviously be conducted extremely carefully because it is volatile and can even become an extension of the sexual harassment if not done properly. In addition, mediation should never be used in situations of severe harassment or sexual assault or with people of different ranks within the agency.

When complainants select mediation to resolve their complaint informally, the procedure must be voluntary on the part of both the complainant and the respondent. Both must agree to the process and state that they will comply with the details of whatever settlement is achieved. Of course, the complainant can choose another option, such as the formal complaint procedure, if the outcome is unsatisfactory. There is typically no formal involvement by the employer during the mediation process.

Other Informal Complaint Procedures

While several models for informal complaint procedures have already been discussed, there are additional possibilities for ways in which employees can bring issues of sexual harassment to the attention of their agency.

Hotlines

Agencies should consider establishing a hotline to receive complaints anonymously and to answer questions regarding sexual harassment and other forms of workplace discrimination. The hotline can be operated by the ombudsperson program, the contact person program, or the department with responsibility for receiving formal complaints (e.g., Human Resources, Equal Employment Opportunity).

Focus Groups and Climate Surveys

Agencies should periodically hold focus groups with employees who may experience sexual harassment or other forms of workplace discrimination. Another method of gaining input is to conduct anonymous climate surveys of employees, as discussed in greater detail in other chapters.

Employee Organizations

Management should also encourage employee organizations such as labor unions and professional associations for women and minorities to help identify problems in the system and encourage employees to report incidents of harassment. Regular meetings can be scheduled between members of the administration and representatives of these employee organizations to collect their information and input. However, unions should not be the only employee organization to be utilized; in law enforcement and firefighting, for example, some of the problems faced by women have been largely ignored by their unions.

FORMAL COMPLAINT PROCEDURES

A formal complaint process includes an investigation and the possibility for discipline as well as an appeal process, which is preferably made to an outside arbitrator, a peer review panel, or a board of appeal. For a number of reasons, formal complaint procedures are best operated by the personnel division, whether this is located within the police or fire department itself or in the external government structure (city, county, state, or federal). For one thing, experts in personnel usually have a thorough understanding of the issues involved in workplace discrimination and harassment and are therefore better equipped to handle these complaints than investigators in Internal Affairs or other units within the agency. In addition, complaints of discrimination and harassment are emotionally charged and often have political implications, so personnel experts are often the best ones to act as neutral fact finders.

Separate Discrimination Units

In our opinion, the most effective mechanism for investigating and resolving complaints of discrimination and harassment is a special discrimination investigation unit. Such specialized units are most effective if they have the following characteristics:

- They are separate from the Internal Affairs division and have the authority to investigate complaints from all sworn and civilian personnel regarding sexual harassment and other forms of workplace discrimination, such as that based on sex, race, national origin, age, sexual orientation, disability, or other protected status.

- They are located off-site to provide maximum confidentiality for complainants and respondents.

- They are headed by a commanding officer of the same rank as the commanding officer of the Internal Affairs division.

- They are structured to report directly to the chief administrator of the organization.

- They are staffed with civilian experts in personnel issues who have expertise in the areas of sexual harassment and employment law.

- They are provided with ongoing training by community experts on the issues of employment discrimination, such as gender, race, sexual orientation, disability, and age.

- They are given direct access to legal advisors with expertise in the law pertaining to employment discrimination.

- They coordinate their actions with related agency divisions and selected personnel, especially Internal Affairs, Human Resources, Equal Employment Opportunity (EEO), behavioral sciences, and training.

Other Alternatives

If an agency cannot create a separate unit, there are various other configurations for assigning investigators to complaints of sexual harassment and other forms of workplace discrimination.

Internal Affairs

Investigators in Internal Affairs are accustomed to investigating employee misconduct, and they can therefore be assigned responsibility for handling complaints of sexual harassment and other forms of workplace discrimination. However, they must first be thoroughly trained in the legal issues involved, and they must understand the dynamics of sexual harassment and the reasons why victims are typically reluctant to report this behavior. Moreover, complaints of discrimination and sexual harassment must be clearly differentiated from other cases of officer misconduct and must be appropriately classified and separately tracked. One of the biggest hurdles to overcome when assigning discrimination complaints to the Internal Affairs division is that those personnel are trained to look at a finite issue, so they often do not understand or appropriately investigate problems such as those that arise in hostile workplace situations. For example, when a complainant reports two or three things that have occurred at different times in the workplace, Internal Affairs investigators tend to look at each one as a stand-alone issue instead of dealing with all of them together as a single situation and also looking at the workplace to determine if there are more examples of harassing behaviors.

Detective Division

Detectives assigned to sex crimes or child abuse cases may make good investigators for harassment complaints, given their understanding of the dynamics of sexual victimization; however, they must be thoroughly trained in the laws pertaining to sexual harassment and other forms of workplace discrimination to be effective.

EEO Coordinator

Alternatively, the agency could appoint an EEO coordinator in the office of the chief administrator (chief, sheriff, director, etc.). This person must be trained in discrimination and sexual harassment law and then given the necessary resources to conduct effective investigations. This would include a private office that is physically removed from that of the chief administrator.

External Agency

For some police and fire departments, the complaint procedure is located outside the agency in a governmental (city, county, state, or federal) agency. In some situations, this can create the perception that investigators are more objective and therefore more credible. By locating the complaint procedure outside the agency where the harassment or discrimination is occurring, this arrangement may also decrease fears regarding confidentiality and retaliation.

IMPLEMENTATION OF THE COMPLAINT PROCESS

There are several steps that should be taken in the implementation of the complaint process.

Establish User-Friendly Procedures

Regardless of whether someone files a complaint through the informal or formal procedures, the location for reporting should be user-friendly. For example, complainants should not be required to go to headquarters or some other location to file their complaint. Obviously, complainants should not have to report to their supervisor's office, and the original report should not be audiotaped or videotaped because this would have a devastating effect on the likelihood of victims coming forward to file a formal complaint of sexual harassment.

Allow Complainants to Bring Advocate

In both informal and formal procedures, complainants should be allowed to bring an advocate when reporting. This advocate can provide moral support to the complainant during the process and also witness the response of the person receiving the complaint. In addition, the advocate can help the complainant to document information such as the next steps in the complaint process. Depending on the particular complaint procedures implemented by the agency, this advocate could be a contact person or ombudsperson, or even a friend or coworker.

Communicate that Complaints Are Taken Seriously

In one study of employees who filed a complaint of sexual harassment in their organization, only half (55 percent) indicated that it was taken seriously and that some action was taken as a result. In fact, about one in four felt that their integrity was questioned (24 percent) and that they were not believed (23 percent); 14 percent felt they were blamed for the situation. Not surprisingly, only one-third of these individuals indicated that they were satisfied with the complaint process (Reese & Lindenberg, 1999). Another study replicated this finding in a federal agency, in which "47 percent of those who lodged a formal complaint … received an unfavorable response" (DuBois, Faley, Kustis, & Knapp, 1999, p. 209).

The lessons from this research are clear: Agencies must make sure that complaints of harassment and discrimination are taken seriously and are referred to the appropriate personnel. Complainants must be treated with respect and not suspicion, and their complaints must be investigated thoroughly, fairly, and objectively.

RESPONSES TO COMPLAINTS

Regardless of the specific type of complaint procedure that is implemented, the following measures are necessary when an employee files a complaint of sexual harassment or workplace discrimination.

Address Immediate Safety

It is critical that agencies respond to all complaints of harassment or discrimination by determining whether the complainant feels safe remaining in the current assignment. This is especially important in law enforcement and firefighting because retaliation may be life-threatening. In law enforcement, retaliation may take the form of failure to provide assistance in emergency situations; in firefighting, it may include tampering with necessary safety equipment. Safety may be a particular concern in situations in which either the complainant has been threatened with violence or the allegations include physical contact.

Separate Parties

For complainants who do not feel safe in their current assignment, the agency must take immediate steps to ensure their safety; however, these steps must carefully balance the rights of the complainant and the respondent. Legal counsel is always recommended. There are three options for responding to this situation.

1. Remove respondent from workplace.   When serious allegations of harassment are raised, some organizations respond by transferring the respondent or placing the respondent on administrative leave pending the outcome of the investigation. However, this action must be considered very carefully, with particular attention to the provisions of labor contracts and personnel policies. In addition, removing the respondent from the workplace may cause other employees to assume that a determination of culpability has already been made, which has the potential of seriously damaging the reputation of an innocent person. However, if there are serious allegations, such as sexual assault or threats of violence, the safest option is probably to place the respondent on administrative leave during the course of the investigation.

2. Remove complainant from workplace.   Sometimes the complainant will ask to be transferred or put on leave pending the results of the investigation. If this occurs, we recommend granting the request whenever possible. However, complainants may sometimes ask to be moved because they are afraid of retaliation. In such a situation, it is important to talk to complainants to make sure that they truly do wish to be reassigned. We have seen some cases in which complainants asked to be reassigned and then later claimed that the reassignment was an act of retaliation. They said they were reassigned to a less desirable position or were "forced" to agree to the reassignment. Clearly, agencies should not just automatically remove the complainant from the workplace because this could be perceived as retaliation. Many complainants do not want to have their life disrupted by being transferred, and this may even increase the damage to complainants and their careers. In many cases, complainants want to remain with their coworkers for the support they can provide during the difficult process of an administrative investigation. We recommend that complainants be given some choices in writing and that they be asked to make a choice and sign the form. Hopefully this will prevent later allegations that they were unfairly treated. A sample form of such a letter is provided at the end of this chapter.

3. Remove both employees from workplace.   Some organizations have a policy to transfer both of the involved parties (complainant and respondent) pending the results of the investigation. Of course, this approach raises all the issues discussed in the first two options.

When the respondent is a coworker, we believe that it is generally best to ask complainants if they feel comfortable remaining in their current work assignment. If they do, complainants can typically remain in the current assignment as long as the supervisor closely monitors the workplace for potential retaliation. If a complainant does not feel comfortable remaining in the current work assignment, however, agencies must consider temporarily reassigning either the complainant or the respondent, or both, as described above. In these situations, we recommend using the sample letter at the end of this chapter (and consulting with legal counsel).

However, if the respondent is the supervisor of the complainant, the complainant *must* be removed from the respondent's supervision and reassigned to a different supervisor. Of course, this raises all the complicated issues discussed above, but we nonetheless recommend that this reporting arrangement be immediately changed to protect the complainant and to prevent allegations of retaliation.

Advise Complainant

The complainant must be ordered not to discuss the issues with anyone in the organization other than the investigative personnel assigned to the case. Complainants should then be contacted on a regular basis throughout the investigation to make sure that they are not experiencing any retaliatory actions.

Inform Immediate Supervisors

Steps must also be taken to inform the immediate supervisors of both the complainant and the respondent about the allegations and to notify the supervisors that they will be held responsible for ensuring that no retaliation occurs in the workplace. They should be instructed to monitor the workplace and to immediately stop any conversations about the situation. Rumors are detrimental to the workplace and should be quashed as quickly as possible.

Inform Respondent

The respondent must also be notified of the complaint and explicitly prohibited from taking any type of retaliatory action against the complainant. The respondent should then be advised to stop the behavior in question and ordered not to discuss the issue with anyone in the organization other than investigative personnel assigned to the case. The respondent should also be told that any contact with the complainant should be kept to a minimum and that the interaction between the two must be on a professional level.

Explain and Begin Investigative Process

The investigator must take care to thoroughly explain the investigative process to both the complainant and the respondent. Complainants should also be advised of their right to file a complaint with the state and federal civil rights agencies and informed of the statute of limitations for filing such a complaint. At that point, the investigator can begin the investigative process by interviewing the parties and gathering the evidence. These steps are described in detail in the chapter on the investigation.

EXAMPLE 10–1

Sample Form for Complainant to Select Temporary Work Arrangements

To: Complainant
From: Agency Director
Re: Assignment During Investigative Process

We understand that filing a complaint against another employee is not an easy decision to make. We will work to complete the investigation as soon as possible and get the situation resolved. We want you to be comfortable with the process and offer you the following options in an effort to assist you:

1. Assignment. You may choose any of the following options for assignment during the time the investigation is taking place:

    a. You may remain in your current assignment. Command staff will monitor the workplace to ensure that you are not exposed to any harassment or retaliation. This option will allow you to continue with your normal work schedule and be among coworkers who know you and who can provide support to you.

    b. You may request a change in work hours so that you are not at work at the same time as the person against whom you have filed the complaint. You may return to your prior working hours at any time.

    c. You may request reassignment to another unit during the time the investigation is taking place. This option will remove you from the workplace where you are experiencing problems and hopefully reduce any stress you may be experiencing. If you choose this option, we will provide you with some alternatives for where you can be assigned. You may return to your prior assignment at any time.

    d. You may request a temporary leave of absence with pay during the time the investigation is taking place. This option will completely remove you from the workplace if you feel that you need some time away from work. You may return to work at any time.

2. Employee assistance. The following services are available to you: [List services such as counseling, peer support, mentoring, etc. Give contact names and numbers.]

3. Investigation updates:
    Investigator _____ has been assigned to investigate your complaint.
    You may reach Investigator _____ at this telephone number. Please feel free to call to receive updates on the progress of the investigation or to provide additional information.

If you have any questions or requests for further assistance, please contact _____ at _____ [supply phone number].

Chapter 11

Selecting an Investigator

Employees who are assigned to investigate complaints of harassment and discrimination must be carefully selected, screened, and trained. Administrators must therefore make a number of important decisions about who should serve as an investigator and whether they should be drawn from inside the organization or hired from the outside.

REQUIREMENTS FOR A SUCCESSFUL INVESTIGATOR

Successfully investigating a complaint of harassment or discrimination requires establishing trust with people who are upset and who are providing conflicting information, maintaining that trust while asking extremely sensitive questions, and protecting the rights of people with polarized interests at stake (Oppenheimer & Pratt, 2003). Obviously, investigators must therefore possess a wide range of knowledge, skills, and abilities:

- Relevant training, experience, abilities, and personal integrity
- Objectivity (both actual and perceived), strength to resist taking sides in the investigation, impartiality, and open-mindedness
- Knowledge of relevant laws, rules, and practices (including civil rights laws and contractual obligations under collective bargaining units)
- Knowledge of both the employment problems faced by women and minorities and the reasons these problems might not be reported
- Ability to communicate effectively (even regarding sensitive and sexual matters) with people of different rank and from diverse backgrounds

- Ability to actively listen, analyze, and document both verbal and nonverbal behaviors while a person unloads months or even years of painful memories
- Ability to elicit information from people, even those who want to block the investigation, using open-ended questions and other techniques
- Self-control and mature judgment, even when faced with sexually explicit language, personal criticism, and volatile emotions
- Integrity to keep information from the investigation confidential
- Ability to accurately recall information from note taking
- Ability to collect and analyze information from a variety of sources (including some that may be sensitive and/or controversial)
- Writing skills to produce clear and concise reports
- Knowledge of how to interview despite a code of silence

Investigators must also be able to do work that not everyone will like or appreciate, knowing that at least one of the parties—and possibly both—will be unhappy or even angry with the result. Given the difficulty of the task, investigators may need to have a trusted advisor (preferably someone from outside the agency); they can then discuss the case confidentially and can test out their theories and ideas about workplace behaviors with this advisor.

SELECTION, SCREENING, AND TRAINING OF INVESTIGATORS

In the chapter on the complaint process, we discussed a variety of options regarding where to locate staff who are responsible for receiving and investigating complaints of harassment and discrimination. These options included a separate discrimination unit, an Internal Affairs unit, a detective division, a Human Resources Department, an Equal Employment Opportunity (EEO) coordinator, or an external government (city, county, state, or federal) agency. Regardless of where this complaint process is located, however, steps must be taken to select, screen, and train investigative staff to be successful.

Selection and Screening

At minimum, selected investigators must be screened for potential bias against women and minorities. This screening can be conducted either by a panel of experts in an oral group interview procedure or by a qualified psychologist. Of course, anyone who has participated in discriminatory or harassing behaviors must *not* be selected as an investigator.

It is ideal if the investigative staff can be diverse in terms of both gender and race. Some complaints may even be best handled by a team of investigators, especially if the team includes both a man and a woman or people of different racial or ethnic backgrounds. This may improve the quality of the investigation and make it appear more impartial.

When interviewing someone with rank, it is desirable for the interview to be conducted by someone of a higher rank. If there is no person of a higher rank who is trained to conduct these investigations, it is a good idea to at least have someone of a higher rank present in the room when the interview takes place. On the other hand, the chief administrator should *never* be the one to investigate a complaint or conduct an interview. In fact, the investigator probably should not be anyone within top command unless that person has specialized training in conducting sexual harassment investigations.

Recruit Volunteer Investigative Teams

In addition to the options discussed in the chapter on complaint procedures, agencies can consider constructing volunteer investigative teams, with personnel recruited from throughout the agency with different ranks. These volunteer investigators can include members of both sexes and various racial or ethnic backgrounds to incorporate different views and to increase the investigators' perceived credibility. In fact, the process of recruiting and training volunteer investigators can be part of the organization's educational campaign. The training can therefore have benefits throughout the entire organizational structure, as investigators bring their training and expertise back to their units and workgroups. In addition, these individuals will be particularly well suited to provide feedback on the effectiveness of the policies and procedures that are implemented by the agency.

Volunteer investigators can thus be used for situations of sexual harassment as long as they are well trained in and well integrated into the formal complaint process. If volunteers are utilized, however, it is critical that they be held to the same standard as Human Resources professionals and others with more formal authority for conducting internal investigations, with all the attendant protections for the confidentiality and rights of those involved. The use of volunteer investigators is a particularly viable option for smaller agencies that do not have the resources to assign sexual harassment investigators to internal investigations on a full-time basis.

Training

Once the investigators have been selected and screened, they must receive thorough and ongoing training from qualified experts in the area of discrimination law, labor contracts, and equal employment opportunity. In addition, specialized training must be provided on how to interview victims of sexual harassment (including sexual assault). Investigators must first be trained in-depth and then provided continuing education to ensure that their skills and knowledge are up-to-date. This is particularly important in the area of sexual harassment and workplace discrimination because laws and standards are constantly evolving. Any training that is attended by the investigators should be documented in their personnel file.

For example, the Americans for Effective Law Enforcement (AELE) Legal Center provides a training program on internal investigations and discipline for law enforcement, public safety, and corrections personnel. More information is available at www.aele.org. There is also a training manual for sexual harassment investigators available in a book written by Salisbury and Dominick (2004) titled *Investigating Harassment and Discrimination Complaints: A Practical Guide.*

TYPES OF INVESTIGATORS

There are three options when selecting an investigator for a complaint procedure: internal investigators, external investigators, and attorneys.

Internal Investigators

When investigators are drawn from inside the agency, the primary advantage and disadvantage are the same: They have knowledge about the organization and the people involved. On the one hand, this means that they can get up to speed on the situation more quickly than an external investigator who would need to spend time learning the structure and language (relevant lingo) of the organization.

On the other hand, this also means that they might have preexisting opinions about the people involved and personal assumptions about the behavior or situation described in the complaint. For example, someone from inside the agency may not see behaviors as a problem if they are commonplace in the organization. For this reason, the investigation is not usually conducted by the complainant's supervisor but instead is forwarded to someone in Human Resources or another investigative unit. Investigators from inside the organization may also be hoping for a promotion or an assignment to a specialty unit and may therefore be reluctant to find misconduct against a higher-ranking officer.

The organization must therefore take pains to communicate that investigators drawn from inside the agency are serving as impartial fact finders without any interest in the outcome of the investigation. To effectively convey this message, persons selected as investigators must be (and appear to be) unbiased, they must avoid any conflict of interest, and they must be assigned to Internal Affairs, Human Resources, or some other neutral unit.

Employees will typically judge the fairness of the investigator based on such issues as friendships and alliances within the organization. When an internal investigator is assigned, it is therefore a good idea to ask both the complainant and the respondent if they are comfortable with that investigator. If either person expresses concerns, the agency should seriously consider assigning another investigator because this perception will negatively affect the quality and credibility of the investigation. In some situations, this perception may even be sufficient cause to hire an external investigator to ensure that the investigation is—and is seen to be—thorough, impartial, and fair to everyone.

External Investigators

Agencies may choose to hire external investigators as long as they are highly experienced in dealing with sexual misconduct issues and in conducting discrimination investigations within organizations such as police and fire departments. For example, an external investigator is likely to be the best option when the harassment is particularly severe or the charge is made against someone of high rank. External investigators should *always* be used if the complaint is made against the chief administrator of the organization (e.g., Sheriff, Chief, or Director).

If external investigators are used, legal counsel must review the provisions in the Federal Trade Commission's Fair Credit Reporting Act that pertain to the use of external investigators in cases of sexual harassment and other forms of workplace discrimination. (For more information, see www.ftc.gov.)

Advantages of External Investigators

Advantages of external investigators include the fact that they may appear to be more objective and often have more experience in handling these unique situations. In addition, the external investigator may be better able to testify in court if there is litigation and may have fewer assumptions about the situation and the people involved. Because a thorough investigation can damage working relationships and possibly affect the investigator's chances for promotion or other job benefits, external investigators are sometimes better able to listen to the various sides of the issue without becoming personally involved and without experiencing any negative consequences.

There are ways that the agency can maximize the benefits of using an external investigator. For example, the agency can use the external investigator as the lead investigator and assign an internal investigator as an assistant. This option combines the expertise of the external investigator with the internal investigator's in-depth knowledge of the organization. It must be clear, however, that the external investigator is in charge of the investigation and is the decision maker. The final report should be prepared by the external investigator.

Another option is to conduct an internal investigation but have it reviewed by an external investigator. With this type of arrangement, the external investigator should have the authority to mandate additional investigative steps, such as interviewing other witnesses and examining other evidence. The external investigator should also be the one to make the determinative findings.

Disadvantages of External Investigators

One of the disadvantages of the use of external investigators is the added cost to the organization. Another possible disadvantage is that an external investigator may need help in understanding the structure, terminology, and other unique aspects of the organization. In the end, however, the benefits may far outweigh these costs in many situations.

Attorneys

For agencies that utilize an external investigator, it is generally not advisable to hire an attorney. Although attorneys know the law and how to present a case in court, they are not necessarily good at investigating and interviewing. In addition, any attorney who may be involved in litigation on the case *cannot* be used in the investigative process. On the other hand, it is always a good idea to have the completed investigation *reviewed* by an attorney.

Tips for the Investigator

Upon being assigned to an investigation, investigators need to be sure that their knowledge of the law is current. This type of law is continually evolving, so something that investigators learned last month may not be true this month. In addition to staying continually updated on the legal issues, investigators must take steps to avoid both bias and the appearance of bias:

- When internal investigators are assigned to investigate a case in which they are perceived to have a close relationship with any of the parties or witnesses, it is recommended that they ask to have the case reassigned to another investigator.

- If a conflict of interest is perceived and the case cannot be reassigned, investigators can take the following steps to reassure all parties that the investigation will be done in an impartial manner:

  At the beginning of the interview with the complainant and the respondent and any major witnesses, disclose the fact that a relationship exists and the nature of the relationship.

  Make a pledge to each of these people to do everything possible to conduct an impartial investigation.

  Allow the parties to the investigation to express any reservations they may have about the issue of impartiality.

  Document the fact of the disclosure of this relationship, and document the response of the parties.

  Try to bring in another person who does not have any relationship with the parties as a witness to all interviews.

  Do not make findings or recommendations for resolution; merely report the facts.

  Have the final report reviewed by someone who is perceived to be neutral (an outside expert would be desirable). The report should also be reviewed by a legal advisor.

  Request that management develop a policy for dealing with these kinds of situations in the future.

- When external investigators are assigned to investigate a case, they must overcome the perception that they do not understand the organization and its culture. Here are some ways they can overcome this perception:

  Ask to have a neutral internal person assigned to assist with the terminology or to explain procedures. It is desirable that this person have the authority to order people to cooperate.

(continued)

Tips for the Investigator (*continued*)

Ask to have a copy of the organization's manual of procedures available for reference. If there is no manual, ask for copies of relevant policies and procedures.

Ask to have a copy of any labor agreement for reference.

Develop a trusted advisor in a similar field. For example, if it is an investigation of an employee in a law enforcement agency, find an advisor in a different law enforcement agency to help interpret policies and procedures.

Have a draft of the final report reviewed by someone within the agency who is perceived to be neutral; however, do not compromise on findings of fact.

Have the final report reviewed by the legal advisor for the organization.

Keep a copy of the final report in case of future litigation.

Document the steps taken to obtain input, and have the report reviewed.

Chapter 12

Beginning the Investigation

Once an organization becomes aware of harassing or discriminatory behaviors, a variety of steps must be taken to ensure that the situation is handled appropriately. These steps include initiating an investigation, interviewing the parties and witnesses, and collecting the evidence. Uniform guidelines must be developed by the agency to ensure that the investigation is timely, thorough, and fair.

PROBLEMS IN THE WORKPLACE

There are a variety of ways in which an agency may find out that a problem of sexual harassment or discrimination is occurring in the workplace:

- An employee, supervisor, or manager may observe the problematic behavior.

- A supervisor or manager may hear rumors of the behavior or receive an anonymous complaint from someone inside or even outside the agency.

- The agency may receive a formal or informal complaint filed by an employee or someone outside the agency.

- The agency may be contacted by the Equal Employment Opportunity Commission (EEOC) or a state regulatory agency.

Regardless of the source of the information, the agency must respond to the problem once someone in a supervisory or management position becomes aware of the possibility that harassment or discrimination has taken place. Complaints must be investigated even when they do not appear to constitute a legal violation, the behaviors took place a long time ago, and/or the victimized employee has since left the agency.

Complaints of harassment or discrimination must also be investigated even when they appear trivial or dubious at first. This is true for a number of reasons. First and foremost, the original complaint may not describe the entire situation. Often, the behavior that an employee originally complains about only represents the "last straw" in a long history of abuse. Only after interviewing the complainant can an investigator determine the extent of the problem. Second, harassment or discrimination that took place a long time ago may involve employees who are still working for the agency and the "institutional memory" of the behaviors may continue to poison the workplace environment. For example, if it is common knowledge that women are sexually harassed at the firearms range, female police officers may be anxious about having to report to the range to qualify for their service weapon. This would be true regardless of whether the original victim was still working for the agency. Third, even if the behavior in question doesn't violate the law, it may still violate policy within the agency.

Even if the behavior does not violate any law or policy, it will still need to be addressed because it is obviously upsetting to the employee and therefore disruptive to the workplace. Finally, agency response is needed even when the complainant is seen as someone who is "flaky" or as someone who complains about everything. In fact, it is possible that the employee's "flakiness" is the *result* of the harassment. Remember that the goal of conducting an investigation is not just to avoid litigation but to stop workplace abuses and prevent further harm to employees.

PLANNING THE INVESTIGATION

Once a problem comes to the attention of someone in a supervisory or management position, the courts expect a timely response; in fact, prior court decisions suggest that the agency needs to respond within one to two days of the original complaint. Therefore, agencies must respond quickly to plan the investigation. This planning process may include the following seven steps:

1. Make temporary changes to the workplace during the investigation, such as separating people or work duties and placing someone on administrative leave.

2. Determine both who needs to know what information and how this will be provided during the course of the investigation.

3. Identify which documents will be needed and request copies.

4. List all the people to interview, and specify the best order for the interviews. At a minimum, this would include all complainants and respondents as well as all potential witnesses, unless there is a logical and clearly articulated reason for not interviewing a particular witness.

5. List the questions to ask, and consider the likely responses—especially to difficult issues.

6. Review the sexual harassment policy and procedure for the agency.

7. Gather referral information for counseling and other services that might be appropriate.

When an investigation is initiated, the investigator must promptly advise the respondent to stop the behavior in question; however, there should be no sanction beyond that until the investigation is concluded (Oppenheimer & Pratt, 2003). If this planning does not result in an investigation that begins within one to two days of the original complaint, the reason for this delay must be both reasonable and carefully documented.

INTERVIEWS WITH COMPLAINANT, RESPONDENT, AND WITNESSES

The investigation will then typically proceed with interviews—first with the complainant, then with the respondent, and finally with the witnesses. Detailed guidelines to assist with this process are provided in the chapters on interviewing the complainant, respondent, and witnesses. As described in those chapters, the interviews should be used to identify all the allegations involved, which may include multiple complainants, respondents, witnesses, and others with information. The interviews must also reveal as much information as possible about *all* the allegations, including any complicating factors such as friendships, intimate relationships, or grudges between the people involved. In addition, everyone who is interviewed should be asked about both other people who might have relevant information and other sources of corroborative evidence. If allegations are made that the supervisor is the harasser, it may be necessary to interview the entire work unit. This issue is discussed in further detail in the chapter on supervisory responsibilities.

It is also important to note at the outset that the interview process must include a diligent effort on the part of the investigator to accurately record all the information provided by the parties, witnesses, and others. One method is to take written notes. A better strategy is to take notes and record the interview using a video or audiotape. That way, the investigator is better able to recall information and avoid either forgetting or dismissing details that might later prove to be important.

Additional Evidence

During the interviews with the complainant(s), respondent(s), and witness(es), the investigator must ask questions about the types of documents or records that may support their statements. This could include the following:

- Timesheets or other payroll records to document dates worked, promotions, pay raises, leaves taken, etc.
- Attendance rosters and calendars for meetings or training seminars
- Telephone records to document calls made

- Electronic communications or computer records
- Copies of offensive pictures, cartoons, calendars, letters, cards, memos, emails, etc.
- Copies of journals, diaries, letters, or other writings
- Supervisor files or organizational memos
- Policy statements or other directives on harassment, discrimination, misconduct investigations, confidentiality, and retaliation

The investigator should also review any records pertaining to prior complaints of sexual harassment or discrimination to determine how the agency responded. In some cases, the investigator may need to check with legal counsel before securing documents such as computer records.

It may also be necessary to collect other types of physical evidence, such as gifts or clothing. If these items cannot be physically collected and kept secure, they should be photographed for the file. In addition, the investigator should seek to visit and photograph the scene of the incident (whenever possible) to establish details of the physical location and to identify additional potential witnesses.

ELEMENTS TO ESTABLISH

For situations involving *quid pro quo* sexual harassment and a hostile work environment, the investigator should consult the chapter on law for the pertinent elements to be established. By writing down the elements that must be established, investigators can develop a plan for the investigation to guide their interviews and other evidence-collecting efforts. Investigators must keep in mind that all the complainant's allegations must be addressed during the course of the investigation. These allegations may include other types of gender harassment or discrimination, such as negative job actions and hiring or selection issues.

Negative Job Actions

For complainants who state that they were disciplined, fired, or subjected to some other negative job action as part of the harassment, the investigator must determine the following:

- Whether the negative job action that is described by the complainant actually took place (e.g., discipline, demotion, termination)
- Whether the action was based on gender, gender discrimination, *quid pro quo* sexual harassment (either explicit or implied), or retaliation
- Whether other employees in a similar situation experienced the same negative job action
- Whether the negative job action affected just women or if men were also affected

Hiring or Selection Issues

Alternatively, when the issue is one of hiring or selection for a particular position, then the investigator must determine the following:

- Whether there was an actual vacancy
- Whether the complainant actually applied for the position or otherwise stated an interest in it
- Whether the complainant was qualified to be appointed to the position
- Whether the complainant was, in fact, not hired or selected for the position
- Whether this decision was based on gender, gender discrimination, *quid pro quo* sexual harassment (either explicit or implied), or retaliation
- What reasons were given by the employer for not hiring or selecting the person
- Whether these reasons were legitimate
- Whether other similar individuals were also not hired or selected and whether those individuals were women or men

Regardless of the type of complaint being investigated, writing down the elements that need to be established will help investigators both keep them in mind during the investigative process and avoid getting sidetracked.

ANONYMOUS COMPLAINTS

When supervisors or managers receive a complaint anonymously, the investigator can discuss with them any suspicions they have about who might be involved. Of course, the materials or behaviors involved may also provide clues regarding who is responsible. For example, if someone received an offensive letter, the wording of the letter can be examined to try to identify its source; if an offensive cartoon was posted, the investigator can try to determine by its location who might have posted it; or if the anonymous harassment was done via email, computer experts may be needed to try to determine its source. It is even possible to take more extreme measures, such as installing video surveillance in the area where the harassment occurred, but this would need to be done with the help of legal counsel.

While law enforcement professionals might have experience with these types of investigative techniques when responding to a crime, they do not always utilize them when conducting an internal investigation. Yet they can be equally effective, if not more effective, in this context because the investigator likely has personal experience with the workplace and the people involved. This experience can therefore inform the investigative strategy used.

Even if the person responsible for the offensive material is never identified, it is still important for investigators to find out about the situation. For example, investigators can poll employees about the work environment more generally or ask about specific behaviors that might be involved. Of course, this is a good practice to use occasionally even when no one has complained about sexual harassment. (The importance of climate surveys is discussed in the chapters on training and prevention.) It is also always appropriate to respond by providing training for the entire unit or agency.

UNIFORM STANDARDS FOR THE INVESTIGATION

To ensure that all investigations are conducted in a way that is thorough, fair, and impartial, organizations must develop uniform standards for investigating and documenting complaints of harassment and discrimination. It is best if these guidelines are included in the comprehensive policy on harassment and discrimination; however, they may be elaborated elsewhere in the policy manual or in other guidelines for supervisors, managers, and investigators. At a minimum, these investigative guidelines will need to cover the following issues.

Confidentiality

Standard guidelines for the investigative process must outline who is informed of the complaint as well as how much information is given to the complainant, the respondent, and their supervisor(s). The fact that a complaint has been made should be disclosed only to those who have a need to know:

- Person responsible for conducting the investigation
- Person responsible for supervising the investigation
- Respondent
- Supervisor of the respondent
- Supervisor of the complainant

Confidentiality guidelines should be outlined on a form that everyone involved in the investigation must sign and date. This form must state that any violations of the confidentiality guidelines constitute a separate infraction that will be investigated and that will result in discipline if substantiated. Penalties for violating the confidentiality guidelines should be included on the form, and investigators must monitor the situation for breaches of confidentiality both during the investigation and after its conclusion.

Retaliation

Strong prohibitions against retaliation must be part of any standard investigative process and would include notifying everyone involved in the investigation of the policy provisions against retaliation and spelling out the penalties levied against those found in violation. Prohibitions against retaliation and the penalties for violations should be outlined in a form that everyone involved in the investigation must sign and date. Investigators must then monitor the situation for retaliation and initiate a separate investigation if any retaliatory actions are reported or suspected.

Timeline

It is critical to spell out timelines for conducting and completing the investigation. All complaints of sexual harassment and workplace discrimination should be given priority and completed within a very short time period, such as 30 days. Investigations must generally be conducted as quickly as possible while still ensuring a thorough examination of the issues. However, sometimes things happen that increase the amount of time required for the investigation; in such a situation, these events must be carefully documented. For example, if an important witness is on a three-week vacation, thereby delaying the investigation, this fact should be noted to counter any claims that the investigation was not done in a timely manner.

Notification of Complainant Rights

The investigative procedure must also include procedures for notifying complainants of their rights, relevant statutes of limitations for taking legal action, and resources available to them in both the department and the community.

Documentation

Uniform standards must be outlined for documenting all investigations of sexual harassment and other forms of workplace discrimination. Further guidance on this issue is provided in the chapter on documentation.

Standard of Proof

For this type of administrative investigation, the appropriate standard is a "preponderance of the evidence," which means that the allegation is more likely than not to be true; in other words, it is more likely than not that the incident happened largely the way the complainant described it. This standard of proof must be explicitly stated in the investigative guidelines because this is a common source of errors—especially for those in law enforcement who are more accustomed to the criminal standard of "beyond a reasonable doubt." This is *not* the standard of proof for a sexual harrassment investigation (see chapter 19).

Notification of Outcome

Both the complainant and the respondent must be informed of the outcome of the investigation, but the agency must first thoroughly review the requirements of the state and federal privacy acts and any relevant labor contracts to determine what information can be disclosed. In general, the amount of information given to the complainant should be maximized to the extent possible.

Disciplinary Action

Any appropriate discipline or remedial training should be swiftly imposed and completed. Guidelines for appropriate discipline are discussed in the chapter on that topic, but it is worth noting here that verbal counseling is not typically appropriate except for minor first-time offenses. Timelines for disciplinary actions should be included in the investigative guidelines.

Follow-Up

There should be a routine follow-up interview with complainants within 30–60 days of the conclusion of the investigation to determine if they have experienced any retaliation.

OTHER ISSUES IN THE INVESTIGATION

Before we conclude this chapter on beginning the investigative process, there are two other issues worth considering. These pertain to coordination with external agencies and actions to take if the complainant quits while the investigation is underway.

Coordination With External Agencies

The investigation of a sexual harassment complaint may sometimes need to be coordinated with union representatives, attorneys (for the complainant, respondent, or others), the EEOC, and even outside law enforcement agencies, depending on the nature of the behavior involved. Of course, criminal charges must be referred to the appropriate law enforcement agency and/or the separate investigative channel within the agency (such as the detective division). Even when such coordination is necessary, it is still best to notify as few people as possible to reduce the potential for breaches of confidentiality.

It is important to note that an employer must not abandon the investigation just because the EEOC or a state regulatory agency provides notice that it is also conducting one. For one thing, the outside organization is likely to take much longer to investigate than the agency itself; in addition the agency clearly has its own responsibility to find out what happened and fix it regardless of what outsiders do. In any case, the investigation conducted by an external agency is typically not nearly as complete as one done internally.

Complainant Quits

The investigation also must not be abandoned just because the complainant quits while the investigative process is underway. For one thing, the problems cited by the complainant may affect other employees in the workplace. In addition, the agency clearly has a duty to respond to all complaints of sexual harassment and other forms of workplace discrimination regardless of whether the complainant leaves. Even in situations in which the allegations are ultimately unfounded, there may still be a benefit to clearing the air with a thorough investigation.

Employers must keep in mind that some complainants file a lawsuit citing "constructive discharge" after resigning. This means that the complainant was forced to quit because the environment was extremely hostile and no one did anything about it. To counter this charge, it will therefore serve employers well to note that the investigation continued after the complainant left and that remedial actions were taken.

COMMON MISTAKES

Salisbury and Dominick (2004) have described some of the most common mistakes that are made when investigating complaints of sexual harassment and other forms of workplace discrimination. These are so important that they are worth repeating here. Here is a list of the most common mistakes:

- Failing to interview the complainant
- Failing to interview the respondent

- Failing to interview additional complainants, respondents, or witnesses who are identified as part of the investigation

- Shortcutting the investigation or skipping it altogether if an investigation is initiated by an external agency

- Dragging out the investigation and/or corrective actions for an unreasonable amount of time

- Imposing discipline or even terminating the respondent before completing the investigation

- Failing to investigate additional allegations that are revealed during the investigation

- Documenting the investigative process and findings in an insufficient manner

- Failing to prevent retaliation

- Failing to hold supervisors accountable for participating in or overlooking either the original harassment or subsequent retaliatory actions

- Abandoning the investigation because the complainant either requests it or quits

By following the guidelines throughout this book, investigators will easily avoid such common pitfalls and conduct a successful investigation.

Tips for the Investigator

Preparing for a successful investigation ideally begins long before any specific complaint is received. To be most effective, therefore, investigators should plan to do the following:

- Visit the nearest office of the EEOC or your state's Labor Department to obtain copies of the complaint forms that they use and other helpful documents. Some offices may have investigative guidelines or other tips for the employer.

- Check the Yellow Pages of the telephone book to identify law firms that specialize in employment law; then contact these firms and get on their mailing list for seminars.

- Join a human resources association such as the Society for Human Resource Management (www.shrm.org). These associations often have newsletters or seminars on topics involving employment discrimination.

- Attend conferences sponsored by women's organizations, especially those organizations for women in law enforcement and firefighting, to learn about current issues.

- Conduct Internet research to learn about new books on sexual harassment or investigative techniques.

- Conduct Internet research on websites such as www.findlaw.com to stay current on court decisions.

- Check the websites of the National Employment Lawyers Association (www.nela.org), the EEOC (www.eeoc.gov), and the U.S. Department of Labor's Women's Bureau (www.dol.gov/wb).

Chapter 13

Employee Options for Responding to Sexual Harassment

Investigators must be familiar with the various formal, informal, and legal options that are available for employees to report sexual harassment and discrimination in the work-place. These options exist in addition to the complaint procedures in place within the organization, which are discussed in a previous chapter.

EMPLOYEE RESPONSES TO SEXUAL HARASSMENT

All employees have the right to work in a workplace that is free of sexual harassment. When employees do experience sexual harassment, however, there are typically a number of informal strategies and formal procedures designed to stop it. Because there is a time limit for reporting the problem to governmental agencies or filing a lawsuit, employees who are being sexually harassed may want to use both informal strategies and formal procedures at the same time.

INFORMAL RESPONSE STRATEGIES

As discussed in previous chapters, many employees experiencing sexual harassment decide to pursue informal procedures, whether these are in addition to or in place of the more formal complaint process. For example, an employee may decide to use interpersonal strategies to try to stop the harasser's behavior or to otherwise improve the situation. Even if these strategies fail to end the harassment, they should be documented so that employees can provide evidence of the harassment if they decide either to file a complaint with an administrative agency or to sue their employer. The following sections discuss actions to take in informal complaint procedures.

Verbally Confront Harasser

For some types of sexual harassment, it is necessary to let the harasser know that the behavior is unwelcome in order to establish that the conduct is in fact "sexual harassment." To illustrate, if the harasser is repeatedly asking the employee out for dates, the employee should refuse these requests and tell the harasser to stop asking. Then if the requests continue, it will be clear that they are unwelcome and therefore constitute sexual harassment. For example, the employee could be advised to use one of the following phrases:

"Don't do that to me."

"Don't say that to me."

"I am not interested in any kind of a relationship with you."

"If you don't stop harassing me, I will report your behavior."

One option for employees is therefore to directly inform the harasser that they are offended by the behavior and will not tolerate it. In many situations, this may be sufficient to persuade a harasser to stop the behavior. However, employees should always carefully consider whether this is an appropriate strategy in their particular situation. Such an approach may not be safe or reasonable for anyone experiencing severe forms of sexual harassment or even sexual assault. Furthermore, employees who decide to confront their harasser might also want to consider taking another person along—both for their own safety and for the purpose of documenting the harassment.

Write Letter to Harasser

Alternatively, some people may find it easier to write a letter to the harasser to communicate their disapproval of the behavior. In some situations, this may be enough to put a stop to the harassing behavior; it also serves as documentation of the harassment and the employee's response. However, employees should be advised to not write the letter when they are upset or angry because it is usually more effective to use a direct but polite tone. The letter should consist of three parts:

1. Detailed factual account of each incident of sexual harassment. In it, the employee should simply state what the harasser did or said on each occasion, including dates and places as well as the precise language that was used (whenever possible).

2. Description of ways the harassment has affected the employee. Employees should thus describe their emotional and/or physical responses to the harassing behaviors as well as their thoughts regarding the situation.

3. Actions the employee would like to see the harasser take in order to remedy the situation. For some employees, this might simply be a request that the

harassing behavior stop immediately; however, other employees may have additional requests concerning their employment conditions, in which case these requests should also be included. For example, employees might ask the respondent to stay away from their desk or work area.

For employees who decide to write such a letter, they should keep a copy in order to document their efforts to communicate to the harasser that the behavior was unwelcome.

Keep Journal

Still other employees may decide to make a written record of each incident of sexual harassment in a journal, diary, or work log. In such a written record, they can be advised to describe the harasser's conduct and the ways the harassment made them feel physically and emotionally. The record should also include dates and places as well as any witnesses to the incidents of sexual harassment.

Accompanying this written record should be copies of any medical bills, records of time lost from work, or any other information relating to loss of income due to the harassment. For employees who later decide to file a complaint, this written record will help them to remember each incident in detail; it will also provide powerful corroborative evidence of the harassment even though it is written by the employee.

Talk to Others

For many employees, sharing the ordeal with a friend, counselor, or coworker may make them feel stronger and better able to respond effectively to the sexual harassment—it may even help to repair their self-esteem. However, when employees do tell someone about the sexual harassment, they should be advised to make a written record of the conversation. In many situations, the person who is told of the harassment can provide much-needed support to the employee and may even serve as a valuable witness later during an investigative process.

Employees who experience emotional or physical problems as a result of the situation should also be encouraged to seek help from an employee assistance program or other counseling programs. As described in the chapter on the problem of sexual harassment, these situations can have a wide range of very detrimental effects, and employees will need to take measures to protect their emotional and physical well-being.

Tell Supervisor

Employees can also be advised to tell their supervisor in very clear terms what is happening and that they want it to stop. For example, an employee might say, "John Jones comes to my desk nearly every day and asks me how my sex life is. I want it stopped now."

In many organizations, the supervisor will then have the responsibility to report this situation to the person or unit designed to receive and investigate complaints of sexual harassment. Of course, supervisors all too often fail to meet this responsibility; however, they may still be helpful in addressing the problem by intervening, asking the harasser to stop, or taking other corrective actions. When supervisors do fulfill their duty to report such a complaint, employees will then be routed into the formal complaint process within the organization.

FORMAL COMPLAINT PROCEDURES

In addition to any informal measures that employees might pursue, there are also various types of formal complaint procedures they can utilize:

- Filing a formal complaint with the designated investigative body within the agency (e.g., Human Resources, Internal Affairs, Discrimination Unit)
- Filing a complaint with the Human Resources Department of the governing (e.g., city, county, state, or federal) agency
- Filing a complaint with the agency administrator (e.g., Chief, Sheriff, Director)
- Filing a complaint with the legal department of the governing body (e.g., city, county, or state government)
- Filing a complaint with an elected official
- Filing a complaint with the state's Labor Department
- Filing a formal complaint with the Equal Employment Opportunity Commission (EEOC)
- Filing a sexual harassment lawsuit against the employer

The following sections describe actions to be taken in these various formal complaint procedures.

File Complaint Within Agency

Most employers have a policy and procedures in place for employees to file a complaint about unlawful harassment. These usually direct the employee to report incidents of sexual harassment to the Human Resources Department or to a supervisor or manager.

In some workplaces, however, the labor contract directs employees to file a sexual harassment complaint directly with the labor union. Unfortunately, complaints of sexual harassment are not typically handled very well by union grievance procedures for a number of reasons. First, the contractual language often doesn't specifically address the issue of sexual harassment, and the problem is not well suited to the "meet and confer" procedure often used for other types of employee misconduct. In addition, union procedures aren't typically very effective at protecting the confidentiality of the complainant and the investigative process, and the time limits are often too short for an adequate investigation.

Employees who file a complaint of sexual harassment also often feel betrayed by their labor union, which typically represents the respondent and not the complainant during the process. Worse, research documents that union defense strategies typically focus on attacking the credibility of the complainant or the complaint. In one study with published arbitration cases, such a strategy was used as much as 80 percent of the time (Cohen & Cohen, 1994). Unfortunately, if the labor contract specifically states that sexual harassment complaints must be filed as a grievance first, complainants must go through that procedure or risk losing their opportunity to file a lawsuit.

File Complaint with EEOC or State Agency

As previously discussed, the federal agency that handles sexual harassment complaints is the EEOC. The EEOC was established in 1964 to promote equality in the workplace as well as to investigate and litigate Title VII claims of discrimination on the basis of sex, race, religion, and national origin. The EEOC also investigates and litigates charges of retaliation against anyone filing a formal complaint or participating in an investigative process.

When someone is sexually harassed, one of the options for responding is therefore to contact the nearest EEOC field office. A person can file a complaint within 180 days of the incident, and this can be extended to 300 days if there is a state or local antidiscrimination law that also covers the charge. There is no financial charge for filing a complaint with the EEOC, and employees do not need a lawyer to do so. They can simply call the EEOC to receive information on how to file a complaint, or they can consult the extensive information posted on its website at www.eeoc.gov. After filing the complaint, the EEOC will then provide notice to the employer that a charge has been filed.

Employees can also report their sexual harassment to a state or a local agency for fair employment (such as the Human Rights Commission, Fair Practices Commission, or Labor Department). These state and local agencies function like the EEOC but act on the state or local level by investigating and litigating charges of harassment and discrimination in violation of the state's antidiscrimination laws. For additional information on more than 100 state and local agencies responsible for fair employment, please consult the EEOC website at www.eeoc.gov/employers/stateandlocal.html.

Next, the EEOC and the state's Labor Department will determine whether or not they will investigate the complaint. If so, they will also determine which agency will conduct the investigation. At that point, complainants can also request a "right to sue" letter from the designated agency and go directly to court.

If the EEOC or state agency *does* decide to investigate the charge, the charge can be resolved in several different ways. One of these methods is for the EEOC or state agency to conduct mediation with the voluntary participation of the complainant and the employer. If this process fails, the complaint then returns to the investigative process.

If the EEOC or state agency investigates the charge, this will also include reviewing any complaints or investigative proceedings conducted by the agency itself. If an investigation has already been conducted by the agency, the investigator will certainly be a key witness during this process and the investigative report will be a critically important piece of documentary evidence. Regardless of whether or not the agency has already conducted its own investigation, the employer will also be asked to prepare a response to the complaint. This will be based on evidence gathered during the investigation, including the complainant's statement and other sources. This employer response is not typically as comprehensive as a full internal investigation because its primary purpose is to defend the organization against the charges being made; it is therefore quite different from the type of investigation and documentation described in this book.

After its investigation is concluded, the EEOC can dismiss the case if it failed to find "reasonable cause" to believe that harassment or discrimination occurred. At that point, the person can choose to file an individual lawsuit within 90 days, but most employees will not choose to file a lawsuit if the EEOC has investigated the case and has determined that no violation was committed.

On the other hand, if the EEOC investigation determines that there is "reasonable cause" to believe that the person experienced harassment or discrimination, the EEOC will send a letter explaining its finding. Then the EEOC will either litigate the case or issue a "right to sue" letter for the person to file suit on his or her own behalf. Because of its limited resources, the EEOC only rarely litigates cases of sexual harassment or discrimination. The decision to litigate is typically only made when the EEOC determines that the issues at stake are particularly important to resolve for widespread positive impact.

File Lawsuit

As a final resort, employees experiencing sexual harassment can sue their employers for employment discrimination under Title VII, but federal law requires that they must first file a complaint with the EEOC or a comparable state agency (as in the process described above). Complainants can then file a lawsuit after being issued a "right to sue" letter, regardless of whether the EEOC or the state agency investigates and/or finds reasonable cause to believe that harassment or discrimination occurred.

Employees will hopefully understand that the process of litigation can be extremely difficult, with severe repercussions for their personal, professional, financial, and even physical well-being. However, the employer must be careful to avoid any appearance of dissuading an employee from filing a lawsuit. Of course, the outcome of litigation is always uncertain, and many employees are devastated when they have put everything on the line for a lawsuit that is dismissed or is decided against them. Employees must therefore carefully consider the potential costs and benefits of filing a lawsuit and only do so if they are sufficiently motivated and possess the emotional and financial resources that will be required. Unfortunately, both research and personal experience demonstrate that lawsuits are often the only motivating force powerful enough to create change in traditionally masculine occupations such as law enforcement and firefighting. Therefore, employees who seek to create change via litigation are advised to shore up their personal and financial resources and to network with others who have filed similar lawsuits in agencies across the country. This can be accomplished by contacting professional organizations for women or minorities within their field.

Tips for the Investigator

When investigators receive a complaint of sexual harassment, it is important to take a variety of measures regarding the various options employees have for responding:

- Ask the complainant to describe any interpersonal strategies and informal procedures used to stop the behavior, and provide any documentation of these efforts that might be available. Often, a formal complaint is only the last step in a long process of trying to put an end to the offensive behaviors. If so, this is important to document.

- Determine whether the complainant has filed a complaint with a federal or a state agency. If so, obtain a copy of the complaint.

- Check with legal counsel to determine who will be coordinating with the EEOC or the state agency for fair employment practices. Contact that person to arrange to receive any information that may be pertinent to the investigation.

- Keep in mind that the employer's response to a charge filed with the EEOC or a state agency does not constitute a thorough investigation. This response will be based on the complainant's statement and other evidence but will not typically be as comprehensive as the investigative process described in this book. Also, the purpose of the employer response is to defend against the charges rather than to conduct an objective fact-finding investigation. Therefore, the employer's response should never be considered sufficient for the investigation and documentation of a complaint, and the investigative process should never be abandoned simply because the EEOC or another external agency is conducting its own investigation.

- Consult the Internet for more information on the process for filing a complaint either with the local office of the EEOC (www.eeoc.gov) or with the more than 100 state or local agencies regulating fair employment practices based on state and local antidiscrimination laws (www.eeoc.gov/employers/stateandlocal.html).

Chapter 14

Preparing for the Complainant Interview[1]

The interview with the complainant is perhaps the most important component of any sexual harassment investigation, but a number of common dynamics of sexual harassment often interfere with the ability of investigators to be successful. Preparation is therefore the key. This chapter is designed to both explore how these challenges can hinder the investigation of a sexual harassment complaint and provide investigators with detailed guidance on how to prepare to overcome them during the complainant interview.

COMMON CHALLENGES

Cultural Stereotypes

We have previously discussed how cultural stereotypes suggest that "real" victims will respond to sexual harassment by verbally protesting, confronting the harasser, and immediately reporting the situation. Yet the research clearly indicates that most victims of sexual harassment actually respond with more indirect strategies and that very few file a formal complaint. Even when victims do report sexual harassment, they often do so only after considerable delay. Unfortunately, all these common behaviors are often used against complainants because many people see this as evidence either that the incident didn't take place or that it was really "no big deal."

To overcome the negative effects of these stereotypes, investigators must use the complainant's interview to elicit detailed information about exactly what happened, how complainants responded to the situation, and what they were thinking and feeling at the time. When complainants describe all their thoughts and feelings during the incident, the investigator can reconstruct the whole context of the experience. This can be very helpful in understanding why complainants responded the way they did and why they did not verbally protest, actively confront the harasser, or immediately tell a supervisor. Listed below are several helpful techniques for interviewers.

Avoid Questions That Might Sound Blaming

One particularly important technique is to allow complainants to describe the experience in their own words, which will avoid any implication that the complainant should have responded in a particular way. For example, investigators should never ask the complainant questions such as "Did you tell him to stop what he was doing?" and "Why didn't you file a formal complaint right away?" Questions like these imply to the complainant that there is a correct response to sexual harassment, so complainants may feel that they are being judged and/or that their claim is viewed with suspicion. In general, it is best to avoid the use of "why" questions with complainants because those questions can make it sound like the investigator is questioning their behavior or motivations (Oppenheimer & Pratt, 2003).

Use Open-Ended Questions

Investigators should provide the complainant with open-ended prompts such as "What did you do next?" and "What were you thinking at that point?" and "What were you feeling when he did that?" These types of questions allow complainants to talk about their thoughts, feelings, and experiences during the incident. Investigators are often surprised by the information that complainants provide in response to such open-ended prompts; details are revealed that would not have been elicited if the questions had been posed differently. This strategy also avoids any problem with leading questions (when the investigator suggests to the complainant what the "right" answer might be).

Document Complainant's Reactions

Another way to overcome this challenge is to document in detail how the complainant actually reacted to the situation. This full description can often go a long way toward explaining why the complainant did not react in ways that people expect based on stereotypes of "real" sexual harassment victims. For example, even though complainants might not have reported the situation immediately, they may have used a variety of strategies to address the problem, such as avoiding the harasser and talking with coworkers.

In general, investigators should always try to document any statements that the complainant made to others in the aftermath of the incident. It is especially important to interview the *first* person that the complainant told about the situation because this person will provide unique information regarding the complainant's initial demeanor, behavior, and statements. In the interview with the complainant, investigators therefore need to ask about anyone who was told about the sexual harassment so that these individuals can be interviewed.

Inconsistent or Untrue Statements

Another challenge often faced by sexual harassment investigators is the fact that complainants often make statements in their interview that are inconsistent or untrue. Complainants may also provide only partial information, omitting facts that are unflattering or unfavorable to them. There are a number of reasons for this:

1. Some complainants make inconsistent or untrue statements out of confusion or even trauma resulting from the sexual harassment.

2. Other complainants make inconsistent or untrue statements because they are uncomfortable in the interview situation. Even when investigators are competent and compassionate in their interactions with the complainant, the interview situation is inevitably going to be uncomfortable (if not upsetting) for most people.

3. Complainants might also make statements that are inconsistent or untrue because they are afraid they will be doubted or blamed for the sexual harassment. In order to be believed and taken seriously, complainants sometimes make untrue statements to make their experience sound more like "real sexual harassment." For example, complainants may attempt to minimize their relationship with the harasser or deny their own participation in sexual banter or crude language.

In these cases, it is important for the investigator to emphasize to complainants that they must tell the truth or their credibility will later be questioned. Making the environment safe and nonjudgmental will go a long way toward removing the incentive for complainants to be untruthful. Investigators should also explicitly state that they are not there to judge the complainant's behavior but to find out exactly what happened. Again, open-ended prompts in a complainant interview are one of the best tools for eliciting the whole story—including those behaviors of the complainant that might be seen as unflattering or unfavorable.

Myth of False Allegations

It is perhaps inevitable that the statement by the complainant will likely include some information that is either inconsistent or untrue. Any inconsistencies or untruths are likely to be used against the complainant if they are not handled appropriately during the investigation, so the investigator should respond by realizing that such inconsistencies or untruths are often understandable and should not be confused with a "false" allegation. This is so significant that it bears repeating: *It is critically important that the investigator realize that these inconsistencies or untruths are understandable and should not be confused with a "false" allegation.*

Unfortunately, there is a common myth in society that women routinely file false allegations of sexual harassment, and this myth can make investigators inappropriately suspicious of female complainants. As a result, when the complainant has provided some partial, inconsistent, or even untrue information, many investigators focus on that as proof that the entire complaint was fabricated.

Appropriate Response

While investigators do need to remain aware of the possibility that a complaint *could* be based on false allegations, they must also keep in mind the many reasons why complainants may provide partial, inconsistent, or even untrue information. The appropriate response is therefore to first address the inconsistencies or suspected untruths in the complainant's statement by exploring the issue gently and nonjudgmentally. For example, the first response to any inconsistency in the complainant's statement should be to point it out and ask for clarification. It is entirely possible that the complainant simply made a mistake or that the investigator misheard or misunderstood what the complainant was saying.

It is also important to gently explain to complainants the impact of inconsistencies on their credibility and the quality of the administrative investigation. In many cases, this will be enough to clarify the issue and resolve the inconsistency.

Inconsistencies

If the inconsistency remains, investigators can then explain that conflicting information has arisen and ask for the complainant's assistance in making sense of it. For example, an investigator could say, "I need to ask these questions because I have to write a report on this, and I want to get every detail correct." Or investigators can blame themselves. This technique might work best with complainants who continuously change their story. For example, the investigator could say, "I'm sorry, but I'm confused. I thought you said you didn't tell anyone about the situation." While attempting to clarify, however, it is important that the investigator not get into an argument with the complainant. No matter how volatile the emotions might become, investigators must maintain a demeanor that is calm, professional, and neutral.

If the inconsistency seems to result from the complainant's attempt to make the situation sound more like "real" sexual harassment, investigators need to address the complainant's underlying fear of being doubted or blamed. Investigators can also emphasize the importance of complete truthfulness and create a safe, nonjudgmental environment that encourages honesty even regarding unflattering behavior. The conclusion that a complaint is actually based on a false allegation should be made only when there is evidence to support it.

The Bottom Line

Complaints of sexual harassment—like any other complaint of employee misconduct— should be considered valid and investigated thoroughly until the evidence suggests otherwise. Unfortunately, the myth regarding false allegations has all too often fueled the misperception by investigators that sexual harassment complaints should be treated differently from other types of complaints and should be presumed to be illegitimate from the start.

Decision to Tape or Not Tape

It is also possible that inconsistencies in the complainant's statement are actually due to misunderstanding or inaccurate documentation by the investigator. To increase the accuracy of documentation during the complainant interview, investigators can therefore consider the possibility of audiotaping or videotaping complainant interviews. This is a controversial issue, and agencies should weigh the advantages and disadvantages before consulting with legal counsel and implementing a policy.

Potential Advantages

The primary advantage of taping a complainant interview is that it provides a reliable method of documentation and can therefore reduce the number of interviews needed. If the investigator is using a tape recorder or video camera to record the interview, the written report can obviously be double-checked for consistency with the audiotape or videotape. Many of the inconsistencies in complainant statements actually arise because the investigator failed to record the information accurately. Taping can also record more details than those summarized in a report, which benefits the quality of information and reduces the likelihood of inconsistencies. This can be especially important in complicated cases because inconsistencies can be explored by comparing details in the complainant's account with that of the respondent or those of other witnesses.

Because taping more accurately records all the details of an interview, it can have the additional benefit of protecting the interviewer if a complaint or misunderstanding should arise as a result of what was said. Finally, taping can better convey the immediate response of complainants to the situation. Investigators sometimes have the opportunity to talk with complainants while their emotions are raw. Their words and demeanor—angry, withdrawn, in shock, etc.—can be important in conveying the complainants' actual responses to the situation. Complainants often act very different later in the process of an administrative investigation, so taping can document their immediate responses to the situation. Obviously, taping provides the best evidence in the case of a later lawsuit.

Potential Disadvantages

One potential disadvantage of taping, however, is that it can undermine the credibility of complainants when their demeanor does not fit the stereotype of a "real" sexual harassment victim. Complainants may also make statements in the interview that could be used against them. As previously discussed, the complainant might omit important information or provide partial truths in order to make the experience sound more like "real" sexual harassment. Complainants also sometimes make a statement that they may have caused or somehow deserved the harassment because they have internalized cultural myths that blame the victims of sexual harassment rather than the harassers. In these cases, the investigator's report can help to explain the complainant's behavior and put it in the context of any underlying fears, concerns, or other motivations.

Other disadvantages include the fact that being tape-recorded may be intimidating to those being interviewed, especially the complainant. It is also time-consuming for the investigator to rely on tape recordings as a method of keeping track of information. Of course, if the decision is made to tape the complainant interview, the interviews must also be taped with the respondent, the witnesses, and anyone else involved in the investigation.

If agencies do implement a policy of taping interviews, it is critically important to obtain informed consent before doing so. This right is typically guaranteed by the Peace Officer Bill of Rights—legislation that has been enacted in many states to govern the rights of officers involved in an administrative investigation. While the Peace Officer Bill of Rights varies by state, many of the provisions are fairly standard. For example, all officers being taped during their administrative interview must be informed that they are being taped. Second, officers must be provided a copy of their tape-recorded interview if they request one; however, legal counsel should be consulted in such a situation.

Legal counsel should also be consulted when an interviewee wants to tape-record the session on a personal recorder. Our recommendation is to allow the employee to tape the interview as a means of building trust. In that situation, however, the investigator should certainly tape the interview as well.

Conclusions Regarding Taping

Obviously, there are a number of important advantages and disadvantages to taping interviews of the complainant and others involved in a sexual harassment investigation. Agencies must therefore consult their own legal counsel to make the final determination and request guidance with the decision-making process regarding how the tapes will be stored and when they will be destroyed. We recommend that any tapes be maintained until the statute of limitations for filing a lawsuit has expired. In general, legal counsel should also be consulted whenever employees request a copy of their taped interview, bring in a personal recorder, or raise other issues regarding the audiotaping or video-taping of interviews.

If interviews are taped, it almost goes without saying that investigators must be especially vigilant in their interviewing techniques and documentation. When the interview is being taped, investigators must carefully explore inconsistent or untrue statements made by the complainant, appropriately frame the complainant's response and statements within the realistic dynamics of sexual harassment, and document any information from other sources that may be inconsistent with the taped interview.

Investigator Gender

Because of the nature of sexual harassment, many organizations try to assign female investigators to interview these complainants. Although this might be possible for some police and fire departments, it may not always be feasible. In fact, it may not always be desirable, depending on the capabilities of the male and female investigators who are available. It is therefore important that all personnel with the responsibility for investigating complaints of employee misconduct receive appropriate training in how to respond effectively to sexual harassment. For one thing, the female investigator may not always be available to handle the sexual harassment complaint. More importantly, the primary issue is not whether the investigators are male or female but whether *they are good at what they do*. It is clear that competence and compassion are more important than gender in determining success in a complainant interview.

Male Investigators

As we've concluded, both male and female investigators can certainly conduct effective sexual harassment investigations, but male investigators must be aware of the unique issues that may arise because of their gender:

- Male investigators often have trouble identifying with the reactions of the sexual harassment complainant—who is typically a woman—because women's reality and behavior often differ from men's.

- It can be particularly challenging for men to make sense of common behaviors such as not protesting, not confronting the harasser, or not reporting the situation immediately. Women and men obviously have very different scripts for socially acceptable behavior, particularly in sexual situations.

- Male investigators may also be more likely than female investigators to believe that women routinely fabricate allegations of sexual harassment. Some male investigators may even fear being falsely accused of sexual harassment or at least can identify with the threatening possibility.

- Some male investigators may feel uncomfortable with a complainant who becomes extremely emotional during the interview or other investigative procedures.

- Some complainants may not feel comfortable talking to a male investigator after experiencing serious sexual harassment at the hands of a male employee.

For all these reasons, male investigators face unique issues when responding to sexual harassment situations involving a female complainant; however, successful investigation requires that the interviewer fully document the perspective and actions of the complainant when seeking to understand the situation.

Female Investigators

Female investigators often share with their male counterparts a difficulty in understanding the behavior of sexual harassment complainants:

- Female personnel, particularly in police and fire departments, have often been exposed to sexually harassing behavior themselves, so they may have a hard time taking the complaint seriously or may want to take the side of the respondent rather than the complainant.

- Female investigators may have the added challenge of wanting to distance themselves from the complainant. Women sometimes focus on reasons to blame the complainants of sexual harassment to convince themselves that by avoiding such behavior, they can guarantee that they will never be similarly harassed.

- Some female investigators have also personally experienced sexual harassment. By comparing other experiences with their own, female investigators who have been sexually harassed may sometimes perceive that a complaint does not represent "real" sexual harassment like their own.

Female investigators must be aware of these unique challenges and ensure that they communicate effectively and empathetically with complainants.

Conclusions Regarding Investigator Gender

Because few agencies will implement a policy of assigning female investigators to all complaints of sexual harassment, all investigators with the responsibility for handling complaints of employee misconduct must be trained to effectively handle situations involving sexual harassment. Male and female investigators must both be trained to conduct a successful sexual harassment investigation, with the understanding that their gender does affect how they perceive and react to these situations.

TIPS FOR SUCCESSFUL INTERVIEW WITH COMPLAINANT

Given the importance of the complainant interview, it is critical that it not consist simply of asking the traditional who, what, when, where, and why questions. This is particularly important to keep in mind when the investigator is someone from within the police or fire department. Law enforcement and firefighting personnel tend to be action-oriented people, yet interviews with sexual harassment complainants require patience for a long, detailed, and often emotionally difficult interview. In addition, law enforcement personnel have often "learned" how to conduct interviews by directing a number of rapid-fire questions to establish basic information or by using a confrontational style that is inappropriate for this type of interview.

In contrast, a sexual harassment investigation requires the time and patience to conduct a lengthy interview designed to elicit detailed information from the complainant. Throughout the interview, investigators must carefully examine the complainant's story for any aspect that can be corroborated. Even if the detail is not relevant for establishing the truth of the specific allegations, anything that the complainant states as a fact can be documented in order to seek corroboration for describing the entire context of the situation, and the same is true for interviews conducted with the respondent and other witnesses. Following are several pointers for the interview with the complainant.

Avoid Two Common Errors

Two of the most common errors that interviewers make are interrupting too often and asking too many questions. These errors may be particularly likely when the investigation is being conducted by a law enforcement professional. To illustrate, a research study was conducted with police detectives who stated that they were aware that constantly interrupting was a common interviewing mistake, but they denied that they personally did so during interviews. Only after listening to an audiotape of their own interviewing technique did these detectives realize how often they did interrupt victims and witnesses. Then they became motivated to correct the error (Fischer, 1995).

Do Not Use Interruptions or Rapid-Fire Questions

Obviously, interruptions and rapid-fire questions can disconcert the complainant in a sexual harassment investigation. Not only does this disrupt rapport, but it can also decrease the amount and accuracy of information obtained during the interview. To illustrate this problem, the same study of police detectives described above revealed that the typical interview contained only 3 open-ended questions and 26 short closed-ended questions. Furthermore, when asking the open-ended questions, the detectives interrupted the witness's response after *7.5 seconds*. This is an average of four interruptions per response. Worse, the close-ended questions were asked in a staccato, rapid-fire style with less than a 1-second pause between the witness's response and the next question. "In none of the interviews was the witness permitted to complete his or her narration without being interrupted" (Fischer, 1995, p. 735).

To improve one's interviewing style, it may be helpful to imagine what it feels like to be interrupted every 7.5 seconds and never allowed to complete a response. It is easy to see how this might be especially troubling for someone reporting something as difficult and sensitive as sexual harassment.

Avoid Inappropriate Sequencing

Turning yet again to the study of police detectives, another almost universal error was seen with the inappropriate sequencing of questions. First, the detectives typically asked questions in the order in which they appeared on their form for reporting criminal offenses. Obviously, this may not represent the order in which information is stored in the witness's memory or the order in which events happened.

Second, the detectives typically asked questions in a "lagging order," addressing something that was indicated in a previous response rather than the current one. This probably happens because the detectives lagged behind in taking notes or because they wanted the witness to elaborate on a previous point. However, these questions too frequently "appeared in the middle of the witness's description of another component of the crime, so that the follow-up question interrupted the witness's train of thought and cut short any possible elaboration on the current topic" (Fischer, 1995, p. 735).

To correct these errors, questions should be asked in a way that reflects the complainant's recall of events. For example, questions about the harasser should be asked together rather than interspersed throughout the interview. If the complainant skips over sexual details in the initial narrative, the investigator can avoid delving into these issues immediately but rather follow up with more specific questions later. In other words, investigators may have to hold off asking questions that they currently have in mind and ask them later when it is more appropriate in the context of the complainant's response (Fischer, 1995). This doesn't necessarily come naturally to investigators—and it takes extra mental effort—but the payoff can be great in terms of rapport with the complainant as well as the quantity and quality of information obtained.

ENDNOTE

1. Sections of this chapter were based on the document entitled: *Successfully Investigating Acquaintance Sexual Assault: A National Training Manual for Law Enforcement.* It was developed by the National Center for Women & Policing (2000), with support provided by the Violence Against Women Office, Office of Justice Programs (grant #97-WE-VX-K004).

Chapter 15

Interviewing the Complainant[1]

The interview with the complainant is perhaps the most important component of any sexual harassment investigation. This chapter is designed to provide investigators with detailed guidance on how to be successful, with recommendations for how to proceed before the interview, at the start of the interview, during the interview, and at the conclusion of the interview.

BEFORE THE INTERVIEW

For most investigations, it is appropriate to interview the complainant first, then witnesses and others with relevant information, and finally the respondent. By using this sequence, the investigator will have gathered a great deal of information by the time of the respondent interview; however, it is sometimes necessary to interview the respondent earlier due to "leaks" about the existence of the investigation or because of specific provisions in the labor contract.

In general, the interview with the complainant should be scheduled as soon as possible after the initial complaint is received. This reassures complainants that their complaint is being taken seriously. Before this first interview takes place, it is important for investigators to plan the standard instructions, prepare the necessary paperwork, and select an appropriate location.

Plan Standard Instructions

Investigators should always write down standard instructions that need to be provided in the complainant interview in order to make sure that nothing critical is overlooked. This standard information will likely address the following:

- Purpose of the investigation

- Role of the investigator as an objective fact finder

- Complainant's right to take breaks and ask questions throughout the interview

- Expectation that the complainant will cooperate fully and provide truthful information

- Complainant's right to have a private attorney or support person present during the interview if a union representative will not be there

- Process for the interview, including the fact that the investigator will take notes, prepare a written summary, and ask the complainant to review that summary and make corrections before signing it

- Confidentiality guidelines, including the fact that the person cannot discuss the issues with anyone inside the agency

- Prohibition against retaliation, as well as the process for reporting any retaliatory actions that the complainant may experience

- Reminder that complainants and others must not conduct their own investigation into the incident, spread rumors about the incident or the people involved, or take any other action with respect to the investigation

- Complainant's right to copies of the any tape recording or transcript of the interview (if the interview is tape-recorded)

- Explanation of the entire investigative process, such as interviewing witnesses, interviewing the respondent, and gathering evidence

Complainants should also be given an estimate of when the investigation will be concluded and how they will be notified of the results.

Prepare Necessary Paperwork

In preparation for the first interview, investigators should make sure that they have a copy of the sexual harassment policy, contact information, and appropriate referrals to give to the complainant. The investigator must also prepare a copy of the written agreement to be signed by the complainant regarding the confidentiality guidelines and the prohibitions against retaliation.

Select Appropriate Location

The complainant interview must take place in a location where the complainant will feel safe and comfortable. At a minimum, the location must be quiet, private, and free from distractions. The investigator should not accept any phone calls; it is best if phone calls can be held so that even the ring does not interrupt the interview process. It is also nice to provide complainants with coffee, water, tissues, or other items to increase their comfort level in the interview. Ideally, the interview should be conducted in a location that protects the confidentiality of the complainant, so one possible strategy is to conduct the interview somewhere outside the agency. If so, the interview should never be held in a restaurant or a hotel room—both because of the lack of privacy and the inappropriate message that would be conveyed to complainants. Instead, a more neutral location should be identified. Some agencies have even taken steps to locate a separate unit for discrimination investigations in a different building. (This possibility is discussed in the chapter on the complaint process.) If such a facility is not available, it may be possible to use an office or a conference room in a governmental (city, county, state, or federal) agency.

If the interview is to be conducted within the agency, it should take place in a room that is private and that minimizes the possibility of the complainant being seen entering or exiting.

AT THE START OF THE INTERVIEW

Once the investigator has carefully prepared for the interview, it is time to make the initial contact with the complainant. This initial contact should always be made in person or on the phone, never by email, by mail, or through a third party. During this initial contact, the investigator can schedule the interview and also address basic issues of confidentiality so that the guidelines are clear from the outset (McQueen, 1997). The interview process begins by determining who will be present; by providing explanations, preliminary information, and assurances; and by addressing some of the complainant's basic concerns.

Determine Who Will Be Present in Interview

In most cases, police and fire department personnel have a right to union representation for interviews only if they could potentially lead to discipline, so the complainant will not typically have a union representative present. However, research has documented that "the experience of participating in an investigative process can be as emotionally and physically stressful as the sexual harassment itself" (Paludi & Paludi, 2003, p. 186). It is therefore appropriate for the complainant to have a support person present during the interview, as long as this person can provide support without interfering with the investigative process.

Complainants should always be advised of this right to have a support person at the beginning of an interview, if a union representative, a private attorney, or another support person is not present however, it is not appropriate for this support person to be a spouse or a significant other. Complainants often find it difficult to provide sensitive information in their presence, so this can inhibit candor in responding. In addition, a spouse or a significant other may be interviewed at a later stage of the investigation as a witness to the complainant's reaction to the harassment. Better options for a support person might include a coworker or a friend from outside the agency.

If the complainant does bring in someone—or if the interview is rescheduled for a time when the complainant can have a representative or a support person present—the interview can then proceed with a preliminary discussion of the ground rules and confidentiality guidelines.

Explain Purpose of Interview

At the beginning of the interview, the investigator must explain the purpose of the interview to the complainant; specifically, the purpose of the interview is to collect information to determine exactly what happened. The investigator can state that the agency is conducting the investigation because it cannot ignore any allegation of sexual harassment—that every allegation must be investigated and kept confidential.

Provide Standard Instructions and Information

The beginning of the interview is also the appropriate time for the investigator to provide standard instructions and other information to the complainant. This is when the investigator may find it especially helpful to have prepared notes ahead of time on these standard instructions (see the section above on planning the standard instructions). At this point, the investigator needs to make sure that the complainant has a chance to ask questions regarding the interview and the larger investigative process, including potential outcomes.

Address Concerns Regarding Confidentiality

Typically, one of the primary concerns of complainants is how this will affect their workplace and their relationships with coworkers. Complainants are often particularly concerned about what will happen once the respondent is contacted. To address this concern, investigators can provide a copy of the confidentiality policy to complainants, with provisions regarding who will be notified of the complaint and who will have access to the investigative file. Complainants can be reassured that every effort will be made to protect the confidentiality of all the parties involved in an investigation.

Investigators can also highlight that everyone involved in the investigative process will need to read and sign the confidentiality provisions and that several witnesses will likely be interviewed, so it will not be obvious exactly which people provided what information. However, confidentiality can never be guaranteed, and complainants must be informed of the realistic limits on the confidentiality protections. For example, the policy will likely require that the complaint be formally reported even in cases in which this is against complainants' wishes. In addition, criminal behavior such as acts of stalking and threats of violence, will likely require coordinated effort within and even outside the agency.

It is critically important for investigators to take these concerns regarding confidentiality seriously and to ask complainants what can be done to make them feel more comfortable during the investigation process. For example, the investigator can tell complainants when the respondent will be informed of the investigation so that they can prepare themselves and possibly take the day off. It may even be appropriate to offer complainants administrative leave for that day, so they do not need to be in the workplace when the respondent is notified of the complaint.

Some complainants may be so emotionally upset or frightened by the situation that they are not able to do their jobs. If this is the case, the investigator should assist complainants in securing a temporary paid leave until they are able to return to their work. There may also be situations in which the allegations are so serious that the respondent must be immediately separated from the complainant or placed on leave until the investigation is completed. These would include situations in which the respondent is the complainant's supervisor or an actual sexual assault has occurred.

Address Concerns Regarding Outcomes of Investigation

Complainants are also typically concerned about the consequences of providing a statement. They are often worried about the implications of filing the complaint, not only for themselves and the respondent but also for the larger work unit or the agency as a whole. Of course, investigators cannot guarantee any particular outcome of the investigative process; however, the investigator can address this concern by explaining to complainants that the agency takes complaints of sexual harassment seriously and that the investigation will be conducted as quickly, fairly, and thoroughly as possible.

This concern may be particularly important in those cases in which a sexual harassment investigation is conducted without the victim having filed a formal complaint. For example, a situation of sexual harassment may come to the attention of a supervisor or be reported by a coworker of the victim. In these cases, the victim may not want to cooperate with the investigation or see any discipline levied against the respondent.

Yet police and fire department personnel are typically *required* to participate in the investigation of any complaint regarding employee misconduct, including sexual harassment. The parties therefore do not have the right to refuse to participate in the interview or other investigative procedures, but a great deal can be done both to increase their comfort level during the process and to address concerns regarding the outcome of the investigation.

In this type of situation, complainants should be told of the agency's responsibility to investigate any allegation of sexual harassment, and they should be reassured that the agency will strive to prevent retaliation and to quickly and fairly resolve the situation. If complainants continue to resist giving information, the investigator has no choice but to order them to cooperate with the investigation. In some ways, this actually takes the onus off complainants. At that point, complainants can truthfully say that they were ordered to tell the truth about the situation. Nonetheless, it is especially important in these situations to take steps to prevent retaliation (these steps will be discussed in a later chapter).

Acknowledge Difficulty of Investigation Process

It is generally best for investigators to begin the interview with the complainant by introducing themselves, if they are not personally acquainted, and acknowledging the difficulty of filing a sexual harassment complaint and participating in the investigation. Although investigators need to remain unbiased in their presentation, they can also convey sympathy by stating, "I'm sorry that we had to meet under these circumstances" or "I realize that this process must be very difficult for you."

By acknowledging the difficulty of the situation with the complainant, the investigators can establish rapport and create an open and nonjudgmental atmosphere. As a result, it is likely that the complainant will provide better information to enhance the investigation. In addition, it is helpful to thank the complainant for having the courage to come forward and provide information so that the agency can make the workplace better for everyone. This attitude will reinforce the complainant's decision to report.

Allow Complainant to Vent Emotions

When the complainant expresses emotions in an interview, it is appropriate to allow him or her to vent these emotions while validating that the feelings are both normal and appropriate. Using a calm, reassuring voice, the investigator can communicate empathy and establish rapport, but an investigator should never get "hooked" by the complainant's emotions and start expressing anger or disgust at the respondent. The investigator's tone can be calm and reassuring while still remaining professional and unbiased.

Communicate Empathy

It is crucial to communicate empathy during a complainant interview because it establishes rapport with the complainant, facilitates cooperation, and ultimately creates an environment that will yield the most information for a sexual harassment investigation. Perhaps the single most important thing an investigator can do to communicate empathy, however, is to simply ask complainants how they are doing and *really listen* to the answer. For example, victims of sexual harassment often blame themselves for the situation and excuse the harasser, so investigators can allow complainants to vent this emotion before redirecting back to the purpose of finding out exactly what happened. The investigator could simply prompt the complainant to "Tell me what happened next."

On the other hand, complainants may feel very angry at the respondent, other coworkers, and the agency as a whole. They may feel betrayed that the agency allowed the harassment to take place or that coworkers participated or sided with the respondent. In response, the investigator could simply reply, "I can hear how angry you are."

When a union is involved, the complainant may feel particularly betrayed because the union will typically represent the respondent, not the complainant. Again, the investigator can simply acknowledge this anger. In general, it is important for complainants to be allowed to vent these emotions so that they can then focus on the purpose of the interview: determining the facts.

Build Rapport

By acknowledging the difficulty of the complaint process and communicating empathy, the investigator will have gone a long way toward building rapport with the complainant. Another good way to build rapport is by explaining the purpose of the interview and other administrative procedures to the complainant. Providing such information not only builds rapport but also establishes the complainant's role as an active participant in the investigative process.

Another effective technique for building rapport is asking complainants if they have any questions about the interview or the investigative process and taking the time to address these questions thoroughly. All of these measures will help to increase rapport and thus the quality of information provided by complainants.

DURING THE INTERVIEW

After providing such information about the investigative process, the investigator can then begin the interview with general questions about the complainant's work history and relationships with coworkers. Not only does this provide an easy beginning to the interview, but it also allows the investigator to establish a baseline for how the complainant responds to neutral questions. This can then be used as a comparison for later responses that may be more sensitive, difficult, or even evasive.

Set Pace and Tone of Interview

At the beginning of the interview, complainants should be informed that they can feel free to stop the interview at any time to take a break or ask a question. Because the purpose of the interview is to get all the facts of what happened, complainants should be encouraged to interrupt at any time to ask about a particular question, include a fact, or correct a mistake.

Although it is hard to estimate how long the interview will last, the complainant should be reassured that the investigator is available for as long as it takes. The investigator should also determine if there are any time constraints that the complainant is facing, such as another appointment or scheduled transportation home. In that situation, it may be necessary to schedule an additional interview for another time in the near future to complete the process.

In general, investigators should move the interview along at a pace that is comfortable for the complainant, allowing time for breaks. Often, upon returning from a break, the complainant will remember information that pertains to a previous question. Well-timed breaks can therefore be useful for both the complainant and the investigator.

Address Questions Complainant Cannot Answer

In the course of the interview, complainants may be asked questions that they do not know how to answer. Sexual harassment complainants often react negatively to this situation because they are concerned that the investigator views them with skepticism or even blames them for the situation. Complainants may even guess or provide incorrect information just to provide an answer to the question.

To address this issue, investigators can inform complainants at the beginning of the interview that they may be asked some questions that they don't know how to answer. Complainants should be told that it is appropriate for them to say "I don't know" or "I don't remember." In fact, complainants should be explicitly cautioned against guessing. Investigators can reassure complainants that they may not know the answers to all of the questions but that the purpose of the interview is to obtain as much *accurate* information as possible.

During the course of the interview, investigators can strive to avoid asking several questions in a row that complainants don't know how to answer. For example, if complainants don't know the answer to two consecutive questions, the investigator can try to ask a third question that they will know how to answer. Depending on the nature of the question, it may even be helpful to ask complainants to act out or otherwise demonstrate the behavior to clarify exactly what happened.

First Stage: Complainant's Narrative

In the first stage of the interview, the investigator should begin by asking complainants to describe what happened in their own words and at their own pace.

Use Open-Ended Prompts

It is particularly important that the first stage of the interview begin with open-ended prompts and sufficient time for complainants to tell their story in their own words and at their own pace. The investigator should avoid interrupting and asking leading questions but rather ask questions only to clarify details or to prompt further narrative. The investigator must then listen carefully to the responses and take accurate notes for inclusion in the report. By allowing complainants to take the lead in telling their story and not interrupting them, the investigator can increase the amount of information obtained.

Allow Time for Silent Pauses

When complainants pause in their narrative, investigators should remain silent or provide an encouraging prompt for them to continue rather than asking a question that may sidetrack or discourage complainants from telling their story in its entirety. Silence often allows complainants a moment to collect their thoughts or to regain their composure, which is especially important during an interview situation. Although this can be difficult, it is important for investigators to allow complainants these silent pauses and not to leap in with a question. Complainants must be allowed to complete their narrative before moving into the second stage of the interview, at which time follow-up questions are appropriate.

Maintain Eye Contact and Appropriate Body Language

The investigator should generally look directly at the complainant during the interview, even if that individual does not return the eye contact. This communicates that the investigator is comfortable with the complainant and the information that is being discussed. Investigators should always try to maintain direct and comfortable eye contact to communicate that they are actively engaged in the process of listening to the complainant's story. This does not mean that investigators should stare at the complainant but rather that they should use eye contract to express interest and empathy.

Investigators can also express their attention and interest through body language, by nodding or otherwise indicating that they are following what the complainant is saying. It is best, however, to avoid feedback that might be interpreted as being evaluative (e.g., "That's good" or "That's right").

The investigator should use smooth movements and speech style, thereby expressing patience, friendliness, and support. It is critical that the investigator's voice remains calm and reassuring throughout the interview, no matter how volatile the emotions of the complainant might become.

It is particularly important for the investigator to maintain this comfortable demeanor when the complainant is using sexual language or describing sexual behavior. An investigator's discomfort with sexual language will be clearly communicated to complainants and make them feel less comfortable in the situation. It is also generally best for the investigator to avoid touching the complainant, especially if the investigator is male and the complainant is female.

Monitor Complainant's Body Language

As for the body language of complainants, investigators can watch this as an additional source of information about their level of comfort during the interview. When complainants communicate with their body language that they are uncomfortable or upset, it may be a particularly appropriate time to ask if they would like to take a break. For example, complainants may begin to fidget excessively or breathe too quickly. The investigator can also allow the complainant to skip certain questions if the questions become too difficult and return to them later when the complainant appears more comfortable.

When complainants' body language communicates discomfort, this is a good time to reassure them how important their cooperation is and how vital their role is in the investigative process. It is also important that the investigator avoid any preconceived notions about body language that might lead to the conclusion that the complainant (or the respondent or a witness) is not telling the truth. Such nonverbal behavior is important to monitor as a source of information, but it cannot be used to automatically conclude that the person is lying. For example, people may fidget, avoid eye contact, or cross their arms in an interview situation, not because they are lying but because they are understandably uncomfortable in the situation or have cultural differences in nonverbal expression.

Use Reflective Comments

Investigators should exhibit active listening at all times; for example, reflective comments can be used to encourage continued narrative by the complainant. Such comments reflect back to complainants some of what they said, in summary form. This reflecting will encourage the complainant to keep talking, as long as it is done in a way that elicits continued narrative rather than a closed-ended response. To illustrate:

> Complainant: "I had worked with him on a few shifts, but I didn't know him well."
>
> Investigator: "He was someone you knew casually?"

Complainant: "Yeah, so that was why I was surprised when he started showing up at my locker every day when I started my shift."

In this example, the investigator has reflected back to the complainant the essence of what was said in order to focus the complainant's attention on the point and to encourage further elaboration.

Clarify and Summarize

To make sure they are following the details of the complainant's story, investigators can clarify and summarize what they have heard after each segment. Investigators should not interrupt the complainant to clarify points, but when complainants pause after completing a segment of the narrative, investigators can use this opportunity to clarify a particular issue or summarize the events and facts in that segment. To do this successfully, investigators must make notes of their questions while listening.

After summarizing the complainant's account, the investigator should ask a question to invite clarification or elaboration by the complainant. For example, the investigator's summary of events could be followed with a question, such as "Do I have that part right?" or "Is that the way it happened?" This process both ensures that the investigator understands the details and allows complainants to verify that they are communicating clearly. However, detailed follow-up questions should not be used until the next stage of the interview, after complainants have completed telling their story in their own words.

Take Breaks as Needed

If the investigator suspects that a break might be useful, it is appropriate to ask the complainant if he or she would like one. In situations in which a union representative, a private attorney, or another support person is present during the interview, that person can also help the investigator to monitor the complainant's demeanor to determine when it might be helpful to take a break. In most instances, however, the actual decision to take a break should be left to the complainant.

Complainants might want to take a break after particularly difficult sections of the interview, for example, after the description of any sexual comments or sexual acts involved in the situation. Breaks are particularly useful for complainants to regain their composure and prepare for the remaining questions. Taking a break can even facilitate rapport between the investigator and the complainant because it demonstrates concern for the complainant's comfort and well-being during the interview.

In general, investigators should ensure that the complainant gets to take a break at least once an hour. This gives the investigator and the complainant a chance to stretch, and it can be used as a defense in any situation in which the complainant later alleges being subjected to unreasonable periods of interrogation. For this reason, breaks should always be documented in the investigator's notes.

Investigators can also suggest taking a break at any point during the interview when the complainant becomes overly emotional; however, if the complainant becomes completely overwrought, the interview may have to be rescheduled. In that situation, investigators can help the complainant to connect with resources that might be helpful in coping with emotional issues, such as an employee assistance program or other counseling programs.

Take Notes During Interview

Investigators must always take detailed notes during the interview with the complainant, even if the interview is being audiotaped or videotaped. These notes will form the basis of the investigative file by outlining the allegations and identifying potential sources for corroborative evidence. It is therefore important that the investigator avoid taking notes on personal issues that are not relevant to the investigation because the notes form a part of the investigative record. It is also helpful to make notes on a separate page about questions that the investigator wants to ask later.

Second Stage: Follow-Up Questions

After allowing complainants to tell their story in their own words and without interruptions during the first stage of the interview, it is appropriate to move into the second stage, when the investigator uses follow-up questions to elicit additional information. However, it is still important in this second stage to use open-ended questions and to allow complainants to answer fully before asking the next question. Investigators must also continue to avoid both interrupting and following one question with another so quickly that the complainant does not have enough time to respond.

Complainants must be allowed to describe what happened in their own words and at their own pace, avoiding any break in the narrative until they have finished. Rather than interrupting during this narrative, investigators should focus their attention on carefully documenting everything being said. When a complainant has finished describing what happened, the investigator can go back to clarify points of confusion and elicit additional details with follow-up questions.

Explain Questions Asked

It is critically important that complainants feel they are an active part of the investigative process, and one of the best ways of doing this is by keeping them informed. As previously mentioned, complainants must be informed at the beginning about the purpose of the interview and their role in it. Throughout the interview, investigators should also explain the questions that are asked, especially those dealing with sensitive information such as unflattering behavior. This would include the complainant's participation in sexualized workplace banter or crude language.

Explain Use of Repeated Questions

Investigators can also explain to the complainant that they will sometimes ask questions in several different ways and that this does not mean that they do not believe the complainant or that they doubt the complainant's response. While investigators should not hesitate to repeat a question if it is necessary to clarify a point, it can be helpful to reassure the complainant that this is not being done because they are doubtful about the complainant's behavior or a previous response.

By reminding the complainant that the investigator's job is to make sure that all the information is being recorded correctly and completely, this should explain why the investigator sometimes needs to repeat a question. Investigators must also keep in mind that repeating a question often implies to the complainant that a previous answer was somehow unsatisfactory. As a result, questions should be repeated only when absolutely necessary, and they should be accompanied by an explanation of why they are being repeated to avoid encouraging the complainant to guess or change a response.

The underlying theme is that investigators must keep complainants informed of what is happening during the investigation and why. When investigators ask the complainant about sensitive topics, they need to explain why this information is needed and how it is helpful in interpreting the information uncovered during the investigation. Investigators must always remember that the complainant is carefully watching them for signs of being doubted or blamed, and any question or procedure that might add to the complainant's suspicion needs to be carefully explained to reassure the complainant and ensure his or her continued cooperation.

Obtain Specific Types of Information

In the complainant interview, investigators must obtain information in a variety of areas. If these points are not covered by complainants in their narrative account during the first stage of the interview, these points should be addressed with follow-up questions in the second stage. This information can then be used to establish a chronology of events, which is helpful in making sense of the allegations and the investigative findings. In general, information to obtain during the complainant interview includes the following points.

What Behaviors Are Being Reported. It is important to obtain as much detail as possible about each behavior listed by the complainant. Even if the investigator does not think that the conduct meets the criteria for sexual harassment or any other form of employee misconduct, it is still important to document the behaviors. There is a reason the complainant is providing the information, and the importance of the behavior may become evident at a later time in the interview. The behavior may also have a meaning for the complainant based on his or her social group identification (e.g., gender, race, religion, national origin, sexual orientation) that is not immediately obvious to the investigator but that will become clear during the course of the investigation. It is therefore important to document not only the behaviors that are described by the complainant but also their meaning and interpretation *from the complainant's perspective.*

What Additional Behaviors Took Place. After the complainant has listed the primary allegations, it is important to prompt for further examples of behaviors or situations that were seen as offensive. This is because complainants will often limit their initial account of the harassment to those incidents that were either the most recent and/or the most severe, but an encouraging prompt will elicit more information.

What Exact Dates and Times Were (If Possible).   If the complainant does not remember an exact date, investigators can ask different types of questions to help the complainant attach the date to something: Was it close to a holiday? Was it at the beginning or end of the complainant's workweek? Did it take place at an event such as a training seminar whose date can be obtained elsewhere? Was it just before the respondent left on vacation? There is usually some way to set an approximate date.

Who Was Involved in the Incident(s).   Was it just the respondent and the complainant in a private office? Or was the respondent's partner standing nearby and encouraging the respondent in the behavior? If it was just the respondent and the complainant, who else knew that they were together at that point in time?

What Evidence Exists to Corroborate Account of Incident.   Were there written exchanges? Was a call made on a cell phone? Was something sent by email?

Whether Situation Interfered With Complainant's Work Performance.   One way to ask this question is to say, "What did you do after the incident?" Complainants may describe how the behavior negatively affected their ability to do their job effectively. For example, a complainant may say, "I would often be late handing in reports because I had to wait until I was sure he had left the building."

Whether Situation Created Hostile and Intimidating Work Environment.   This question should not be asked directly at first; instead, initial questions should be more indirect. For example, the investigator could say, "How did you feel when this happened?" For complainants who use phrases such as "hostile work environment," they can be asked, "What do you mean by that? What did you feel was hostile? How did it affect your job?" This may prompt the complainant to describe the situation in more detail.

Who Might Have Witnessed Respondent's Behavior or Have Other Information. This is a particularly important issue to probe. Complainants will often say that no one else witnessed the behavior or that they did not report it. However, skillful questioning may reveal that a secretary sat nearby and could have overheard what was said or that the complainant may have told someone (a friend, a coworker, a family member, a therapist, or a pastor) at least part of the story. Sometimes the complainant may write about the situation in a journal. Even when complainants do not tell anyone about the situation, others may have noticed a difference in their behavior as a result.

What (If Anything) Complainant Did to Communicate that Respondent's Behavior Was Unwelcome.   Again, this is a delicate area of questioning. Sometimes complainants "communicate" that the behavior is unwelcome by completely avoiding any contact with the respondent, some complainants simply make sure that they are never alone with the respondent, and others jokingly tell the respondent to stop. Investigators must keep in mind that the strategy used by the complainant to communicate that the behavior was unwelcome may not immediately seem to be reasonable or appropriate from their perspective, but it may have represented the best the complainant could manage in the situation.

Whether There Was Pattern of Similar Behavior in Past.   This pattern may include behavior by the respondent that was directed toward someone else but witnessed by the complainant. Investigators must therefore be careful about using the word "similar" to describe the different behaviors or labeling them as "sexual harassment." A better technique is to ask complainants if there were other things the respondent said or did that were unprofessional or that made them feel uncomfortable, no matter how minor. When complainants begin to think about other times they felt uncomfortable, this often reveals a pattern of behavior on the part of the respondent or others.

Whether Supervisors Knew of Incident and How They Responded.   Complainants should always be asked a variety of questions about whether supervisors knew about the situation or should have known about it. First, did any of the incidents take place in view of a supervisor? For example, if the complainant was ridiculed during roll call, this would have been witnessed by at least one supervisor as well as other coworkers. Second, did any of the incidents take place where a supervisor should have been able to see or hear what happened? To illustrate, if the complainant and the respondent were standing near the door of the sergeant's office during an incident, this should have been witnessed by the sergeant if he or she was in the office. Third, did the complainant tell a supervisor about any of the behavior? Complainants will sometimes tell a supervisor (but not others) about some of the behaviors, especially the behaviors that are least embarrassing. For example, a complainant may tell a supervisor, "John is really rude sometimes." If the supervisor does not ask any questions about this statement, the complainant may understandably fear giving any more details. Or the complainant may tell the supervisor, "I would appreciate it if you would tell Sgt. Jones to stop getting in my desk," when Sgt. Jones is actually leaving sexually harassing notes in the complainant's desk drawers.

What Complainant Would Like to See Happen.   Again, investigators must be extremely careful with this question because the answer may be that the complainant would like to see the respondent fired. One way to ask this is to say, "What would you consider to be a satisfactory outcome to your complaint?" or "What do you feel the agency needs to do to resolve this situation?" Often, complainants just want the behavior to stop; however, if the situation has gone on for a long time, just stopping the behavior may not be enough to assure them that the situation has been fairly resolved. In either case, it is helpful to know whether the complainant has a reasonable expectation of the outcome of the investigation.

Whether Complainant Received Copy of Policy and/or Training on Sexual Harassment (and If So, When).   Was the policy given to the complainant upon employment or at any other time? Is there any documentation of the receipt of the policy and/or participation in the training program?

Obtain Information on Complainant's Behavior and Relationship with Respondent

In addition to the topics outlined above, the investigator must also ask the complainant about his or her behavior and relationship with the respondent. These questions should address the complainant's and respondent's past history and relationship as well as the respondent's interactions that were seen as sexually harassing by the complainant.

When the complainant is describing any behaviors, it is important for investigators to distinguish between the complainant participating in activities that are voluntary and consensual (e.g., shared jokes or workplace banter) and the complainant "playing along" to avoid creating a problem. For example, the complainant may have smiled at off-color jokes or even joked about the pornographic pictures in the break room to avoid being teased, ostracized, or otherwise targeted for additional harassment. This does not mean that the complainant voluntarily participated in the activity or that it was not seen as offensive.

For this purpose, it can be particularly helpful to ask complainants what they think the respondent will say when confronted with the allegations. The answer to this question can often be revealing about their relationship. For example, a complainant may respond, "He will probably say that I am just angry because he told the sergeant I screwed up on a call." Or the complainant may answer, "He will probably say that I lied because he told me that is what he would say if I reported him."

Whether or not this is actually what the respondent eventually does say in response to the complaint, it provides useful information about the relationship between the complainant and the respondent from the complainant's perspective.

Identify Potential Witnesses and Others Who Were Told About Situation

It is critical that investigators identify anyone who may have witnessed the sexual harassment or who was told of the situation by the complainant. As previously discussed, it is particularly important to find out about the first person the complainant told about the situation because that person can explain the complainant's initial response and demeanor. When asking complainants about potential witnesses, the investigator should always assess whom they told, when they told them, and what they said.

Investigators must also try to find out about others who might have been sexually harassed by the respondent. These people will need to be interviewed, even if they do not work in the organization.

AT THE CONCLUSION OF THE INTERVIEW

At the conclusion of the interview, complainants often look to the investigator for a reaction to their story. The investigator can therefore take this opportunity to reassure complainants by thanking them for their vital cooperation. At this point, the investigator can also ask complainants if they have any additional information that they would like to offer. Sometimes details come to mind during the course of the interview that complainants should be invited to share before concluding. Complainants should also be encouraged to call the investigator or make another appointment if more information comes to mind at a later time.

Explain Future Procedures

Before complainants leave the room, it is important to explain to them the procedures involved in the investigative process. All too often, investigators forget that complainants may not understand the procedures of an administrative investigation, even if they have extensive experience with criminal investigation as part of their law enforcement career. For this reason, investigators must take the time to explain these procedures to complainants as well as outline the reasons underlying these procedures. Investigators should also address any questions or concerns the complainant might have about what is and is not part of the administrative investigation.

When the investigator is explaining the administrative investigation, it is important to avoid false assurances or unrealistic expectations about the process. For example, complainants should not be told that the complaint will likely be substantiated or that the respondent will be disciplined. Instead, complainants should be provided with honest information about the process and possible outcomes, without investigators compromising the appearance of impartiality.

Complainants should also be informed of their rights regarding both relevant statutes of limitations for taking legal action and any resources available to them in the department and the community.

Address Issues of Confidentiality and Retaliation

At the conclusion of the interview, investigators should return to the complainant's concerns regarding the issues of confidentiality and retaliation. Given that administrative investigations take place within an ongoing work relationship, most complainants will understandably have concerns about what will happen when the respondent is contacted about the complaint. It is therefore important for investigators to again mention the protections of confidentiality and the process for reporting any violations by someone who inappropriately shares information about the complaint.

Of course, the complainant must also be cautioned against violating the confidentiality policy by discussing the issues with coworkers. Complainants can be advised to discuss the issues only with friends or family members outside the organization. It is also important to remind complainants that retaliation is prohibited and that they should report any negative behaviors they experience as a result of filing the complaint and participating in the investigation.

It is critical to determine at some point during the interview whether the complainant feels comfortable remaining in the same work assignment during the time it will take to investigate the complaint. For complainants who do not feel comfortable in their current assignment (e.g., because they will have daily contact with the respondent), the investigator must bring this information to the attention of the appropriate command staff so that suitable actions can be taken. On the other hand, it is not a good idea to change the assignment of any complainants who do not want to change. Moving complainants to a different assignment can be perceived as retaliation. These issues are discussed in greater detail in the chapter on the complaint process.

Lay Groundwork for Follow-Up Contact

Investigators must remember that complainants may remember additional details at a later time or may decide that they feel comfortable disclosing more details at some point after the initial interview. Investigators should therefore provide information to the complainant about how to contact them to answer questions or to provide additional information. Alternatively, the investigator may need to follow up with the complainant to clarify information or to ask additional questions. Contact information should always include a phone number or an email address for confidential communication.

Provide Referral Information

It is always helpful for investigators to provide the complainant with referrals for an employee assistance program or other counseling. Investigators can and should convey empathy to the complainant during the investigative process, but it must remain clear that their role is an objective fact finder, so they cannot serve as a therapist or an advocate for the complainant.

Have Complainant Sign Written Statement

Once the interview is complete, the investigator will need to prepare a written statement for the complainant. When this is finished, the complainant should be asked to review this written statement and make any corrections before signing and dating it. A copy of the written statement should then be provided to the complainant, and another copy should be included in the investigative file.

Keep in Touch with Complainant

After the written statement is filed, investigators should stay in touch with complainants and keep them apprised of the status of the investigation. Complainants will typically want to be updated about the process of the administrative investigation, and they must be notified of the ultimate disposition of the complaint and any disciplinary sanctions for the respondent. At a minimum, complainants should be contacted for follow-up within 30–60 days of the conclusion of the investigation to make sure they are not experiencing retaliation and to find out if they are aware of any breaches of the confidentiality agreement.

ENDNOTE

1. Sections of this chapter were based on the document entitled: *Successfully Investigating Acquaintance Sexual Assault: A National Training Manual for Law Enforcement.* It was developed by the National Center for Women & Policing (2000), with support provided by the Violence Against Women Office, Office of Justice Programs (grant #97-WE-VX-K004).

Chapter 16

Interviewing the Respondent

Successfully interviewing the respondent in a sexual harassment investigation requires skilled questioning and rapport building to obtain the necessary information. This chapter provides detailed guidance for interviewing the respondent about a complaint of sexual harassment or discrimination.

PREPARATION FOR THE INTERVIEW

As with the complainant interview, investigators need to prepare for the interview with respondents by developing a list of standard instructions, preparing all the necessary paperwork, and selecting a location that is quiet, private, and free from distractions. Investigators must then review the Peace Officer Bill of Rights, any applicable labor contracts, any policies and procedures regarding internal investigations, and any preliminary information (including the respondent's personnel file and any internal investigation files) before proceeding.

Plan Standard Instructions

Standard instructions are listed in the chapter on the complainant interview and include a discussion of confidentiality and retaliation. These instructions, including an explanation of the process for reporting any breaches of confidentiality or retaliatory actions of which they are aware, should also be provided to respondents.

Standard instructions need to include a general discussion of the process for the administrative interview, including the fact that the investigator will take notes, prepare a written summary, and ask the respondent to note any corrections to that summary statement before signing it. In addition, the investigator must state that the agency has an expectation that the respondent will cooperate fully with the investigation and provide truthful information. The investigator can even remind the respondent that failure to do so could result in disciplinary sanctions. In law enforcement, unlike other professions, personnel can be forced to cooperate with the investigation and to participate in interviews; the penalties for refusing to cooperate can range up to and include termination. Of course, all respondents must be informed of their rights during the investigative process, as specified in the labor contract or the employee hand-book. This will include any relevant provisions from the Peace Officer Bill of Rights.

Review Peace Officer Bill of Rights

Many states have enacted legislation usually referred to as the Peace Officer Bill of Rights, which contains restrictions governing the interview process such as how much time is allowed, how often people can take breaks, how many people should be involved, and what information or materials will be made available to officers. It also typically restricts the types of punishments that will be allowed and outlines the process for appealing sanctions. Investigators must obtain a copy of the Peace Officer Bill of Rights for their state and make sure that they do not violate these rights during the investigative process. For example, some peace officers have a right to the tape and/or transcript of their interview if it is taped. In addition, there are rulings in case law at both the state and federal levels that impact the way investigations are conducted. Investigators must consult with legal experts to make certain that they are aware of all the rulings and laws that control internal investigations and criminal investigations.

Prepare Necessary Paperwork

As was the case for the complainant interview, investigators must prepare the necessary paperwork before interviewing the respondent. The respondent must always be provided with a copy of the confidentiality guidelines and prohibitions against retaliation, which the respondent will be asked to read and sign. It is also a good idea to provide a written statement to respondents that both summarizes the Peace Officer Bill of Rights and acknowledges their understanding of its implications.

Collect Preliminary Information

Before investigators begin interviewing the respondent, they will typically have collected some preliminary information on the allegations and potential corroborative evidence, including statements from potential witnesses. The witnesses may have even been interviewed before the respondent. Based on the information given by the complainant and witnesses, therefore, the investigator may want to gather and review any corroborative evidence, including documents or offensive communications such as emails, memos, cards, letters, pictures, or cartoons.

Review Respondent's Personnel and Investigation Files

Investigators should also review the personnel file of the respondent and any prior investigation files before the interview, if they have not already done so. When reviewing the respondent's files, it is particularly important to determine whether there are prior complaints of sexual harassment or other forms of employee misconduct. It is also important to identify any documentation indicating that the respondent received a copy of the sexual harassment policy or attended training on the topic of sexual harassment prevention.

Supervisor or Manager as Respondent

If the respondent is a person of equal or higher rank than the investigator, it is important to bring a second person into the interview. This person must be of higher rank than the respondent. In law enforcement and fire departments, rank structure is important and carries with it a great deal of authority. To ask a subordinate officer to interview a superior officer is not fair to the subordinate officer. The subordinate officer may feel intimidated by the rank of the respondent or may have valid concerns for his/her future in the department if the superior officer is angry about being accused. Also, having someone of higher rank present can be important if the respondent has to be ordered to answer questions.

Whenever a second interviewer is involved, the team must make a plan for how the interview will be conducted, who will be the lead, and what roles each person will play.

START OF THE INTERVIEW

When investigators have done all the preparation for the interview with the respondent, it is time to start the interview.

Describe Purpose of Investigation

While the investigator must always describe the general purpose of the investigation to respondents, this may not initially include information about the specific allegations or the identity of the complainant. Rather, this description might be limited at first to a statement that the investigator is looking into "some things that may have occurred in the workplace." To illustrate, the investigator might say the following:

> I have been assigned to look into some things that may have occurred in the workplace (division/department, etc.). I will tell you about the event and then ask for your recollection of it. It is important that you provide as much information as you can remember so that my investigation will be thorough.

At this initial stage of the interview, the identity of the complainant should not be revealed to respondents unless it is necessary for the successful completion of the interview process. (This issue will be discussed in greater detail later.) Of course, by the end of the interview, respondents must be given the chance to respond to each and every allegation that is made by the complainant, but this can sometimes be done without identifying who the complainant is. It is also important to review the labor contract and the applicable state laws because some rules mandate that the officer be told who is complaining about the behavior in question.

Allow Representation During Interview

Within police and fire departments, employees typically have the right to have a union representative or some other advocate present during an investigative interview if it could result in disciplinary sanctions. The respondent may even bring a private attorney to the interview, and this is appropriate as long as it is clear to everyone that the attorney is there only as a witness and will not be allowed to conduct the interview. On the other hand, it is not appropriate to have a spouse or a significant other present; another coworker or a friend from outside the agency is a better choice.

If respondents do not bring someone with them to the interview, they must be notified of their right to representation, consistent with the Peace Officer Bill of Rights and/or provisions of the labor contract. The interview may even need to be rescheduled so they can bring an appropriate representative—but this should be scheduled to take place as soon as possible so the investigation can proceed in a timely fashion.

Open with General Questions

After discussing the standard instructions and other preliminary issues, respondents should be asked if they have any questions about the process. Then it is typically best to begin the interview with general questions about the organization and the respondent's work history, both to collect basic information and to establish a baseline for neutral responses. If the investigator suspects that the respondent is evading questions later on during the interview, the behavior can be compared with that shown during these initial baseline responses.

Never Assume Guilt or Innocence

Because investigators will typically conduct the interview with the complainant first, it is easy for them to develop a picture of what happened from the complainant's point of view—along with a very negative image of the respondent. However, investigators must *never* assume the respondent's guilt or innocence at the beginning of an investigation. Rather, investigators must actively work to maintain a neutral orientation and an open mind about the complaint because they have not yet heard "the other side of the story." In addition, personal biases will be sensed by the respondent and will negatively influence the integrity of the investigation.

Establish Rapport

Not surprisingly, most respondents will be extremely defensive at the beginning of the interview, so the investigator must work to establish rapport with respondents and put them at ease. Most important, respondents must understand that the investigator is a neutral fact finder who has no preconceived ideas of what happened. The investigator can accomplish this by providing the standard instructions and other preliminary information and by asking the opening questions with a demeanor that is objective and impartial. Rapport is perhaps best established, however, by reminding respondents that the purpose of the investigation is to find out exactly what happened and by highlighting that their cooperation is needed to get the complete picture.

Protect Confidentiality

As previously stated, the respondent must be informed of the charges at some point during the interview and given the opportunity to respond to every single allegation being investigated. The investigator should also reassure the respondent that the agency will endeavor to keep the complaint and investigative information confidential.

To make sure that respondents are informed of the confidentiality provisions, they should be asked at some point during the interview to read and sign a statement of the agency's policy regarding confidentiality. It is particularly important to stress to respondents that they must not discuss the complaint with coworkers or try to conduct their own investigation. The investigator can also highlight the fact that actions that go against the confidentiality policy constitute separate violations that will be taken seriously and investigated and that those actions may result in disciplinary sanctions if they are substantiated.

Of course, the respondent will undoubtedly want to know the details of the allegations and the identity of the complainant, but the investigator must redirect these questions and not answer them. Rather, the underlying concern of respondents can be addressed by acknowledging how difficult the process must be for them and by reassuring them that they will have the opportunity to respond to each of the allegations in detail before the interview is completed.

Even though the investigator cannot answer specific questions about the identity of the complainant, the respondent will typically know who complained or at least will have a pretty good idea by the end of the interview; often, this information is apparent from the specific questions that are asked. Therefore, it is critical for the investigator to reiterate the importance of confidentiality, stating that the respondent is not allowed to discuss the issues with other employees or to retaliate against the complainant or anyone else who might cooperate with the investigation.

On the other hand, respondents may react to the investigation with surprise, saying that they simply want to straighten out this issue with the complainant. Respondents should be told that they are to have no contact with the complainant about this issue until the investigation is completed and it is determined how the situation will be resolved.

Prevent Retaliation

It is also critically important that the respondent be cautioned against retaliating against the complainant or anyone else providing information during the investigation. As with breaches of confidentiality, any such retaliatory actions will constitute a separate violation of policy that will be taken seriously and investigated, and those actions will result in discipline if they are substantiated.

DURING THE INTERVIEW

Investigators should never hesitate to go over the above issues several times with the respondent during the interview process because the respondent must thoroughly understand the information provided. At the same time, investigators must maintain a neutral attitude toward the respondent, no matter how volatile his or her emotions become during the interview. For example, it is never appropriate for an investigator to argue with someone during an interview. Other guidelines for the respondent interview are consistent with those for the complainant interview. During the interview process, investigators should strive to do the following:

- Keep the goals of the interview in mind.
- Maintain visual contact as much as possible, and use appropriate body language.
- Use active listening techniques, including reflective comments and statements to clarify and summarize.
- Repeat questions when necessary to clarify a point.
- Check for consistency if a respondent's answer doesn't seem to fit with previous answers.
- Ask the respondent to demonstrate if it will be helpful to understand what happened.
- Establish a chronology of events.
- Repeat facts back to the respondent to confirm that they are recorded accurately.
- Identify anyone else who might be a witness or who might have information about the incident.
- Avoid drawing any conclusions or making any promises that cannot be kept.
- Take accurate notes, whether or not the interview is taped.

During the interview, many respondents will want to know whether they will be called back for more information and what will happen as a result of the investigation. Of course, the investigator cannot answer these questions or make any promises about what will happen. Investigators should therefore respond by saying that the agency takes complaints of sexual harassment seriously and that the investigation will be conducted as quickly, fairly, and thoroughly as possible. Respondents can also be reassured that they will be notified when the investigation is completed and that if any further action is to be taken, they will have another opportunity to be heard.

Maintain Focus on Issues

While it is sometimes difficult to keep the respondent focused on the issues at hand, this is critically important to a successful interview. For example, the respondent may try to use the interview as a way to find out more information about the investigation or to vent angry feelings about the workplace or the people involved. Yet it is important to keep respondents focused and not let them take over the interview. In such a situation, it may be helpful to take a break; then begin again with a clear statement about the focus of the interview and the direction of the questions. It is desirable, however, to let respondents vent their emotions to some degree. Their venting may reveal a motive for the actions they took, or it may reveal a desperate need for further training.

Document Evasive Behavior

If the investigator is uncertain about the truthfulness of any response, it is often best to simply wait silently. People who are not telling the truth usually become very nervous with a long pause and may volunteer information just to break the silence. Investigators should also be on the lookout for signs of verbal evasion. This could include the respondent not answering a question directly, especially if he or she answered previous questions in a direct way.

For example, the respondent may answer "No" to several questions in a row and then respond with "I don't recall." This may be an indicator that the person being interviewed is evading the last question asked. Alternatively, the respondent may give very detailed answers to several questions and then suddenly answer with a curt response, which may be an indication of the respondent either lying or not feeling comfortable discussing the issue. A good investigator will probe into those areas. Whenever an investigator suspects verbal evasion, it is usually a good tactic to respond directly by noting the suspected evasion and repeating the question. For example, an investigator might say, "Officer Brown, it appears that you are reluctant to answer my question. Let me rephrase it for you." Investigators must continue to ask the question directly until they receive a straightforward answer.

It may also be effective to stop the interview and read the agency's policy on cooperating with an investigation and being truthful. No accusation needs to be made directly. Often the investigator can simply review the policy and then state, "Let's go over the prior question again to make sure I understand your answer." In many cases, this approach will bring about a more truthful response.

Another way to detect evasion is by evaluating whether the response makes common sense. For example, it may be reasonable for respondents to indicate that they don't recall whether they told the complainant that she looked nice in a particular outfit; however, it is not reasonable for respondents to fail to recall asking the complainant to engage in sexual intercourse (Salisbury & Dominick, 2004).

When the respondent gives a far-fetched answer or account of events, investigators should still respond directly by stating that they have concerns about the truthfulness of the story. This provides the respondent with the opportunity to either explain the far-fetched story or dig in deeper (Oppenheimer & Pratt, 2003). Of course, it is always important to document any such attempts at verbal evasion by respondents because these instances are critical for evaluating respondents' credibility later.

Law enforcement professionals often make the mistake of assuming that the purpose of the interview is to get the respondent to "confess." In fact, a confession is not typical in a workplace investigation of sexual harassment, and it is not required to substantiate the allegations based on the standard of "a preponderance of the evidence." This issue is discussed in greater detail in the chapter on making a determination and imposing discipline.

Obtain Specific Information

After providing the standard instructions and addressing other preliminary issues, the interview with respondents can then continue with specific questions about what happened in the alleged incidents. This is different from the interview with the complainant, who was allowed to first detail the allegations in a narrative response. In the interview with the respondent, specific questions are needed to address the individual allegations and to gather information regarding the following issues.

Date, Time, and Place of Each Event. The interview with the respondent should be used to confirm the information provided by the complainant and the witnesses. For example, if an incident was described as taking place on a particular day, it will be important to confirm that the respondent was working that day and was actually present at the place where the event took place.

Names of Witnesses to Any Event. Investigators must also find out from the respondent additional names of people who were present at any of the events. Particular care must be taken to include civilian employees as well as any supervisors or command staff who may have been present.

Respondent's Version of Events. This is a good place to let respondents tell their story without interruption. It can even be a good idea to have respondents relate their story several times to see if it is consistent. The investigator can then use techniques described in the chapter on interviewing complainants, such as repeating back what the respondent said and asking if that is correct. The investigator could say, "I want to be sure that I understand what happened. Will you go over it again for me?"

Corroborating Evidence for Respondent's Account. Were there written exchanges? Were telephone calls made? Was something sent by email?

Respondent's Stated Reason for Behavior. For respondents who admit to the alleged behavior, they will often come up with one of the reasons listed below in the section on common defenses to allegations of sexual harassment. If so, it is best for the investigator to let respondents explain the reason for their actions without interruption. It is also good to have respondents relate this information more than once, again to test its consistency.

Complainant's Response. Respondents should also be asked about how the complainant reacted to the behavior. What did the complainant say or do?

Complainant's Indications of Unacceptable Behavior. If there is evidence that the complainant found the behavior unacceptable, investigators must obtain details of this event. Exactly *how* did the complainant communicate that the respondent's behavior was unwelcome?

Respondent's Receipt of Copy of Sexual Harassment Policy. It is critical to ask respondents whether they received a copy of the sexual harassment policy and whether they read it. Was the policy posted in the workplace? Was it given to the respondent upon employment or at any other point? This answer can then be compared with documentation in the respondent's personnel file or in other agency records. While the failure to receive or read the policy does not constitute a defense to sexually harassing behavior, it is important information to obtain to design appropriate corrective actions for both the respondent and the agency.

Respondent's Attendance at Any Training Classes on Sexual Harassment.   Again, the investigator must first ask the respondent about training classes and then compare that answer to documents that have been gathered from personnel files or other agency records. This information is useful for understanding the incidents being investigated, and it can provide feedback on the effectiveness of the training program.

Respondent's Understanding of Sexual Harassment Policy.   During the interview, the investigator can then seek to determine whether the respondent understands the agency's policy on sexual harassment. For respondents who say they do not understand the sexual harassment policy, investigators should ask what it is they do not understand. While the interview is not the appropriate time to educate respondents about the policy, it is important to document what aspects of the policy respondents say they do not understand. Respondents who say they do not understand the policy should also be asked if they have ever asked for clarification or additional training. For respondents who say they do understand the policy, they should be asked whether they think their behavior is acceptable according to the policy.

Common Respondent Defenses to Allegations of Sexual Harassment

In any case of sexual harassment, there are a number of defenses that the respondent might raise during the interview process to explain or justify the behavior described in the allegations. It is important to note that each of these defenses includes an admission that the behavior took place, so they all can serve as the basis for resolving the complaint as substantiated. However, the defenses may sometimes be relevant for designing an appropriate corrective response.

For example, if the respondent in the example above admits to the behavior but states that he did not mean to harass Jane, the complaint can be substantiated. Even behaviors that are not intended to offend can nonetheless be quite offensive and can constitute sexual harassment. However, the intentions or motivations of the respondent may be a factor to consider when designing the appropriate discipline. In this example, the comment may have been a first-time offense that would not be repeated if the respondent were required to attend remedial training in sexual harassment issues. Some of the most common defenses to a complaint of sexual harassment are described below.

"I Was Joking. I Certainly Didn't Mean to Harass Her."   The courts do not recognize this as a valid defense, so it should not be considered a valid defense in an administrative investigation either. Establishing a claim of sexual harassment requires only determining that the behavior took place and that it created or contributed to a hostile work environment.

EXAMPLE 16-1

Illustration: What This Might Look Like

To illustrate, the steps in an interview with a male respondent that addresses a single verbal comment made to a female complainant might resemble this sample dialogue:

1. "Do you know Jane Doe? How do you know her? How long have you worked with her? What is your working relationship with her?"

These questions get the respondent on record early in the investigation about his attitude toward Jane. If he says he has a good working relationship with her and then later accuses her of bad intentions toward him, he is being inconsistent. On the other hand, if he says he has a poor relationship with Jane, he should be asked to describe why there is a poor relationship. What are the events that contributed to the poor relationship? Does he believe that she has some ulterior motive for filing a complaint against him?

2. "On March 2, 2005, you and Jane Doe attended a meeting to discuss the new company program on child care. Do you remember attending that meeting?"

If the respondent does not recall attending the meeting or denies being at the meeting, the investigator can show him documents that confirm his attendance or tell him about witness statements confirming that he did in fact attend the meeting.

3. "Do you remember sitting next to Jane at the meeting? Do you remember making a statement to Jane about child care? What did you say?"

If the respondent admits to making a statement, the investigator must be sure to accurately record exactly what he claims he said. If he denies making any statements or says he cannot recall any statements, the investigator can then ask the next question.

4. "Did you say, 'If women are going to spread their legs and get pregnant, they should stay home and take care of the kids'?"

If the respondent admits making the statement, the investigator can then ask, "What did you mean by that? Why did you make that comment?" On the other hand, if he denies making the statement, the investigator should simply sit quietly for a few moments to see if he volunteers any additional information. If not, the investigator can ask, "Did you say anything similar to that statement?" Finally, if the respondent volunteers any statement, the investigator must write down his exact words and repeat them back by saying, "I want to make sure that I understand what you said. Did you say _____? Did you say anything else?"

5. "What was Jane's response to your comment?"

The investigator must get the respondent to provide details about the complainant's responses, both verbal and nonverbal/physical.

6. "Did anyone else hear your comments? Who? How did they respond?"

The investigator must get names and additional information from the respondent.

7. "Did anything happen after the meeting in regard to your comment? Did anyone talk to you about it? Did Jane ever discuss this with you at any time after the meeting?"

The investigator must obtain as many specific details as possible about events after the meeting in question.

When the investigator has obtained all the information that the respondent is willing to give regarding a specific allegation, the interview can then proceed with similar questions about the next event. The interview is completed once all the allegations have been addressed. If the respondent denies all or most of the allegations, investigators should ask why the complainant would have made them. This question may help provide insight as to what is going on in the workplace. For example, the respondent could be asked, "Why would Jane make these allegations about you if they are not true?"

The investigator must carefully document the respondent's statements and evaluate whether they are consistent with information provided by the respondent himself, the complainant, and other witnesses.

The respondent's admission that the behavior took place is therefore sufficient to substantiate the complaint. However, this defense highlights the importance of determining whether the respondent was given a copy of the sexual harassment policy or received training in sexual harassment. If the comment was a first-time offense, mandated training or counseling may be an appropriate corrective response.

"I Have a Right to Free Speech. I Can Say What I Want."   This is a defense that the courts only rarely accept because one person's right to free speech cannot infringe on another person's right to work in an environment that is free of harassment and discrimination. Therefore, the investigation should focus on whether the respondent admits making the statements.

"But I Didn't Say Anything Sexual to Her."   While this may be true, the courts are clear that words or actions do not have to be sexual to create a hostile work environment; the fact that the person is being harassed on the basis of gender is sufficient. Again, investigators must document whether the respondent has been provided with a copy of the sexual harassment policy and has received sexual harassment training.

"I Wasn't Even Talking to Her. I Was Talking to My Friends." As reviewed in the chapter on legal issues, this is not a valid defense because a bystander can also complain if the workplace is hostile. The behavior does not have to be directed at the complainant to create or contribute to a hostile work environment. Again, the policy and training issues must be documented.

"But She Was Joking, Too!" This issue may be the most difficult one. Just because complainants may have "participated" in similar behavior in the past does not mean that they want to continue to participate. In this instance, an investigator must try to determine whether the complainant was an active participant in the behavior or simply an onlooker. The investigator must also consider if the complainant was "forced" to participate in the behavior through peer pressure or presence of a supervisor. The investigation must focus on determining whether the behavior was truly unwelcome and therefore constitutes a violation of the sexual harassment policy and law. The investigator can ask several questions to explore the issues involved:

1. Exactly how did the complainant participate? Did she laugh? Respond approvingly? Tell another joke?
2. What was her behavior, and what were the words she used?
3. Who was there and witnessed the event?
4. Had the complainant participated in prior situations? What were they?
5. Had the complainant ever indicated that she did not wish to be exposed to this type of behavior?
6. How often had these types of situations occurred between the respondent and the complainant?

"She Obviously Didn't Mind. Just Look at the Way She Dresses, Sleeps Around, Etc." A complainant's activity outside the workplace is seldom pertinent to such workplace issues. Although respondents often use the complainant's personal behavior or manner of dressing as an excuse, it is not an accurate indication that the complainant will find any particular behavior in the workplace welcome. Here again, the issues of policy and training must be documented.

"But No One Ever Told Me about Sexual Harassment." When respondents raise this type of defense, it is important to find out if they were aware of the agency's policy. Is the policy posted? Has it been distributed? Did the respondent sign a form acknowledging receipt of the policy? Is this signed form kept in the respondent's personnel file? Has the respondent attended any training on the topic of sexual harassment? How long ago?

CONCLUSION OF THE INTERVIEW

After the investigator has asked questions about each allegation and believes that all the relevant information is documented, the interview can be concluded by asking the respondent several final questions:

1. Do you have any further information about the events that we have discussed?
2. Do you have anything else you want to say about the investigation?
3. Have you been given a copy of the employer's policy about sexual harassment? Have you read it?
4. Have you received any training about sexual harassment?
5. Do you have any other questions?

Remind Respondent About Issues of Confidentiality and Retaliation

When the interview is completed, the investigator must remind the respondent not to discuss the issues with coworkers and not to engage in any kind of retaliatory actions against the complainant or others.

Have Respondent Sign Written Statement

After the interview, the investigator must type up a written statement and give it to the respondent to review for accuracy. Any corrections must be made before the statement is signed and dated by the respondent. A copy should then be given to the respondent, and a copy should also be placed in the investigative case file.

Maintain Follow-Up Contact With Respondent

The investigator will need to have follow-up contact with the respondent. The respondent should be notified of the timeline for the completion of the investigation; respondents should also be urged to contact the investigator if they remember any other relevant information after the interview.

Later, the respondent must be informed of the results of the investigation and of any action to be taken by the employer. Any disciplinary action will, of course, be conducted according to the rules of the employer and any applicable labor agreements.

Chapter 17

Interviewing Witnesses

This chapter provides detailed guidance for interviewing witnesses and others with information relevant to the investigation. Issues regarding the code of silence are examined, and suggestions are made for dealing with that situation.

TYPES OF WITNESSES

When identifying different types of witnesses to be interviewed in a sexual harassment investigation, it is important to keep in mind that they may have different kinds of information that are relevant (Oppenheimer & Pratt, 2003):

- Witnesses may have direct knowledge about an incident if they saw or heard all or part of it. These are the most important people to interview in any investigation.

- Witnesses may also be termed "outcry witnesses" if the complainant told them of the incident either immediately afterward or sometime prior to filing the complaint. These people are also important to interview because their information may or may not corroborate the account of the incident given by the complainant.

- Witnesses may have information about similar behavior by the respondent, even if they don't have direct knowledge of the incident or knowledge of the complainant's description of the incident. While these people are not as critical to the investigation as the other types of witnesses, they can sometimes be helpful—especially if there are no witnesses with direct knowledge of the incident and no "outcry witnesses."

- Character witnesses are not likely to be useful in this kind of investigation, unless they have specific information of the kind described above. They should not generally be interviewed because they will not offer corroborative evidence but will unnecessarily increase the number of people involved in the investigation with confidential information.

As the investigation proceeds, the investigator must keep track of all potential witnesses and others with relevant information. Investigators can then decide which witnesses to interview and in what order. The reasons for interviewing—or not interviewing—any witnesses on the list should be recorded to protect against the appearance of bias. Unfortunately, gathering information from witnesses can be difficult due to the code of silence that operates in many law enforcement agencies.

CODE OF SILENCE

When attempting to deal with sexual harassment or any other form of workplace misconduct, most law enforcement agencies continue to face problems in dealing with the code of silence. For those who are not familiar with it, the code of silence is an unwritten mandate that law enforcement officers not provide any information that will harm another officer. Even though this code of silence is unwritten and most officers will deny that it exists, it creates huge problems for investigators. A similar code of silence also operates within fire departments, with firefighters often extremely reluctant to "rat on" fellow firefighters.

In most cases, it is fairly easy to see when the code of silence is operating. The clearest signals are sent when officers admit that they were present at a particular place and time when something occurred but deny that they saw or heard anything. For example, a female officer may report that a male officer made a sexual comment to her at roll call. During the investigation, one other male officer admits that he heard the comment; however, all the other officers who were in the room at the time deny that they heard anything, even though some of them were sitting quite close to the people involved. This is a good example of the code of silence in operation.

Some investigators may wonder why the code of silence is so strong in law enforcement. We believe there are several reasons. First and foremost, officers have to rely on each other for backup in emergency situations, and this creates a very strong bond between officers, sometimes referred to as the "brotherhood" or the "blue wall." In addition, police culture often supports the perception that the public, the press, the politicians, and the "brass" are all "out to get them" for any little mistake they make. Both these factors combine to create a mentality of "us versus them" that breeds the code of silence. The result is that officers often band together and tacitly agree that they will support each other no matter what. An officer who violates the code of silence can be penalized by being ostracized, being shunned, and even not getting backup in emergency situations.

Agency Response

Many police agencies have struggled with how to handle the code of silence. Unfortunately, some administrators simply put their heads in the sand and refuse to face the problem, but the only way to break the code of silence is to make the consequences of *adhering* to the code more severe than *breaking* the code. For example, the leader of the agency must make it clear that failure to report misconduct or fully cooperate in any internal investigation will lead to severe discipline, including termination. Of course, this must be followed up with actual disciplinary sanctions when officers do fail to either report misconduct or cooperate with an investigation. This gives officers a face-saving way to cooperate with an investigation, by telling themselves and others, "It was either cooperate or lose my job."

Investigator Response

When it comes to investigating complaints of employee misconduct such as sexual harassment, the best way for an investigator to deal with the problem during an interview is to directly confront officers with the fact that they are adhering to the code of silence. Sometimes this can be done by pointing out that officers are highly trained and skilled in observation, so it is hard to believe that they did not see or hear what took place. Other times, it can be effective to read to officers the section in the policy manual requiring them to be truthful.

One law enforcement agency we know of even gives the investigators the authority to order officers to take a polygraph examination to determine if they are telling the truth. That agency believes that it has been effective in breaking the code of silence. However, requiring officers to take a polygraph is prohibited in some states in the legislation commonly referred to as the Peace Officer Bill of Rights (see the chapter on the respondent interview for more detailed information). There are also legitimate concerns regarding the validity of polygraph examinations because they are based on detecting physiological responses to stress, rather than lies. Therefore, the decision to give an officer a polygraph should be made only with the assistance of legal counsel.

INTERVIEW PROCESS

Even before an investigation begins, it is important to keep in mind that most witnesses will be extremely reluctant to talk about the allegations under investigation. In some cases, this will be due to the code of silence, with officers refusing to provide information that might harm a fellow officer. In other cases, the witnesses are simply being pulled in two different directions—by the complainant and the respondent. They may even have long-term friendships with either or both parties. It is therefore not surprising that witnesses often resent being drawn into an investigation.

Address Witness Concerns

To address these concerns, witnesses must first be reassured that the agency has a policy against retaliation and that this policy will be enforced. While no one can guarantee that retaliation will not take place, witnesses can be assured that the agency will take proactive steps to prevent it and that they should immediately report any retaliation that they do experience. Witnesses should also be informed that retaliation is a separate violation of policy that will be taken seriously and investigated thoroughly and that any substantiated claims will result in discipline.

Second, witnesses must be told that the agency is taking the complaint under investigation very seriously and that the investigator wants to learn *the truth* about what happened. This is especially important if the information the witnesses have to give may harm the employer in a lawsuit. They may have fears about losing their jobs or harming their careers if they give information to the investigator. Third, witnesses must be assured that their name and the information they provide will be kept confidential to the extent possible. Fourth, the investigator must explain to witnesses the investigative process and the way in which the information they provide will be used.

In some situations, it may be necessary to order the witness to cooperate with the investigation and to provide truthful information in order to avoid charges of insubordination. While this strategy should be pursued only as a last resort, it can sometimes be helpful for witnesses by taking the onus off them for breaking the code of silence. They can then say that they had to cooperate with the investigation for fear of losing their job.

Protect Identity of Complainant

When interviewing witnesses, it is often possible to obtain the necessary information without revealing the identity of the complainant or any specific details of the allegations. For example, the investigator may be able to ask witnesses only general questions about the working environment rather than specific questions pertaining to the allegations. This strategy is especially likely to be used when a supervisor is accused of creating or condoning a hostile work environment. In such a situation, it is almost always recommended that the investigator interview everyone working in that unit. Not only does this strategy provide the most information on the working environment, but it also serves to conceal the identity of the complainant. In fact, this type of investigation can even be conducted without anyone (but the respondent) realizing that a complaint has been filed. Inquiries can be made in a general way, as if the agency is simply surveying employees about their workplace environment.

In other situations, it may be possible to disguise the identities of the specific people involved by asking questions about others who are not involved in the investigation. In other words, the same question could be asked about everyone in a similar position, thereby not singling out any one person or workgroup. For example, when a complaint is filed against one sergeant in a particular unit, the investigator could ask witnesses about the behavior of all the sergeants in that unit. By asking about all the sergeants, the investigator can frame the interview as an evaluation of supervisor effectiveness rather than a sexual harassment complaint. Again, this strategy can be used to conceal both the identity of the complainant and the fact that a formal complaint was filed. In addition, asking a question in this way may reveal other issues that may be contributing to a hostile work environment by gathering more information about the working environment in that unit.

Give Instructions Regarding Confidentiality

When witnesses are questioned in regard to the complaint, they must be instructed not to share this information with other employees. There are a number of valid reasons for this. First, the investigation must be based on the individual recollection of each person; by discussing the facts with other employees, the investigation becomes tainted. Second, any discussion of the investigation may cause further harm to the complainant or the respondent. As was done with the complainant and the respondent, witnesses must therefore be asked to read and sign the agency's policy on confidentiality. The investigator can note that any violations of the confidentiality policy will be taken seriously and investigated—and may result in disciplinary actions if they are substantiated.

Follow General Interview Guidelines

In any investigation, witnesses will have information that could benefit either the complainant or the respondent, but the approach to witnesses on both sides of the issue must always remain neutral and unbiased. As was done with the complainant and the respondent, the investigator should use open-ended questions and avoid communicating the "right answer" to witnesses. Other interviewing guidelines discussed in the previous chapters are also relevant here:

- Planning the standard instructions
- Reviewing the Peace Officer Bill of Rights
- Preparing the necessary paperwork (including the policies on sexual harassment, confidentiality, and retaliation)
- Selecting an appropriate location that is quiet, private, and free from distractions
- Explaining the purpose of the interview in general terms, without identifying the complainant (whenever possible)
- Addressing concerns regarding confidentiality and the outcome of the investigation
- Asking witnesses to read, sign, and keep a copy of the policies on sexual harassment, confidentiality, and retaliation
- Building rapport, and establishing a tone of respect
- Setting the pace of the interview, and taking breaks as needed
- Using open-ended prompts, and allowing time for silent pauses
- Maintaining eye contact and appropriate body language
- Using active listening, such as comments that are reflective and statements that clarify and summarize
- Repeating a question if necessary in order to clarify and accurately record information
- Documenting evasive behavior, and responding directly to suspected untruths
- Taking notes, and preparing a written statement to be reviewed by the witness

When interviewing witnesses, it is generally best to offer as little information as possible about the incident and the investigation. While witnesses will certainly want to know the details of the allegations and the identity of the complainant, investigators must redirect such questions and not answer them. Investigators must also avoid discussing any opinions or conclusions with witnesses or otherwise giving the appearance of taking sides regarding the complaint.

Provide Standard Instructions

As was the case with the complainant and the respondent, investigators must discuss with all witnesses the standard instructions, such as the general process for the administrative interview and the agency's expectation that employees will cooperate fully with the investigation and provide truthful information. The investigator can even remind employees that the failure to do so could result in disciplinary sanctions. All employees involved in an investigation should be given a copy of the policy on harassment and discrimination, and they should be asked to read and sign the agency's policies on confidentiality and retaliation. It is particularly important to remind witnesses that they have a right to be free from retaliation and to inform them of the process for reporting any retaliatory actions that they may experience. It is best if this process has the witness report retaliation directly to the investigator rather than go through the more formal complaint channels.

Finally, during the investigative process, witnesses must be informed of their rights, as specified in the labor contract, the employee handbook, and the Peace Officer Bill of Rights. While witnesses may request representation during the interview, this is not typically their right unless the interview could lead to disciplinary sanctions for them. However, it may still be appropriate to allow witnesses to have a representative in the interview if it will allow the investigation to proceed quickly and smoothly—as long as the representative can avoid disrupting the interview process.

Identify Types of Information to Obtain

When interviewing witnesses, the primary information to obtain is their recollection or other information that might corroborate either the complainant's or the respondent's version of events. Witnesses must therefore be asked about the exact dates and times of events as well as any complicating factors such as friendships, intimate relationships, or grudges between the people involved. Witnesses should also be asked about both documents or other evidence that might pertain to the incident or investigation and identities of any other potential witnesses.

The interview with witnesses can typically begin with general questions about their job and their relation to each of the parties (the complainant and the respondent), and it can conclude by asking them if they have any other information that is likely to be relevant to the incident or investigation. Witnesses can even be asked if they are aware of the sexual harassment policy and if they have attended any training on the subject.

Elicit Names of Other Witnesses

During the interview with witnesses, they will be asked to provide names of employees or other people with information relevant to the investigation. These people should be listed by the investigator and be evaluated with respect to the type of information they can provide. In most cases, it is desirable to interview everyone that either the complainant or the respondent lists as a witness or someone with pertinent information. Failing to do so may result in allegations that the investigator is biased.

Sometimes it may even be necessary to interview everyone in a particular unit, especially if the complainant alleges that there is a hostile work environment or if the supervisor is the respondent in the complaint. In such a situation, it is better to interview too many people than to miss one important witness—particularly because such a strategy can also be used to protect the identity of the complainant as previously discussed.

Obtain Additional Information from Supervisors

For supervisors who are interviewed, they must be asked additional questions to determine whether they have received a copy of the sexual harassment policy and whether they have read it and understand it. Supervisors must also be asked whether they have attended a training class in sexual harassment and whether they understood the information provided.

Respond to Confidentiality Breaches

If the investigator gets the sense that any witnesses have discussed the incident or investigation, it is important to question them and determine to whom they have talked about the investigation. If they learned information from another employee who was previously interviewed and who was ordered not to discuss the case, then the investigator should reinterview the employee who is violating the confidentiality policy to determine if charges should be brought. Of course, this is always a delicate issue, but it is especially difficult when the complainant is the one who talked to another employee about the case. Charges brought against the complainant will most likely be seen as retaliation for having filed the complaint; therefore, discipline should be pursued only with the consultation of legal counsel.

Conclude Interview

At the conclusion of the interview, witnesses should be reminded not to discuss the investigation or incident with coworkers. They can also be given an estimate of how long the investigation will take. In addition, it is helpful to encourage witnesses to call the investigator with any additional information they may remember after the interview.

Maintain Follow-Up Contact

After the witness's statement is prepared, it should be given to the person who was interviewed to make sure the statement is accurate. The witness can then make any corrections before signing and dating the statement. A copy of the statement should be placed in the investigative file.

Tips for the Investigator

Investigators who are involved in interviewing should do the following:

- Attend seminars. There are many seminars available on investigative techniques. Investigators should attend regularly to stay up-to-date on interviewing information.

- Role-play situations. It is sometimes helpful to role-play with other investigators; choose situations dealing with issues such as the code of silence or the evasive answers of witnesses.

- Join associations. There are associations for Internal Affairs investigators and for investigators of sex crimes. These associations often provide training seminars or newsletters that are helpful for keeping up-to-date on investigative techniques. The associations also provide a good place to meet other investigators and to develop mentoring relationships.

Chapter 18

Documenting the Investigation

Once the investigation is complete and the determination made, investigators must communicate this information accurately and effectively. Documentation will include the final investigative report and an investigative case file (with interview statements and other materials).

FINAL INVESTIGATIVE REPORT

When preparing a final report on the results of the investigation, investigators must keep in mind that it will need to serve many purposes. In a case involving sexual harassment or workplace discrimination, the final report will have many uses:

- Factual account of the allegations, interviews, and findings of the investigation
- Basis for possible discipline of employees
- Tool to identify training needs
- Defense to any lawsuits alleging improper handling of sexual harassment complaints

The process of writing the report forces the investigator to analyze the evidence that supports or challenges each allegation and can even reveal missing information, which the investigator may decide to address by following up with one of the parties or collecting additional evidence.

Once the final report is drafted, it should then be reviewed by someone other than the investigator before being finalized. It is best if this secondary reviewer is a female supervisor or manager who can provide feedback on the investigative process and the final report. Although some agencies require the investigator to recommend disciplinary sanctions or other corrective actions, we do not believe this is an appropriate role for the investigator; instead, we believe these decisions are best left to those with supervisory and management authority. Of course, for investigators who are required to formulate disciplinary sanctions or other corrective actions, these must be carefully articulated in the final report and supported by the evidence contained in it.

Contents of Final Investigative Report

Brief Overview

The final investigative report should begin with a brief overview of the allegations and findings. This part will include the names of the complainant, respondent, and witnesses. The name of the investigator(s) should also be included, along with the dates of the investigation.

Summary of Complainant Allegations

In this second section, the complainant should be identified and each of the allegations listed. This more detailed summary should also include dates and times of all alleged incidents as well as a general summary of the statement provided by the complainant. However, the more detailed written statement by the complainant will appear in the investigative case file, which is different from the final investigative report. The investigative case file is discussed in greater detail later in the chapter. Investigators must keep in mind that this initial summary of the complainant's allegations should be written *from the perspective of the complainant* and not include the analysis or interpretation by the investigator.

Summary of Witness Statements

In the next section, it is helpful to provide a summary of each witness's statement. If desired, a code number or other confidential identifier may be used to refer to witnesses so those reading the report will not know their names. This section of the investigative case file should contain only a summary of the information obtained from the witnesses and any statements made. Their entire written statements will be included in the investigative case file, not in the final investigative report. As with the complainant's allegations, this initial summary of the witnesses' statements must be written *from the perspective of the witnesses themselves* and not include any analysis or interpretation on the part of the investigator.

Summary of Respondent Statements

The statements of the respondent should then be provided in summary form. As with the other parties, this summary must be written from the perspective of the respondent and the entire written statement included in the investigative case file, not in the final investigative report.

Report of Investigative Steps Taken

The report should next detail the steps taken by the investigator to look into each of the allegations and should include the evidence gathered, the witnesses interviewed, and the determinations made. Depending on the similarity of the allegations or their relationship in time, it may sometimes be easier to combine the investigative steps for all the allegations in a single chronology; however, in other cases it is best to list the steps taken for each allegation separately. In either case, the report should present a clear description of the many important steps of the investigative process.

Analysis and Interpretation

In this section, the report must describe a detailed analysis of the evidence supporting and challenging each allegation, which serves as the basis for subsequent findings. This analysis will include a determination of credibility made by the investigator regarding the people interviewed and the documents reviewed. In some cases, it will also address additional issues or potential violations that were uncovered during the investigation, which might warrant further action but are beyond the scope of the current investigation. These should be referred to the appropriate personnel for subsequent action.

Determinative Findings

Depending on agency regulations, investigators may be asked to assign a specific classification to each allegation and its findings. For example, some agencies require investigators to use terms such as "unfounded," "sustained," and "not sustained" to describe the findings with respect to each allegation. Others require a summary of overall findings, such as "Behavior that violates the sexual harassment policy did occur." Still other agencies do not allow the investigator to make findings; the investigator simply reports on the results of the investigation but does not record any determinative findings.

While each of these strategies may be appropriate in some instances, we believe it is best for the investigator to stick to "regular language" to describe the alleged behaviors and findings, as summarized in the chapter on making a determination. In other words, investigators should avoid using legalistic terms and simply describe their findings in their own language. In some cases it is necessary to make a determination for each allegation seperately. In cases of a hostile work environment, however, investigators are advised not to make a determinative finding with respect to each separate act of harassment. Such an approach would be nearly impossible in some situations in which the behavior took place over months or years, with numerous individuals responsible, so in such cases the finding must be based on the totality of circumstances uncovered by the investigation.

List of Exhibits

The investigative report should conclude with an appendix listing the evidence gathered and describing any copies that are attached for the convenience of the reviewer. These materials are then included in the investigative case file, but they do not constitute part of the final investigative report.

Guidelines for Final Investigative Report

In general, the final report must not contain any bias or unsupported conclusions. The final investigative report should (1) be clear, concise, complete, and accurate because any inconsistency will undermine the credibility of the report and the entire investigative process; (2) avoid jargon or acronyms that might make the report difficult to read by people outside the agency; and (3) use quotation marks for direct quotes to preserve the original language of those interviewed to the extent possible.

INVESTIGATIVE CASE FILE

While much of the information gathered during the investigation is presented in the final report, there is a great deal of additional material that is included in a larger investigative case file. To put it succinctly, everything that is uncovered during the course of the investigation goes into the investigative case file. On the one hand, the final investigative report may be provided to the complainant, the respondent, and others, so it is important that it not include information such as the identity of witnesses or others providing information; it should only include summaries of witness statements or other information. On the other hand, all written statements in their entirety should be included in the larger investigative case file. This is *not* given to complainants or respondents.

Contents of Investigative Case File

The investigative case file will likely contain the following materials:

- Table of contents (and/or a chronology of events)
- Summary of the allegation(s)
- Time frames for the alleged incidents
- Statement from the complainant and any witnesses named by the complainant
- All documents and records from the complainant and witnesses named by the complainant
- Statement from the respondent and any witnesses named by the respondent
- All documents and records from the respondent and witnesses named by the respondent
- Observations and analysis of the investigator
- List of witnesses and others interviewed (with their contact information)
- Other relevant information and documents (e.g., relevant laws, comparative cases, description of the work site, attendance records, training records)

- All communications with those involved in the investigation (e.g., emails, letters, memos)

- All materials pertaining to any administrative measures taken during the course of the investigation (e.g., removing the complainant and/or the respondent from the workplace)

- Documentation of any follow-up activities with the complainant, the respondent, or others

The investigative case file should be clearly labeled and easily indexed, as it constitutes the official record of the investigative process. It should also include the investigator's original notes to avoid the appearance of the investigator hiding something. In fact, we recommend that the investigator keep no notes other than those included in the investigative case file because it does constitute the official record of the investigation.

CONFIDENTIALITY ISSUES

There are two issues that need to be mentioned at this stage of the investigation (when the investigative report is being written and the investigative case file is being prepared). Those issues pertain to copies of interview statements and participant confidentiality.

Copies of Interview Statements

Copies of the complainant's and the respondent's written statements should be placed in the investigative case file; in addition, both the complainant and the respondent should be given a copy of their own written statement if they want one. The investigator can even give witnesses a copy of their own statement if they request one, but they do not need to be offered a copy proactively. If witnesses are provided with a copy of their written statement, they must be informed that they cannot show it to others within the organization during the course of the investigation.

Participant Confidentiality

The final investigative report and the investigative case file are both confidential and should be made available only to those who absolutely need to know. This group would include the person with responsibility for supervising the investigation, the person responsible for imposing disciplinary sanctions and other corrective actions, and the chief administrator for the agency. If the report must be provided to others, it may need to be redacted to protect the confidentiality of people mentioned by name. Obviously, the final investigative report should never become a matter of public record, and the entire investigative case file should not be provided to the complainant and the respondent.

Tips for the Investigator

To maximize their effectiveness at documentation, investigators should do the following:

- Develop a standard format for conducting and documenting investigations of sexual harassment and other forms of workplace discrimination.
- Be sure that the final report is comprehensive enough so that the people who will make decisions about the outcome and possible discipline will have all the facts.
- Have another investigator, as well as a female supervisor or manager, review the report before submitting it.

Chapter 19

Making a Determination and Imposing Discipline

After the investigator has interviewed the parties and the witnesses and has collected all the evidence, it is time to make a determination that will be used as the basis for imposing disciplinary sanctions or other corrective actions.

REVIEW PERSONNEL FILES

As part of the process of collecting evidence, the investigator will need to check the personnel files of both the complainant and the respondent as well as any prior investigative files for the respondent.

Review Personnel File of Complainant

It is helpful to review the complainant's work history as long as the investigator avoids developing any prejudice regarding the complainant's "good" or "bad" reputation within the organization. Investigators must keep in mind that any negative performance evaluations or other indicators of poor work performance on the part of the complainant may actually be the *result* of sexual harassment rather than a cause for doubting credibility.

When reviewing the complainant's personnel file, investigators should therefore look for obvious changes in performance. For example, if the complainant has received adequate or outstanding performance evaluations and then suddenly begins receiving negative performance evaluations, investigators can look for a connection with the sexual harassment complaint. The question to ask is whether the performance evaluations changed after the event(s) described by the complainant took place. A drastic change in performance can some-times indicate either that the supervisor was unfairly critical about the complainant's per-formance or that the event had a deleterious effect on the complainant's job functioning.

Complaints about the performance of the complainant must be analyzed with particular care. For example, if the complainant had no prior citizen or supervisor complaints in the file and then suddenly several complaints appear, it may be a sign of retaliation. Respondents have been known to enlist friends in filing complaints as a form of retaliation against complainants and others involved in the investigation.

Review Personnel and Investigative Files of Respondent

When reviewing the personnel and investigative files of the respondent, investigators must obviously pay particular attention to whether there are prior complaints of sexual harassment or other forms of employee misconduct—regardless of whether these complaints were made by the same complainant or someone else in the organization. Investigators also need to find out how the agency responded to these complaints in order to help determine disciplinary sanctions and other corrective actions in this instance. The respondent's investigative file must be examined with particular care to see if there are complaints from citizens about similar types of behavior, such as rude conduct (especially to women) or a pattern of complaints. The personnel file can also be used to determine whether the respondent received a copy of the sexual harassment policy at any time and/or participated in a training program for sexual harassment prevention.

WEIGH THE EVIDENCE

Once the interviews have been conducted, the evidence has been collected, and personnel files have been reviewed, it is time to weigh the evidence and make a determination. At this stage, the investigator may find it helpful to make a page for each allegation and to list all the evidence supporting the allegation and challenging it. This process may identify additional information that is needed, which can be addressed in a follow-up phone interview with any of the parties or witnesses. Then a determination can be made by analyzing corroborative evidence (direct and indirect), identifying contradic-tions or other inconsistencies, determining the credibility of individuals and documents, and identifying ulterior motives of the parties and the witnesses.

Analyze Corroborative Evidence

Evidence gathered in the investigation may provide corroboration—whether direct or indirect—for the account given by the complainant or the respondent. *Direct corrob-oration* is provided by individuals who witnessed the incident, although their memory of the event is likely to be less complete than that of the parties involved. In most situations, events do not have the significance for witnesses that they have for the complainant and the respondent, so the memory of witnesses' may not include details of their personal interaction. Such corroborative evidence must therefore be evaluated by taking into account whether there were any factors limiting the capacity of the witnesses to observe or remember the event. This might include a witness's blocked view of the incident, hearing impairment of a witness, factors that would have diverted a witness's attention, etc. To make this determination, it is often helpful for the investigator to visit the site in order to evaluate the ability of any witnesses to observe the events in question (Salisbury & Dominick, 2004).

On the other hand, *indirect corroboration* is provided by individuals who did not witness the event but who were told about it by the complainant or others. Indirect corroboration is also provided by witnesses who observed changes in the behavior of the complainant following the event.

The determination of any charge will therefore be based in large part on the extent to which the complainant's allegations are corroborated, both directly and indirectly, by witnesses or other evidence. To illustrate, the courts have accepted each of the following as corroboration of sexual harassment allegations (Salisbury & Dominick, 2004, p. 120):

- The complainant told someone about the incident(s) at about the time they occurred and said that she or he did not welcome the behavior.
- The complainant took steps to avoid the accused by seeking a transfer, staying out of a particular work area, passing up overtime opportunities.
- The complainant's performance, attendance, attitude, or health deteriorated.
- Other individuals experienced similar behavior from the accused.
- Other individuals witnessed all or part of the offensive behavior.
- Other individuals witnessed the effects of the behavior on the complainant.
- The complainant documented significant incidents or events in a diary, journal, or work log.
- The complainant tape-recorded the incidents.
- The accused admitted part or all of the behavior but said she or he was "just kidding."

As discussed in the chapter on the respondent interview, any admission that the behavior took place can be used to substantiate the allegation regardless of the specific excuse or explanation given.

Identify Contradictions or Other Inconsistencies

The process of weighing the evidence will also take into account any contradictions or inconsistencies that might be evidence that a party or a witness is being untruthful; however, they may also be the result of confusion, poor memory, or other simple human errors. Therefore, interviews must be conducted to comprehensively question the parties and the witnesses, and inconsistencies that are identified must be documented so that the individuals can be reinterviewed to clarify the issue.

When inconsistencies are detected, it is sometimes difficult to assess which version is correct. However, the content and the context of the inconsistency must be evaluated to determine whether it undermines the credibility of one of the parties or if it was the result of understandable human error (e.g., poor memory for trivial details). In other words, some inconsistencies are inevitable because no one has a perfect memory for all the details of an event. However, some inconsistencies matter more than others. If it pertains to a trivial detail, the inconsistency does not even need to be resolved in order to make a determination. If the inconsistency is more significant or central to the allegations, however, every attempt must be made to clarify the issue, even if it requires follow-up interviews. The issue must be considered as a factor when evaluating the credibility of the individuals and the plausibility of their account of events.

Of course, any evaluation of consistency in a person's statement must be applied equally across interviews. For example, it would be inappropriate for an investigator to minimize one small inconsistency in the account of the complainant while highlighting an equally minor inconsistency in the respondent's account of events (Salisbury & Dominick, 2004).

Make Determinations of Individuals' Credibility

Investigations of sexual harassment and other forms of workplace discrimination often rest heavily on determinations of credibility for each of the parties and witnesses involved. Such credibility determinations should be based primarily on corroborative evidence, as long as the investigator keeps in mind that the evidence does not need to confirm the entire account of the complainant to support its validity. In fact, witnesses will rarely recall the incident with the same level of detail as the complainant because the incident wasn't as significant to them. Other witnesses will not even have direct knowledge of the incident at all; instead, they may be asked for information about the events leading up to the incident or taking place afterward. The weight of the evidence must therefore take into account the perspective of witnesses and the likelihood that their memory is accurate.

Determining the credibility of individuals will also require an evaluation of contradictions or other inconsistencies (as discussed above) as well as any evidence that the person has been untruthful in other situations. This usually should not include an evaluation of character evidence unless it pertains directly to the question of the individual's reliability and/or truthfulness as a witness. It is also important to decide whether the account of events given by each individual is plausible. Specific guidance in each of these areas has already been discussed in previous chapters on interviewing.

Assess Credibility of Documents

Just as the people involved in the investigation must be evaluated with respect to their credibility, so must the documents and other evidence that are collected. For example, documents can be viewed with greater credibility if they are

- Prepared by someone other than the complainant or the respondent.
- Created at the time of the event and not at some later time.
- Created for some routine process rather than for the complaint or the investigation.
- Maintained with a clear chain of custody.
- Consistent with other documents prepared by the same person or for the same purpose.

Credibility determinations must therefore be made for any documents or other evidence that are collected in order to evaluate whether they are legitimate or if they have been created or altered in order to influence the results of the investigation.

Identify Ulterior Motives of Parties or Witnesses

Of course, investigators must always evaluate the motives people may have for lying. While it is extremely rare for a complainant to completely fabricate a story, it is not uncommon for the story to be exaggerated or told in a way that makes the complainant look good and the respondent look bad—this is just human nature. It is also common for the respondent and any supervisors to minimize the alleged misconduct. These issues are discussed at length in the previous chapters on interviewing.

It is worth noting in this context that witnesses and others may also have ulterior motives that merit consideration when making a determination. These motives may include various forms of bias, favoritism, and self-interest. While such ulterior motives are not likely to be proven, they must be taken into account when evaluating the credibility of individuals and their version of events.

MAKE A DETERMINATION

Once the investigator has gathered and reviewed all the evidence and made the appropriate credibility determinations, it is time to make a final conclusion regarding the validity of the complaint. This will include a determination of whether the behavior took place and whether it is prohibited by agency policy. For cases of harassment and discrimination, there are a number of possible conclusions:

1. The incident(s) took place basically as described in the allegation(s).
2. Some of the allegations took place as described, but others did not.
3. The incident(s) took place as described, but the complainant's interpretation was inaccurate or unreasonable.
4. The allegation(s) is (are) not true; the complainant fabricated the story.
5. No determination is possible in the situation.

Even after doing everything right, investigators may still not have 100 percent certainty that they are making the correct determination. However, 100 percent certainty is not the standard required in a sexual harassment investigation; the law requires only that the investigative process be fair and thorough and be conducted in good faith. Additional guidelines will help the investigator to achieve this standard; these are discussed below.

Use "Regular Language"

As described in the chapter on documentation, we recommend that investigators use "regular language" for writing the final determination rather than more legalistic language, which may not describe the results of the investigation as clearly. This is especially important for investigators who are not responsible for assigning disciplinary sanctions and other corrective actions because they can simply describe the findings from the investigation and leave the more legalistic disciplinary conclusions to others.

Avoid Taking Easy Way Out

We also caution investigators against taking the easy way out by concluding that no determination is possible, unless this is absolutely necessary. All too often, investigators simply conclude that no determination can be made because there are no direct witnesses to a situation. In fact, sexual harassment may often be a situation of "he said, she said." However, even in this type of situation, there are likely to be witnesses with information that can corroborate at least some of the details of the incident, and there may be outcry witnesses who can speak to the response of the complainant immediately afterward. In addition, there may be documents that support the version of events given by the complainant or the respondent.

Do Not Consider Consequences

Investigators must make their determination without considering the consequences. Most importantly, investigators must not be afraid to conclude that the incident likely occurred as the complainant described it out of fear that the respondent will be disciplined or even terminated. Rather, conclusions about the incident must be made on the basis of the evidence weighed against the relevant standard of proof.

Use Appropriate Standard of Proof

For this type of administrative investigation, the appropriate standard of proof is not "beyond a reasonable doubt" (as in criminal cases) but rather a "preponderance of the evidence" (as in civil litigation). This standard simply means that the allegation is more likely than not true—it is more likely than not that the incident happened largely the way the complainant described it. Another way of stating this is that the investigator has at least 51 percent certainty that the allegations are true, as long as this certainty is supported by the evidence gathered.

Whatever standard is used, it must be stated clearly within the policy or manual of procedures for investigators, and it must be implemented consistently. For example, the standard of proof should not be based on the severity of the complaint so that more proof is required to substantiate more serious allegations.

Who Makes the Determination of Charges?

In most cases, we believe that investigators should not be the ones to determine whether the allegations have been substantiated; rather, investigators best serve as neutral fact finders, with the determination of findings left to the agency administrator. Of course, this does not mean that investigators are prohibited from offering opinions on credibility or other issues. However, we do not recommend that investigators make the final determination on the charges or recommend disciplinary sanctions and other corrective actions because this is better handled by agency management.

For each allegation, we recommend that the investigator simply list all the factors that support the complainant's version of events and all the factors that do not support the complainant's version. This allows the decision maker to review the documentation and to make a final determination. However, in cases of a hostile work environment, it is not desirable for investigators to make a determination on each separate allegation; instead, they should look at the facts that support the complainant's allegations (as a whole) and then make a determination as to whether those facts taken together violate the sexual harassment policy.

IMPOSE APPROPRIATE DISCIPLINE

When an investigation has substantiated an allegation of harassment or discrimination, appropriate sanctions should be levied in a timely manner. While some agencies require that the investigator make a recommendation for disciplinary sanctions, we believe this is an inappropriate role for the investigator. We believe that any decisions regarding disciplinary sanctions and other corrective actions are best left to those with supervisory or management authority. Regardless of who makes the determination, however, the purpose is to stop the harassment or discrimination (and ensure that it will not recur) as well as correct the negative effects on the complainant and the workplace. In general, the options for disciplinary sanctions will include the following:

- Reprimand/verbal counseling
- Suspension
- Demotion
- Reduction in pay
- Transfer/reassignment
- Remedial training
- Performance monitoring
- Termination

Selection of a particular disciplinary sanction will then depend on a number of factors, including severity of the offense, existence of prior offenses, and remorse on the part of the respondent. For first-time offenders who commit relatively minor infractions, it is probably appropriate to simply require that they be reprimanded and that they participate in either verbal counseling or another form of remedial training. This is particularly true if the respondent expresses remorse and a willingness to correct the situation. However, reprimands, counseling, and training are appropriate only in situations in which there is no evidence of previous misconduct on the part of the respondent. The investigative findings and corrective actions must therefore be documented in the respondent's personnel file in case there are future problems.

More severe discipline is called for when the misconduct is serious and/or repeated. This would include situations in which the harassment was perpetrated by a supervisor, it included physical contact or intimidation, it involved multiple harassers, or it targeted an individual rather than a group. For example, demotion is often the appropriate response when the respondent is a supervisor involved in a single incident. However, termination is required in situations in which either the harassment is particularly severe and/or repeated or other sanctions are not likely to correct the situation. In sum, when determining the appropriate disciplinary action, it is important to consider not only the severity of the behavior carried out by respondents but also whether the respondents have engaged in similar behavior in the past and whether they recognize their wrong-doing and express remorse and a willingness to correct the situation.

Charge Appropriately

Respondents who have clearly violated the sexual harassment policy should be charged with that violation. Some departments attempt to downplay the incident by charging the respondent with some "catchall" violation such as "standard of conduct" or "conduct unbecoming" or "bringing discredit upon the organization." This is not advisable. First of all, there will be no way to track the number of sexual harassment complaints and determine how discipline has been imposed for those violations. As a result, discipline will most likely not be consistent. It is also a subterfuge to hide those types of complaints and not admit to the fact that complaints have been made. It should be seen as a credit to employers when they appropriately investigate and discipline. But even more serious is the impact such a move would have on the complainant. For complainants to see their allegations downgraded may very well have a detrimental effect on their morale. It will also send the wrong message to other employees, letting them know that the administration does not take complaints of sexual harassment seriously and does not appropriately punish offenders. Of course, it also does not look good in court if a lawsuit should result.

Do Not Reward Employee Who Harassed Others

Once an employee has been disciplined for engaging in sexual harassment or discrimination, it is critically important that the agency not reward the employee with highly desirable job assignments, promotions, Officer of the Year Awards, or other similar benefits. This is so important that it is worth repeating: *Officers who have been disciplined for serious harassing or discriminatory behavior should not be rewarded with highly desirable perks.* In our experience, we have all too often seen lawsuits resulting from a situation in which agencies have quickly promoted the offender, appointed the offender as a field training officer or an academy trainer, or even assigned the offender to investigate sexual harassment complaints. Not only is this a slap in the face of the complainant, but it sends a loud and clear message to the rest of the organization that sexually harassing or discriminatory behavior is not only condoned but rewarded.

Hold Supervisors Accountable

If a supervisor or manager knew about the behavior, it is critical to address disciplinary sanctions or other corrective actions toward them as well. Their involvement may warrant discipline, and it certainly requires providing them with a copy of the sexual harassment policy and training manual so that their response to future incidents will be more appropriate. If the supervisor was aware of serious misconduct and did not follow the agency's policy, for example, it is clearly appropriate to demote him or her. Those in the position of supervisor are acting as an agent for the organization and can create a huge liability if they do not properly perform their job.

Design Other Corrective Actions

In addition to disciplinary sanctions, agencies may seek to take other measures to correct the situation or reverse its negative impact. Depending on the circumstances of the situation, corrective actions can be designed either to address any negative job consequences experienced by the complainant or to change the work environment so as to improve the situation for the complainant. Such actions could include the following:

- Rehiring the complainant if terminated or constructively discharged, without any loss of pay, seniority, or benefits
- Purging the complainant's personnel file of negative records resulting from the sexual harassment
- Promoting the complainant if a promotion was denied due to discriminatory actions
- Restoring sick leave or vacation days
- Paying back wages
- Providing training opportunities
- Covering attorney fees and other costs (e.g., medical expenses, psychotherapy)

When designing corrective actions, the decision maker must look at how the agency has responded to previous incidents, whether a supervisor or manager knew about the behavior, and whether the harasser had received training and clear messages that such behavior was inappropriate. Of course, implementing any corrective actions must be done very carefully, in strict accordance with the provisions of the labor contract and the employee manual. Legal counsel is always recommended in this type of situation.

We also recommend that management discuss with the complainant how to make a positive outcome result from the situation. For example, the agency may need to make changes to its policies and procedures, and the complainant could be involved in the process of revision so that similar problems are not experienced by others in the workplace.

Protect Complainant from Retaliation

Regardless of the specific corrective actions taken, it is extremely important to protect complainants from retaliation and not bring them back into a work environment that is hostile toward them. This is especially important when the complainant is rehired after quitting or being terminated. In such a situation, management must make a concerted effort to help the complainant to reenter the workplace, as it also will do with complainants whose allegations resulted in serious discipline for the respondent. While reintegrating these complainants into the workplace, the agency must make it clear to all employees that the complainants were exercising a constitutional right by complaining and that the agency supports their commitment to improving the agency. In other words, the agency must not only prevent retaliation but also take affirmative steps to make sure that the complainant feels welcome in the workplace.

Use Unsubstantiated Complaint in Positive Way

Sometimes, the complaint may not be substantiated, but the agency can still use the investigative process as an opportunity to provide training and to highlight the philosophy of zero tolerance. For example, the investigator may conclude that the incident was truly a good-faith misunderstanding—perhaps the complainant misheard a comment or incorrectly interpreted a gesture. In such a situation, discipline is not warranted, but it still may be helpful to provide a copy of the sexual harassment policy and/or provide training to everyone in the unit.

The same is true in situations where there simply is not enough information to make a determination. To illustrate, perhaps the complaint is based on a single comment or joke that was not heard by anyone else, and the complainant and the respondent are equally credible. In such a situation, the appropriate response might again be to provide a copy of the sexual harassment policy and/or provide training to everyone in the unit. Even if the complaint was not substantiated, however, steps must still be taken to prevent retaliation against the complainant and others who cooperated with the investigation.

Address Other Problems

Sometimes an investigator may conclude that sexual harassment did not occur, but there are other serious problems in the unit that need to be addressed. For example, it is not uncommon for people to use the sexual harassment complaint procedure for problems that are serious but not actually sexual harassment. This is not necessarily an appropriate use of the complaint procedure, but it does not constitute a false accusation that should result in discipline. Rather, the complaint should be forwarded to the appropriate personnel with the responsibility for investigating and responding to such problems.

FOLLOW UP WITH COMPLAINANTS AND RESPONDENTS

After the determination is made and disciplinary sanctions or other corrective actions are implemented, it is necessary to follow up with both complainants and respondents. This should include both written communication and an in-person meeting.

Draft Follow-Up Letter

In preparation for a meeting with the complainant and the respondent, a follow-up letter should be drafted to summarize the complaint, findings, and corrective actions taken. This is also a perfect opportunity for the agency to highlight its commitment to preventing sexual harassment and prohibiting retaliation against those who report it. The letter can also include a copy of the agency policy. After drafting the letter, investigators can make sure that it is reviewed by legal counsel before it is sent. For example, there may be restrictions about how much information can be given to the complainant, and an attorney can provide the appropriate guidance. This letter can then be given to the complainant and the respondent during their individual meetings with the investigator.

Meet with Complainant

When the investigator meets with the complainant, it is important to discuss the process and outcomes of the investigation. For example, the complainant can be informed of how many interviews were conducted (without compromising the confidentiality of witnesses), what type of evidence was collected, and what factors were used to make a determination. If the complainant believes that something was overlooked in the investigation, this must be seriously considered. If it is a significant issue, it should be further investigated.

If, however, the issue raised by the complainant is minor or redundant (e.g., another character witness), the complainant should be redirected to focus on the actions taken by the employer in response to the investigation. For example, the disciplinary sanctions and other corrective actions can be described and discussed with the complainant to ensure that they are appropriate and likely to be effective. The complainant should also be asked about any retaliation and be reminded about the process for reporting any retaliatory actions. As always, the meeting should be carefully documented (Salisbury & Dominick, 2004).

Meet with Respondent

When meeting with the respondent, the discussion may require more than one meeting, particularly if the allegations are substantiated. The respondent will typically want to hear a description of the investigative process (without compromising the confidentiality of witnesses), which should include a discussion of the agency's policy and relevant laws. Disciplinary sanctions and other corrective actions must then be carefully explained, along with the expectations for future behavior and progress evaluations. The respondent can also be provided with training (either in a workplace group or as an individual) and referrals for counseling or other employee assistance (Salisbury & Dominick, 2004).

Monitor for Retaliation

Finally, the unit needs to be monitored after the investigation is concluded to determine whether there are any leaks of confidential information or retaliatory actions. It might again be appropriate to provide training to the workplace or unit on the topic of sexual harassment and other forms of workplace discrimination. As part of this monitoring effort, the investigator should regularly check with complainants and other key witnesses to make sure they are not experiencing retaliation. This should be done frequently at first and then taper off over time.

Chapter 20

Other Issues

Investigators must have a working knowledge of a variety of other issues that pertain to the subject of sexual harassment: same-gender harassment, harassment based on sexual orientation, harassment of civilian women, bystander harassment, and harassment committed against and by nonemployees. Investigators must also be knowledgeable about forms of workplace harassment targeting members of social groups that are protected by local, state, and federal laws as well as organizational policies. Another issue for investigators to consider is the increasing use of computers for harassment purposes.

SAME-GENDER HARASSMENT

As discussed in the chapter on law, the Supreme Court has made it clear that illegal sexual harassment can take place between two people of the same gender. While approximately 90 percent of sexual harassment involves a male perpetrator and a female victim, the remaining 10 percent includes a large number of incidents involving two people of the same gender. Research clearly documents that this problem is particularly common among men: Only 2 percent of female victims are harassed by another woman, whereas male victims are equally likely to have a male or a female harasser (Berdahl, Magley, & Waldo, 1996; Waldo, Berdahl, & Fitzgerald, 1998). In fact, one study has found that men were 33 times more likely to experience same-gender harassment than women were (Stockdale, Visio, & Batra, 1999).

Clearly, men are more likely than women to experience same-gender harassment. While the research suggests that male victims do not typically experience the same distress as female victims of sexual harassment, worse outcomes are seen among male victims who are harassed by another male as opposed to women harassed by a woman (Berdahl, Magley, & Waldo, 1996; DuBois, Faley, Kustis, & Knapp, 1999; Waldo, Berdahl, & Fitzgerald, 1998). Among men, such harassment often consists of "ritualized male hazing" (DuBois, Faley, Kustis, & Knapp, 1999). Gender harassment is also frequently targeted against men whose behavior does not conform with the stereotypic male gender role (Stockdale, Visio, & Batra 1999).

In many situations, men are subjected to harassment based on the perception that they are homosexual—regardless of whether this perception is accurate. Unfortunately, this type of harassment can quickly become physical, as male colleagues "test" the strength of the officer who is perceived to be gay. Investigators must therefore be particularly careful not to chalk this type of behavior up to horseplay or roughhousing. These behaviors have no place in a law enforcement agency, and this characterization is often used to excuse conduct that is actually abusive, illegal, and dangerous. This type of behavior must be quickly stopped.

In our experience, employees who are harassed by someone of their own gender are particularly likely to find offensive items in their lockers or be exposed to pornographic materials in shared locker rooms or restrooms, so a good test of the climate in any workplace is to inspect the locker rooms and restrooms to see if there are materials displayed that could lead to complaints of sexual harassment. No workplace should have any type of pornography or sexually suggestive materials displayed, and the prohibition against such materials must be strictly enforced because their presence sends a message of permissiveness throughout the organization.

It should not come as any surprise that victims of same-gender harassment are particularly reluctant to file a formal complaint. The research documents, for example, that men who are sexually harassed are less likely to come forward with a complaint than are female victims (DuBois et al., 1998). The very act of coming forward may be perceived as being cowardly or weak, and the fear of retaliation among male victims is often very strong; therefore, investigators must take extra precautions to ensure that these complaints are handled appropriately, investigated thoroughly, and accompanied with proactive measures to prevent retaliation. The courts have made it clear that employers can be held liable for failing to protect their employees from sexual harassment, regardless of the gender of the harasser and the victim.

HARASSMENT BASED ON SEXUAL ORIENTATION

Unlike same-gender sexual harassment, harassment based on sexual orientation is not prohibited in the 1964 Civil Rights Act. It is sometimes prohibited by local and state laws, but regardless of whether it is illegal, it is clearly a problem and has a wide range of negative consequences for both the individuals and the organizations involved. Therefore, harassment based on sexual orientation should be investigated and taken seriously by organizations even when it is not explicitly prohibited by law. For example, many people assume that talking explicitly about sex is okay with someone who is "out" as a gay man or a lesbian. Some people mistakenly believe that when the person talks about his or her partner, he or she is somehow talking about sex. Of course, this is no more true than when the heterosexual person who talks about a husband or wife (Oppenheimer & Pratt, 2003).

Lesbian and gay male officers are also sometimes the victim of harassing complaints and investigations. For example, a coworker may file a false allegation that the officer engaged in domestic violence with a same-sex partner; the allegation may even be made anonymously. While the allegation is not based on fact, the agency is obviously obligated to investigate it. Unfortunately, this can serve to "out" officers who are accused and drag them through the difficult and embarrassing administrative process of investigation. These harassing complaints are particularly damaging when they are made at a time when the person is seeking a promotion or a specialized assignment. In general, officers cannot be awarded such a promotion or a specialized assignment while under investigation, so the harassing complaints can function to stall their career aspirations. Investigators must be alert to this possibility and look into the legitimacy and source of any suspicious complaints made against a lesbian or gay male officer who is seeking a promotion or a specialized assignment.

When it comes to lesbian officers, our experience suggests that they are typically subjected to one of two serious types of sexual harassment. The first type is the constant pressuring for sex by male colleagues. This could include comments such as "You need a real man and you will change." It could also include leaving sexual "toys" for the lesbian officers. The other type of harassment that lesbian women officers often face is being stereotyped as "female men." Lesbian officers are all too often targeted with offensive jokes, sexual comments, and other behaviors on the grounds that they are really "just one of the guys." The women are then placed in the uncomfortable position of either enduring the offensive behavior or filing a complaint and risk being seen as a troublemaker or "rat."

Of course, lesbian officers could be victimized by either *quid pro quo* or hostile work environment sexual harassment based on their gender, and it is sometimes difficult to sort out the harassment they experience as women from the harassment that is based on their sexual orientation. However, this distinction should not matter for the purpose of investigators because they do not need to make the legal determination regarding whether the harassment is in violation of Title VII. The investigator simply needs to determine whether the behavior is in violation of the policies governing appropriate workplace behavior; if there is a violation, the charges can be substantiated and appropriate discipline imposed.

HARASSMENT OF CIVILIAN WOMEN EMPLOYEES

Although all the recommendations in this book are intended to be inclusive of civilian as well as sworn employees, we want to point out that civilian women employees often experience sexual harassment that is much worse than that experienced by sworn women officers. Because civilian women often represent the lowest rung on the hierarchy of the rank structure within law enforcement, they typically have the least power in the workplace; as a result, they are all too often subjected to harassment by *female officers* in addition to the harassment they receive from male officers. This may take the form of female officers joining in the harassment of a particular civilian employee. Sadly, civilian employees, such as dispatchers, records clerks, administrative assistants, and crime prevention specialists, are often extremely reluctant to come forward with allegations of sexual harassment out of fear of retaliation.

The same type of situation is also seen in firefighting and other traditionally male professions in which women represent the minority within the organization and fill roles that are traditionally seen as feminine (e.g., receptionist, administrative assistant). Clearly, harassment of such women is a serious problem that employers must actively work to prevent, investigative, and promptly correct.

BYSTANDER HARASSMENT

The issue of bystander harassment is discussed in some detail in the chapter on the law, but it bears repeating in this context because a person does not need to be the target of sexual harassment in order to file a complaint. The courts have made it clear that bystanders can be victimized by witnessing the sexual harassment of others and that the organization is liable for preventing, investigating, and promptly correcting such situations.

A good example in law enforcement involves civilian employees, as discussed above. In addition to being personally targeted for sexual harassment, civilian women are often exposed to the sexual harassment of female officers. Unfortunately, these civilian women must often hear the harassing comments made to and about the female officers and witness the horseplay to which female officers are subjected. This type of situation can certainly create a hostile work environment—not only for the female officers but also for the civilian employees. Therefore, complaints made by anyone who witnesses sexual harassment must be investigated in the same way as complaints that are made by the target of the harassment.

HARASSMENT OF NONEMPLOYEES

Also cited in the chapter on law is the issue of harassment of nonemployees. Clearly, police and fire departments can be held liable if nonemployees are sexually harassed by someone within the agency. Some examples of potential harassment situations are the citizen who comes to the police precinct to report a crime and the female custodian who comes to the fire station in the evening to clean. In the last several years, newspaper headlines have trumpeted the details of police officers who have sexually harassed or assaulted women who are stopped for traffic violations, women who are the victims of domestic violence, and women who have called the police to report a crime (for a research review of these incidents, see Kraska and Kappelar, 1995). One such case involving the Pennsylvania State Police was recently settled for $5 million. Unfortunately, this problem is not unique to that agency. The possibility of sexual misconduct is something that must be addressed by all law enforcement agencies—both large and small—across the country.

We want to particularly note the problems of sexual harassment that are often seen in Explorer Scouts programs or similar programs. On the one hand, these programs can be a wonderful way to bring teenagers into the law enforcement organization and potentially hire them as officers. On the other hand, we have read all too often about lawsuits in which a police officer has sexually harassed or sexually assaulted young people in such a program. Before assigning anyone within a law enforcement organization to be the coordinator of such a program, a careful examination must be conducted of the applicant, and it should include a psychological fitness examination. In addition, we recommend that there never be just one person assigned as the coordinator; preferably, a team of male and female officers should be utilized as coordinators for any Explorer Scouts program or similar programs. Coordinators should also be required to sign a document warning them about any sexual misconduct with the scouts. This is a very serious issue and one that is too often ignored by law enforcement leaders.

The courts have made it clear that sexual harassment complaints made by nonemployees must be taken very seriously and must be thoroughly investigated. For police agencies, this could mean surveying community members who are stopped for traffic violations, citizens who call to report a crime, and even those who are arrested by the agency. Such a survey should ask questions about the behavior of the officers, so it can identify potential problems such as sexual misconduct. Although this type of survey would be costly to implement, it is clear that the price tag will never be as high as $5 million. In the case of the Pennsylvania State Police mentioned earlier, complaints of sexual harassment filed by citizens and employees were routinely ignored. Managers within police and fire departments cannot afford to ignore the lessons learned from that case.

HARASSMENT BY NONEMPLOYEES

The issue of harassment by nonemployees was briefly covered in the chapter on the law, but it bears repeating in this context. To summarize, the laws that prohibit sex discrimination also hold employers accountable for harassment that employees experience at the hands of nonemployees. In law enforcement and firefighting, this would include harassment by contract workers, such as maintenance workers and garage attendants, as well as others who come into the workplace, such as postal workers, bail bondsmen and bondswomen, court workers, officers from other jurisdictions, and government employees. Any of these individuals could be accused of sexually harassing an employee, and these complaints must be investigated in the same manner as complaints against employees.

The standard for determining whether an agency is liable for such harassment by nonemployees is whether *it knew* or *should have known* about the situation yet did nothing to stop it. When such a complaint is received, the investigation should proceed like any other, by interviewing the complainant and witnesses and by gathering any evidence. This information can be analyzed and summarized in a preliminary report so that management can decide how to respond to the investigative findings with the nonemployee. For example, if the complaint is against a contractor, the company that is providing services can be contacted about the behavior and told that if it does not stop, the contract will be ended. The law enforcement agency can also demand that a particular person not be allowed to work on the contract.

If any criminal actions have occurred in the incident(s), a criminal investigation must be conducted and presented for prosecution. However, if there are no criminal actions alleged and the agency takes effective steps to remove the harasser from the workplace, the final report can document the steps of the investigative process and the corrective actions taken. These findings and results can then be discussed with the complainant to determine if they are likely to be effective.

Even if the complaint is made against someone other than a contractor, the agency must still take steps to correct the problem. For individuals who enter the police facility on behalf of their employer, this employer can be contacted, informed of their behavior, and told that they are no longer welcome in the facility. If the employer cooperates, the problem may be solved; however, if the employer refuses to cooperate, the agency may have to take steps to obtain a restraining order to protect its employee. As with any other type of complaint, a complete investigation must be conducted and documented, and the complainant should be told to report any other violations that may occur.

Unfortunately, sexual harassment by nonemployees is often the continuation of a domestic violence situation in which the employee is being victimized. In these situations, the employer should take reasonable steps to protect employees from domestic violence that is brought into the workplace. There are many places where employers can receive advice on this issue; the best one may be the website for the U.S. Department of Justice, Office on Violence Against Women: www.ojp.usdoj.gov/vawo.

HARASSMENT OF PEOPLE IN PROTECTED CLASSES

The legal criteria for harassment based on race, color, national origin, religious affiliation, age (over 40), and other protected classes are generally the same as they are for sexual harassment. Comments, jokes, or innuendos that are derogatory or demeaning are prohibited, but they constitute illegal discrimination only if they are severe or pervasive enough to interfere with the terms or conditions of an individual's employment. For example, the case of *Etter* v. *Veriflo Corp.* (1988) established that it takes more than "occasional, isolated, sporadic, or trivial acts" to constitute illegal racial harassment. Nonetheless, such behavior should still be considered a violation of agency policy, investigated thoroughly, and disciplined if found to be substantiated.

The same basic standards would also be used for establishing liability for discrimination against any member of a protected class, depending on whether the harasser is a supervisor or a nonsupervisory employee. As discussed in the chapter on the law, there are a number of federally protected classes against whom harassment or discrimination is illegal; however, additional categories of people may be included in local and state laws as well as in the agency's own policies. Any allegation of harassment or discrimination against a member of any of these groups should be investigated following the guidelines provided throughout this book.

While *harassment* of employees based on their disability would be similar to other forms of workplace harassment, there are a host of additional issues pertaining to *discrimination* based on the Americans with Disabilities Act that are beyond the scope of this book. Investigators are encouraged to pursue training in the complex issues pertaining to this act.

Unfortunately, one form of harassment that is becoming increasingly common is based on religious affiliation. On the one hand, employers are legally obligated to make reasonable accommodations for an employee's religious beliefs and practices; on the other hand, this religious expression must not create a hostile work environment for other employees. Often the distinction can be made between private expressions of religion (e.g., taking a day off to observe a religious holiday) and public displays (e.g., posting religious messages or materials in the workplace). Even with public displays, however, a distinction can be made between expressions of religious beliefs that are discreet and positive (e.g., a small religious message or symbol placed on an employee's desk, facing inward) and expressions that are negative or inflammatory (e.g., a quote from a religious text condemning homosexuality posted on the outside wall of a cubical for others to see). This last example would constitute the type of religious expression by one employee that is likely to contribute to a hostile work environment for other employees and should be prohibited. In addition, any comments, jokes, or innuendos that are derogatory or demeaning and that are based on religious affiliation should be prohibited.

USE OF COMPUTERS FOR HARASSMENT

We would like to conclude this chapter with a brief discussion of the increasing role that computers play in the problem of sexual harassment. In recent years, attention has focused on the issues of workplace harassment that involve inappropriate use of computers. This could involve exposure to sexual content on computer screens (through websites, screen savers, and other text or visual images) as well as harassing emails or instant messaging.

Unfortunately, the evidence suggests that the inappropriate use of work computers for sexual perposes is widespread. One study found that 20 percent of men and 12 percent of women have gone online at work for various sexual pursuits (Cooper, Golden, & Kent Ferraro, 2002). Another study found that 28 percent of employees have used their work computer to send sexual materials to coworkers and 31 percent have sent sexual materials to people outside the company. As many as one-third of employees have downloaded pornography at work (Pomeroy, 2004).

Not only can this type of inappropriate computer use contribute to a hostile work environment, but it can also erode the boundaries and norms for appropriate workplace behavior, making other forms of sexual harassment more likely. It is therefore critically important that police and fire departments either include a discussion of these issues in their sexual harassment policy and/or craft a separate policy provision to address issues of inappropriate use of agency computers. Of course, policies and enforcement measures are best designed with input from legal counsel as well as from Information

Technology, Records Management, and Human Resources Departments. Employees must then be informed of the policy, and these issues should be included in any sexual harassment prevention training programs that are implemented. Given the rapidly evolving nature of this legal field, this policy must be updated regularly and employees must be reminded through various means.

Fortunately, inappropriate computer use can be easier to investigate than other forms of sexual harassment because "email, instant messaging and Internet activity form the electronic equivalent of DNA evidence" (Pomeroy, 2004, p. 1). Computer records are often quite easy to investigate, and employers have considerable access to them because the "courts have found that there is no reasonable expectation of privacy in email sent, stored, or received at work" (Cooper, Golden, & Kent-Ferarro, 2002, p. 152). Any allegations of harassment involving inappropriate computer use must be investigated thoroughly and disciplined if they are substantiated; as with other forms of harassment, discipline should become progressively more severe for subsequent offenses. Remedial measures might include putting electronic blocks on the respondent's computer, allowing the respondent only supervised Internet use, or having the respondent leave the office door open when accessing the Internet.

References

ADAMS, K. (2001). *Women in Senior Police Management*. Research report prepared by Australian Centre for Policing Research. Available at www.acpr.gov.au.

BARAK, A. (1994), A cognitive-behavioral educational workshop to combat sexual harassment in the workplace. *Journal of Counseling & Development, 72,* 595–602.

BARGH, J. A., RAYMOND, P., STRACK, F., & PRYOR, J. B. (1993). Attractiveness of the underling: An automatic power—sex association and its consequences for sexual harassment and aggression. *Journal of Personality and Social Psychology, 68(5),* 768–781.

BARTLING, C. A., & EISENMAN, R. (1993). Sexual harassment proclivities in men and women. *Bulletin of the Psychonomic Society, 31(3),* 189–192.

BARTOL, C. R., BERGEN, G. T., VOLCKENS, J. S., & KNORAS, K. M. (1992). Women in small town policing: Job performance and stress. *Criminal Justice & Behavior, 19(3),* 240–259.

BEAUVAIS, K. (1986). Workshops to combat sexual harassment: A case study of changing attitudes. *Signs: Journal of Women in Culture and Society, 12(1),* 130–145.

BEGANY, J. J., & MILBURN, M. L. (2002). Psychological predictors of sexual harassment: Authoritarianism, hostile sexism, and rape myths. *Psychology of Men and Masculinity, 3(2),* 119–126.

BELKNAP, J., & SHELLEY, J. K. (1992). The new lone ranger: Policewomen on patrol. *American Journal of Police, 12(2),* 47–75.

BERDAHL, J. L., MAGLEY, V. J., & WALDO, C. R. (1996). The sexual harassment of men? Exploring the concept with theory and data. *Psychology of Women Quarterly, 20,* 527–547.

206

BLAKELEY, G. L., BLAKELEY, E. H., & MOORMAN, R. H. (1998). The effects of training on perceptions of sexual harassment allegations. *Journal of Applied Social Psychology, 28(1),* 71–83.

BLAXALL, M. C. D., PARSONSON, B. S., & ROBERTSON, N. R. (1993). The development and evaluation of a sexual harassment contact person training package. *Behavior Modification, 17(2),* 148–163.

BONATE, D. L., & JESSELL, J. C. (1996). The effects of educational intervention on perceptions of sexual harassment. *Sex Roles, 35(11/12),* 751–764.

BONI, N., ADAMS, K., & CIRCELLI, M. (2001). *Educational and Professional Development Experiences of Female and Male Police Employees.* Research report prepared by Australian Centre for Policing Research. Available at www.acpr.gov.au.

BROWN, J., & CAMPBELL, E. (1995). Adverse impacts experienced by police officers following exposure to sex discrimination and sexual harassment. *Stress Medicine, 11,* 221–228.

BURNS, S. E. (1993). Evidence of a sexually hostile workplace: What is it and how should it be assessed after *Harris* v. *Forklift Systems, Inc.*? *Review of Law and Social Change, 21,* 357–431.

CAMPBELL, D. J., CHRISTMAN, B. D., & FEIGELSON, M. E. (2000). Improving the recruitment of women in policing: An investigation of women's attitudes and job preferences. *Recruiting and Retaining Women: A Self-Assessment Guide for Law Enforcement.* Report prepared by the National Center for Women & Policing, a division of the Feminist Majority Foundation. Available at www.ncjrs.org.

CHRISTOPHER, W. (1991). *Report of the Independent Commission on the Los Angeles Police Department.* Report prepared by the Independent Commission on the Los Angeles Police Department and available at the website for the Police Assessment Resource Center at http://www.parc.info/reports.

COHEN, C. F., & COHEN, M. E. (1994). Defending your life: When women complain about sexual harassment. *Employee Responsibilities and Rights Journal, 7(3),* 235–243

COMMITTEE ON ACCREDITATION FOR LAW ENFORCEMENT AGENCIES (1991). The Standards Manual of the Law Enforcement Agency Accreditation Program (4th ed.).

CONTE, A. (1997). Legal theories of sexual harassment. In W. O'Donohue (Ed.), *Sexual Harassment: Theory, Research, and Treatment* (Chapter 4, pp. 50–83). Needham Heights, MA: Allyn & Bacon.

CORTINA, L. M., & MAGLEY, V. J. (2003). Rising voice, risking retaliation: Events following interpersonal mistreatment in the workplace. *Journal of Occupational Health Psychology, 8(4),* 247–265.

CULBERTSON, A., & RODGERS, W. (1997). Improving managerial effectiveness in the workplace: The case of sexual harassment of Navy women. *Journal of Applied Social Psychology, 27(22),* 1953–1971.

DANTZKER, M. L., & KUBIN, B. (1998). Job satisfaction: The gender perspective among police officers. *American Journal of Criminal Justice, 23(1),* 19–31.

DRISCOLL, D. M., KELLY, J. R., & HENDERSON, W. L. (1998). Can perceivers identify likelihood to sexually harass? *Sex Roles: A Journal of Research, 38(7/8),* 557–589.

DuBois, C. L. Z., Faley, R. H., Kustis, G. A., & Knapp, D. E. (1999). Perceptions of organizational responses to formal sexual harassment complaints. *Journal of Managerial Issues, 11(2)*, 198–212.

DuBois, C. L. Z., Knapp, D. E., Faley, R. H., & Kustis, G. A. (1998). An empirical examination of same- and other-gender sexual harassment in the workplace. *Sex Roles, 39*, 731–749.

Eberhardt, B. J., Moser, S. B., & McFadden, D. (1999). Sexual harassment in small government units: An investigation of policies and attitudes. *Public Personnel Management, 28(3)*, 351–365.

Felkenes, G. T., & Schroedel, J. R. (1993). A case study of minority women in policing. *Women & Criminal Justice, 4(2)*, 65–89.

Fischer, G. J. (1995). Effects of drinking by the victim or offender on verdicts in a simulated trial of an acquaintance rape. *Psychological Reports, 77*, 579–586.

Fitzgerald, L. F., Drasgow, F., & Magley, V. J. (1999). Sexual harassment in the armed forces: A test of an integrated model. *Military Psychology, 11*, 329–343.

Fitzgerald, L. F., Swan, S., & Magley, V. J. (1997). But was it really harassment? Legal, behavioral and psychological definitions of the workplace victimization of women. In W. O'Donohue (Ed.), *Sexual Harassment: Theory, Research, and Treatment* (pp. 5–28). Boston: Allyn & Bacon.

Fry, L. J. (1983). A preliminary examination of the factors related to turnover of women in law enforcement. *Journal of Police Science and Administration, 2*, 149–155.

Glomb, T. L., Richman, W. L., Hulin, C. L., Drasgow, W., Schneider, K. T., & Fitzgerald, L. F. (1997). Ambient sexual harassment: An integrated model of the antecedents and consequences. *Organizational Behavior and Human Decisions Processes, 71*, 309–328.

Goodson, J. R., Lewis, C. W., & Culverhouse, R. D. (1994). Sexually harassed and stressed out: The employer's potential liability. *Journal of Managerial Issues, 6(4)*, 428–444.

Grundmann, E. O., O'Donohue, W., & Peterson, S. H. (1997). The prevention of sexual harassment. In W. O'Donohue (Ed.), *Sexual Harassment: Theory, Research, and Treatment* (Chapter 10, pp. 175–184). Needham Heights, MA: Allyn & Bacon.

Gutek, B. A. (1985). *Sex and the Workplace.* San Francisco: Jossey-Bass Publishers.

Gutek, B. A., O'Connor, M. A., Melancon, R., Stockdale, M. S., Geer, T. M., & Done, R. S. (1999). The utility of the reasonable woman legal standard in hostile environment sexual harassment cases: A multimethod, multistudy examination. *Psychology, Public Policy, and Law, 5*, 596–629.

Gutek, B. (1997). Sexual harassment policy initiatives. In W. O'Donohue (Ed.), *Sexual Harassment: Theory, Research, and Treatment* (Chapter 11, pp. 185–198). Needham Heights, MA: Allyn & Bacon.

Haar, R. N. (1997). Patterns of interaction in a police patrol bureau: Race and gender barriers to integration. *Justice Quarterly, 14(1)*, 53–84.

Hesson-McInnis, M. S., & Fitzgerald, L. F. (1997). Sexual harassment: A preliminary test of an integrative model. *Journal of Applied Social Psychology, 27(10)*, 877–901.

Horne, P. (1980). *Women in Law Enforcement.* Springfield, IL: Charles C Thomas.

Hulin, C. L., Fitzgerald, L. F., & Drasgow, F. (1996). Organizational influences on sexual harassment. In M. Stockdale (Ed.), *Sexual Harassment in the Workplace* (Vol. 5, pp. 127–150). Thousand Oaks, CA: Sage.

HUNTER-WILLIAMS, J., FITZGERALD, L. F., & DRASGOW, F. (1999). The effects of organizational practices on sexual harassment and individual outcomes in the military. *Military Psychology, 11,* 303–328.

ILIES, R., HAUSERMAN, N., SCHWOCHAU, S., & STIBAL, J. (2003). Reported incidence rates of work-related sexual harassment in the United States: Using meta-analysis to explain reported rate disparities. *Personnel Psychology, 56,* 607–631.

JACOBS, C. D., BERGEN, M. R., & KORN, D. (2000). Impact of a program to diminish gender insensitivity and sexual harassment at a medical school. *Academic Medicine, 75(5),* 464–469.

KOSS, M. P., GOODMAN, L. A., BROWNE, A., FITZGERALD, L. F., KEITA, G. P., & RUSSO, N. F. (1994). *No Safe Haven: Male Violence Against Women at Home, at Work, and in the Community.* Washington, DC: American Psychological Association.

KRASKA, P. B., & KAPPELER, V. E. (1995). To serve and pursue: Exploring police sexual violence against women. *Justice Quarterly, 12(1),* 85–111.

LAFONTAINE, E., & TREDEAU, L. (1986). The frequency, sources, and correlates of sexual harassment among women in traditional male occupations. *Sex Roles, 15,* 433–442.

LATTS, M. G., & GEISELMAN, R. E. (1991). Interviewing survivors of rape. *Journal of Police and Criminal Psychology, 7(1),* 8–16.

LENHART, S. A., & SHRIER, D. K. (1996). Potential costs and benefits of sexual harassment litigation. *Psychiatric Annals, 26,* 132–138.

LILLICH, T. T., WEBSTER, D. B., MARSHALL, E. O., SMITH, T. A., SEAVER, D. C., & SZELUGA, M. A. (2000). The influence of a workshop on dental students' perceptions about sexual harassment. *Journal of Dental Education, 64(6),* 401–408.

LINDEMANN, B., & KADUE, D. D. (1992). *Sexual Harassment in Employment Law.* Washington, DC: Bureau of National Affairs.

MARTIN, S. E. (1989). *Women on the Move? A Report on the Status of Women in Policing.* Report prepared by the Police Foundation. Available at www.policefoundation.org.

MARTIN, S. E. (1994). "Outsider within" the station house: The impact of race and gender and black women police. *Social Problems, 41(3),* 383–400.

MCQUEEN, I. (1997). Investigating sexual harassment allegations: The employer's challenge. In W. O'Donohue (Ed.). *Sexual Harassment: Theory, Research, and Treatment* (Chapter 12, pp. 199–212). Needham Heights, MA: Allyn & Bacon.

MICELI, M. P., & NEAR, J. P. (1985). Characteristics of organizational climate and perceived wrongdoing associated with whistle-blowing decisions. *Personnel Psychology, 38(3),* 525–544.

MORASH, M., & HAAR, R. N. (1995). Gender, workplace problems, and stress in policing. *Justice Quarterly, 12(1),* 114–140.

MORGAN, P. A. (1999). Risking relationships: Understanding the litigation choices of sexually harassed women. *Law & Society Review, 33(1),* 67–92.

MORRIS, A. (1996). Gender and ethnic differences in social constraints among a sample of New York City police officers. *Journal of Occupational Health Psychology, 1(2),* 224–235.

MOYER, R. S., & NATH, A. (1998). Some effects of brief training interventions on perceptions of sexual harassment. *Journal of Applied Social Psychology, 28(4),* 333–356.

MUELLER, C. W., COSTER, S. D., & ESTES, S. B. (2001). Sexual harassment in the workplace: Unanticipated consequences of modern social control in organizations. *Work and Occupations, 28(4),* 411–446.

OFFERMANN, L. R., & MALAMUTH, A. B. (2002). When leaders harass: The impact of target perceptions of organizational leadership and climate on harassment reporting and outcomes. *Journal of Applied Psychology, 87(5),* 885–893.

O'HARE, E. A., & O'DONOHUE, W. (1998). Sexual harassment: Identifying risk factors. *Archives of Sexual Behavior, 27(6),* 561–580.

OPPENHEIMER, A., & PRATT, C. (2003). *Investigating Workplace Harassment: How to Be Fair, Thorough, and Legal.* Alexandria, VA: Society for Human Resource Management.

PALUDI, C. A., & PALUDI, M. (2003). Developing and enforcing effective policies, procedures, and training programs for educational institutions and businesses. In M. Paludi & C. A. Paludi (Eds.), *Academic and Workplace Sexual Harassment: A Handbook of Cultural, Social Science, Management, and Legal Perspectives* (Chapter 7, pp. 175–198). Westport, CT: Praeger.

PARKER, S. K., & GRIFFIN, M. A. (2002). What is so bad about a little name-calling? Negative consequences of gender harassment for overperformance demands and distress. *Journal of Occupational Health Psychology, 7(3),* 195–210.

PERRY, E. L., KULIK, C. T., & SCHMIDTKE, J. M. (1998). Individual differences in the effectiveness of sexual harassment training. *Journal of Applied Social Psychology, 28,* 698–723.

PIERCE, C. A., & AGUINIS, H. (1997). Bridging the gap between romantic relationships and sexual harassment in organizations. *Journal of Organizational Behavior, 18,* 197–200.

POLISAR, J., & MILGRAM, D. (1998). Recruiting, integrating and retaining women police officers: Strategies that work. *Police Chief, 65,* 42, 44, 46, 48, 50, 52.

PRYOR, J. B. (1987). Sexual harassment proclivities in men. *Sex Roles, 17(5/6),* 269–289.

PRYOR, J. B., LAVITE, C. M., & STOLLER, L. M. (1993). A social psychological analysis of sexual harassment: The person/situation interaction. *Journal of Vocational Behavior, 42,* 68–83.

PRYOR, J. B., & STOLLER, L. M. (1994). Sexual cognition processes in men who are high in the likelihood to sexually harass. *Personality and Social Psychology Bulletin, 20,* 163–169.

PRYOR, J. B., & WHALEN, N. J. (1997). A typology of sexual harassment: Characteristics of harassers and the social circumstances under which sexual harassment occurs. In W. O'Donohue (Ed.), *Sexual Harassment: Theory, Research, and Treatment* (Chapter 8, pp. 129–151). Needham Heights, MA: Allyn & Bacon.

PRYOR, J. B., GIEDD, J. L., & WILLIAMS, K. B. (1995). A social psychological model for predicting sexual harassment. *Journal of Social Issues, 51(1),* 69–84.

REESE, L. A., & LINDENBERG, K. E. (1999). *Implementing Sexual Harassment Policy: Challenges for the Public Sector Workplace.* Thousand Oaks, CA: Sage.

ROBB, L. A., & DOVERSPIKE, D. (2001). Self-reported proclivity to harass as a moderator of the effectiveness of sexual harassment prevention training. *Psychological Reports, 88,* 85–88.

ROBINSON, G. V. (1993). *Sexual harassment in Florida law enforcement: Panacea or Pandora's box?* Paper prepared for the Senior Leadership program with the Florida Criminal Justice Executive Institute. Available from the Florida Department of Law Enforcement at http://www.fdle.state.fl.us/FCJEI/publications.asp.

ROSCOE, B., STROUSE, J. S., GOODWIN, M. P., TARACKS, L., & HENDERSON, D, (1994). Sexual harassment: An educational program for middle school students. *Elementary School Guidance & Counseling, 29(2),* 110–120.

ROSELL, E., MILLER, K., & BARBER, K. (1995). Firefighting women and sexual harassment. *Public Personnel Management, 24(3),* 1–7.

ROTUNDO, M., NGUYEN, D., & SACKETT, P.R. (2001). A meta-analytic review of gender differences in perceptions of sexual harassment, *Journal of Applied Psychology, 86(5),* 914–922.

ROWE, M. (1996). Dealing with sexual harassment: A systems approach. In M. S. Stockdale (Ed.), *Sexual Harassment in the Workplace: Perspectives, Frontiers, and Response Strategies* (Vol. 5, pp. 241–271). Thousand Oaks, CA: Sage.

SALISBURY, J., & DOMINICK, B. (2004). *Investigating Harassment and Discrimination Complaints: A Practical Guide.* San Francisco, CA: Pfeiffer.

SBRAGA, T. P., & O'DONOHUE, W. (2000). Sexual harassment. *Annual Review of Sex Research, 11,* 258–276.

SCHNEIDER, K. T. (1996). *Bystander stress: The effect of organizational tolerance of sexual harassment on victims' coworkers.* Paper presented at the American Psychological Association, Toronto, Ontario (Canada).

SEAGRAM, B. C., & STARK-ADAMEC, C. (1992). Women in Canadian urban policing: Why are they leaving? *The Police Chief, 59(10),* 120, 122–128.

SORENSON, R. C., LUZIO, R. C., & MANGIONE-LAMBIE, M. G. (1994). *Perceived seriousness, recommended and expected organizational response, and effects of bystander and direct sexual harassment.* Paper presented at the Third International Conference of Applied Psychology, Madrid, Spain.

STOCKDALE, M. S. (Ed.). (1996). *Sexual Harassment in the Workplace: Perspectives, Frontiers, and Response Strategies.* Thousand Oaks, CA: Sage.

STOCKDALE, M. S., VISIO, M., & BATRA, L. (1999). The sexual harassment of men: Evidence for a broader theory of sexual harassment and sex discrimination. *Psychology, Public Policy & Law, 5,* 630–664.

STOKES, P. P., BELLE, S. S., & BARNES, J. M. (2000). The Supreme Court holds class on sexual harassment: How to avoid a failing grade. *Employee Responsibilities and Rights Journal, 12(2),* 79–90.

THOMANN, D.A., STRICKLAND, D.E., & GIBBONS, J.L. (1989). An organizational development approach to preventing sexual harassment. *CUPA Journal, 40,* 34–43. Cited in R.S. Moyer & A. Nath (1998). Some effects of brief training interventions on perceptions of sexual harassment. *Journal of Applied Social Psychology, 28,* 333–356.

TIMMERMAN, G., & BAJEMA, C. (2000). The impact of organizational culture on perceptions and experiences of sexual harassment. *Journal of Vocational Behavior, 57,* 188–205.

TIMMINS, W. M., & HAINSWORTH, B. E. (1989). Attracting and retaining females in law enforcement: Sex-based problems of women cops in 1988. *International Journal of Offender Therapy and Comparative Criminology, 33,* 197–205.

U.S. MERIT SYSTEMS PROTECTION BOARD (1987). *Sexual Harassment of Federal Workers: An Update.* Washington, DC: U.S. Government Printing Office.

U.S. Merit Systems Protection Board (1981). *Sexual Harassment of Federal Workers: Is It a Problem?* Washington, DC: U.S. Government Printing Office.

Waldo, C. R., Berdahl, J. L., & Fitzgerald, L. F. (1998). Are men sexually harassed? If so, by whom? *Law & Human Behavior, 22,* 59–79.

Wexler, J. G., & Logan, D. D. (1983). Sources of stress among women police officers. *Journal of Police Science and Administration, 11(1),* 46–53.

Wilkerson, J. M. (1999). The impact of job level and prior training on sexual harassment labeling and remedy choice. *Journal of Applied Social Psychology, 29,* 1605–1623.

Williams, C. L., Giuffre, P. A., & Dellinger, K. (1999). Sexuality in the workplace: Organizational control, sexual harassment, and the pursuit of pleasure. *Annual Review of Sociology, 25,* 73–93.

Yoder, J. D., & Aniakudo, P. (1996). When pranks become harassment: The case of African American women firefighters. *Sex Roles, 35(5/6),* 253–270.

York, K. M., Barclay, L. A., & Zajack, A. B. (1997). Preventing sexual harassment: The effect of multiple training methods. *Employee Responsibilities and Rights Journal, 10(4),* 277–289.

Index

A

Abuse of power, 4–5
Accountability
    for prevention, 65–66
    of supervisors and managers, 194–195
Adverse treatment, gender harassment
        and discrimination and, 47–48
African-American women in firefighting, 13–14
Aggravating factors, impact of sexual harassment
        on victims and, 16–17
Anonymous complaints, 121
    response to, 86
Attorneys, as investigators, 114

B

Body language, in complainant interviews, 150–151
Burlington Industries v. *Ellerth,* 31
Bystander harassment, 201

C

Citizens and others outside the agency
    sexual harassment of, 72–73, 201–202
    sexual harassment by, 202–203
Civilian women employees, harassment of, 200–201

Climate. *See* Work environment
Code of silence, 174–175
    reporting sexual harassment and, 21
Complainant interviews, 133–159
    acknowledging difficulty of investigation
        process, 147–148
    addressing questions complainant cannot
        answer, 149–150
    allowing complainant to vent emotions, 148
    audiotaping or videotaping, 137–138
    clarifying and summarizing in, 152
    complainant's narrative in (first stage),
        150–153
    concerns regarding outcomes of investigation
        and, 147
    conclusion of, 157–159
    confidentiality and, 146–147, 158
    cultural stereotypes and, 133–135
    determining who will be present in, 145–146
    empathy and, 148
    explaining purpose of, 146
    eye contact and appropriate body language in,
        150–151
    follow-up contact, 159
    follow-up questions in (second stage),
        153–154

213

Complainant interviews   (*continued*)
    identifying potential witnesses and others
      who were told about situation, 157
    inconsistent or untrue statements in,
      135–136
    information on complainant's behavior
      and relationship with respondent, 157
    investigator gender and,
      138–140
    keeping in touch with complainant, 159
    open-ended prompts in, 150
    preparation for, 143–145
    providing referral information, 159
    providing standard instructions
      and information in, 146
    rapport in, 148–149
    reflective comments in, 151–152
    setting pace and tone of, 149
    silent pauses in, 150
    specific types of information to be obtained
      in, 154–156
    standard instructions for, 144
    start of, 145–149
    taking breaks from, 152–153
    taking notes during, 153
    tips for successful, 140–142
    written statement to be signed by, 159
Complainants
    asking complainant what he or she would like
      to see happen, 95
    explaining investigative procedures and rights
      to complainant, 95
    following up with complainants, 196
    meeting with, 197
    personnel file of complainant, 187–188
    retaliation against complainant or others, 94
    trying to talk complainant out of filing, 94
Complaints of sexual harassment, 98–109. *See also*
    Formal complaint procedures; Informal
    complaint procedures
    anonymous, 86
    failing to listen to and act on, 94
    implementation of the complaint process,
      105–106
    response to. *See* Response to complaints
    summary of complainant allegations, in final
      investigative report, 182
    unsubstantiated, positive use of, 196
    user-friendly procedures, 105–106
Compliments, hostile work environment
    and, 28

Comprehensive sexual harassment policy
    broadened prohibitions in, 72
    complaint procedures for state and federal
      agencies in, 73
    dating and, 76–77
    dissemination of, 75–76
    elements not to include in, 73–75
    elements of, 71–72
    sexual harassment of citizens and, 72–73
    tips for the investigator, 78
Computers used for harassment, 204–205
Confidentiality
    complainant interviews and, 146–147, 158
    documenting the investigation and, 185
    guarantee of, 73–74
    investigation and, 122
    in respondent interviews, 164
    respondent interviews and, 172
    witness interviews and, 177, 179
Consensual sexual relationships, sexual harassment
    policy and, 76
Constructive discharge, 32
Contact person programs, 101–102
Corroborative evidence, 188–189
Costs of sexual harassment, 1
Coworkers
    employer liability for hostile work environment
      and behaviors of, 30–31
    work retaliation by, 54
Credibility
    of documents, 190–191
    making determinations of, 190
Cultural stereotypes, complainant interviews and,
    133–135

D

Dating, sexual harassment policy and, 76–77
Defenses to allegations of sexual harassment,
    168–171
Definition of sexual harassment, 25–27
Determination, making a, 187, 191–193
    weighing the evidence and, 188–189
Determinative findings, in final investigative
    report, 183
Discipline, 123
    appropriateness of, 39
    imposing appropriate, 193–196
    retaliation and, 56–57
Dissemination of a sexual harassment policy,
    75–76, 86–87

Documenting
   complainant's reactions, 134–135
Documenting the investigation, 181–186
   final investigative report, 181–184
   uniform standards for, 123

E

EEOC, filing a complaint with, 130
EEO coordinator, 105
Ellison v. *Brady,* 33
Empathy, in complainant interviews, 148
Employee organizations, 103
   informal complaint procedure, 99–103
Employee responses to sexual harassment,
      126–132
   informal response strategies, 126–129
   keeping a journal, 128
   talking to others, 128
   telling the supervisor, 128–129
   verbally confronting the harasser, 127
   writing a letter to harasser, 127–128
Employer liability, 37
   for hostile work environment. *See* Hostile
      work environment
Employers. *See also* Policies regarding sexual
      harassment
   common mistakes of, 37–39
Equal Employment Opportunity Commission
      (EEOC), 2
Etter v. *Veriflo Corp.,* 203
Evaluation of sexual harassment training,
      87–88
Evasive behavior, in respondent interviews, 166
Evidence
   contradictions or other inconsistencies in,
      189–190
   corroborative, 188–189
Exhibits, list of, in final investigative report, 183
Exit interviews, 65
External investigation and investigators,
      113–114
   coordination with, 124
Eye contact, in complainant interviews,
      150–151

F

False complaints or allegations
   myth of, 135–136
   policy statement regarding, 73

Faragher/Ellerth affirmative defense, 31–32
Faragher v. *City of Boca Raton,* 31, 37
Favoritism, sexual, 77
Female firefighters
   gender harassment and discrimination
      and, 42
   reporting sexual harassment and, 21
Female investigators, 139–140
Female police officers
   gender harassment and discrimination
      and, 41–42
   reporting sexual harassment and, 20
Final investigative report, 181–184
Firefighting, percentage of women who experience
      sexual harassment in, 13–14
Fitzgerald, Louise, 5
Focus groups, 103
Follow-up letter, 196–197
Formal complaint procedures, 98–100, 103–105,
      129–132
   within agency, 129–130
   Detective Division and, 105
   EEO coordinator and, 105
   EEOC or state agency, filing a complaint
      with, 130
   external agencies and, 105
   Internal Affairs and, 104–105
   lawsuits, 132
   separate discrimination units and, 104
   tips for the investigator, 131
Frequency of sexual harassment, 16
Fuller v. *City of Oakland,* 38

G

Gender, sexual harassment and, 17–18
Gender discrimination. *See also* Gender harassment
      and discrimination
   African-American women in firefighting
      and, 14
   federal prohibitions against, 23–24
   sexual harassment as a form of, 23–24
   state and local prohibitions against, 24
Gender harassment and discrimination,
      40–50
   adverse impact and, 48
   adverse treatment and, 47
   common excuses for, 44–47
   examples of, 42
   in firefighting, 13–14, 42
   investigation of, 43–44

Gender harassment and discrimination   (*continued*)
    in law enforcement, 41–42
    more information on, 48–49
    not always sexual, 40
    performance issue and, 45–47
    stereotypes and, 43
Guarantee of confidentiality, 73–74

H

Harris v. *Forklift Systems,* 34
Hazing, hostile work environment and, 28
Hostile work environment, 27–31, 155
    constructive discharge and, 32
    coworker behaviors and employer liability
        for, 30
    determination of "hostile," 29–35
    determination of unwelcome behavior,
        32–33
    elements to establish, 30
    psychological injury not a requirement, 34
    reasonable woman standard and, 33–34
    same-sex sexual harassment and, 34
    supervisor behaviors and employer liability
        for, 31
    third-party harassment and, 34–35
    Weeks v. *Baker & Mackenzie* and, 35
Hostile work environment, examples of, 27–29
Hotlines, 103

I

Inappropriate language, 94
Informal complaint procedures, 99–103
    contact person programs, 101–102
    focus groups and climate surveys, 103
    general training, 102
    hotlines, 103
    mediation, 102–103
    ombudsperson programs, 100–101
Intentions of the harasser, 6
Internal Affairs, 104–105
Internal investigators, 113
Interviews. *See also* Complainant interviews;
    Respondent interviews
    with complainant, respondent,
        and witnesses, 119
    exit, 65
Investigation and investigators, 8, 110–116
    acknowledging difficulty of investigation
        process, 147–148

    additional evidence in investigation,
        119–120
    anonymous complaints and, 121
    attorneys as investigators, 114
    beginning the investigation, 117–125
    common mistakes in, 124–125
    confidentiality and, 122
    coordination with external agencies, 124
    developing a policy on sexual harassment
        and, 78
    disciplinary action, 123
    documentation and, 123
    documenting the investigation. *See*
        Documenting the investigation
    elements to establish, 120–121
    explaining investigative procedures and rights
        to complainant, 95
    external investigators, 113–114
    follow–up, 123
    of gender harassment/discrimination, 43–44
    gender of investigator, 138–140
    hiring or selection issues, 121
    internal investigators, 113
    interviews with complainant, respondent,
        and witnesses, 119–120
    mentors for investigators, 49–50
    negative job actions, 120
    notification of complainant rights and, 123
    notification of outcome and, 123
    planning the investigation, 118–119
    quality of, 38
    quitting of complainant and, 124
    recruiting volunteer investigative teams, 112
    requirements for a successful investigator,
        110–111
    retaliation and, 58, 122
    selection, screening, and training
        of investigators, 111–113
    standard of proof and, 123
    supervisors and managers and, 97
    timelines and, 122–123
    timely response by employers and, 38
    tips for the investigator, 39, 115–116, 125
    training investigators, 112–113
    training program regarding sexual harassment
        and, 89–90
    types of investigators, 113–114
    uniform standards for the investigation,
        122–123
    websites for investigators, 39
Investigative case file, 184–185

J

Job actions. *See also* Tangible job actions
 hostile work environment and, 29
Jokes, as inappropriate aspect of work
 environment, 94
Jokes about the complainant, 55
Journal, keeping a, 128

L

Labor unions, 103
Law enforcement
 focus of this book on, 3
 gender harassment and discrimination in, 41
 percentage of women who experience sexual
  harassment in, 11–12
Laws, federal and state, 23–39
 prohibitions against sex discrimination, 23–24
 summary of employee rights under, 35–36
 summary of employer responsibilities under,
  36–39
Lawsuits, 3–6
 filing, 132
 guidance for agencies based on earlier, 6–9
Liability, employer, 37
 for hostile work environment. *See* Hostile
  work environment

M

Male investigators, 139
Managers. *See* Supervisors and managers
Mediation, 102–103
Mentors for investigators, 49–50
Meritor Savings Bank v. *Vinson,* 24, 25, 27, 32, 37–38
Misconceptions regarding sexual harassment, 5–6
Mitigating factors, 17
Monitoring the workplace, 56
Motivations of harassers, 60
Mutual relationships, misconception about, 5
Myth of false allegations, 73, 135–136

N

Negative job actions, investigation of, 120
Nicknames, hostile work environment and, 28
Nonemployees
 harassment by, 202–203
 harassment of, 201–202
Nontraditional fields, sexual harassment
 of women in, 11

O

Offensive language and jokes, hostile work
 environment and, 28
Ombudsperson programs, 100–101
Oncale v. *Sundowner Offshore Services, Inc.,* 34
Open-ended questions, 134–135
Ostracizing the complainant, 54
Outside experts, monitoring prevention and, 66

P

Peace Officer Bill of Rights, 161
Pennsylvania State Police v. *Suders,* 32
Percentage of women who experience sexual
 harassment in policing, 11–13
Performance
 gender harassment and discrimination and,
  45–47
 holding employees to different standards of, 94
Personal impact of sexual harassment, 15
Personality characteristics of men who sexually
 harass, 59
Personality clash, as common excuse for gender
 harassment and discrimination and, 44–45
Personnel files, reviewing, 162, 187–188
Petrosino v. *Bell Atlantic,* 33
Physical contact, hostile work environment
 and, 28
Policies regarding sexual harassment, 7, 68–78.
 See also Comprehensive sexual
  harassment policy
 common mistakes of employers, 37
 complainant interviews and, 156
 dissemination of, 37–38, 86–87
 goals of, 69–70
 inadequate, 70
 respondent's receipt of copy of, 167–168
 respondent's understanding of, 168
 retaliation and, 55–56
Power, sexual harassment lawsuits and, 4–5
Preventing retaliation, 55–58
Preventing sexual harassment, 59–67
 accountability for, 65–66
 benefits of, 62
 methods of, 62–65
 monitoring of, 66
 perils of not, 61
Prevention of retaliation, supervisors'
 and managers', 96
Professional associations, 103

Professional impact of sexual harassment, 15–16
Professional work environment, promoting a, 63
Protected classes, harassment of people in, 203–204
Psychological injury, not a requirement for hostile work environment, 34
Purpose of harassment, 60

Q

Questions. *See also* Interviews
    follow-up, in complainant interviews, 153–154
    open-ended, 134
    rapid-fire, 141
    that might sound blaming, 134
Quid pro quo sexual harassment, 25–27

R

Rape, victims' failure to report, 18
Rapport
    in complainant interviews, 148–149
    in respondent interviews, 163–164
Reasonable woman standard, 33–34
Recruiting women, 63–64
Referral information, in complainant interviews, 159
Remedial training, 86
Report, final investigative. *See* Final investigative report
Reporting sexual harassment, 7, 18–22
    agency reporting policy, 22
    fears of retaliation and, 19
    indirect strategies for, 19–20
    occupation and, 20–21
    preventing sexual harassment and, 61
    requirement to report, 74–75
    by supervisors and managers, 95–96
    victims' failure to report, 18–19
    work culture and, 21–22
Respondent interviews, 160–172
    collecting preliminary information, 161
    conclusion of, 172
    confidentiality in, 164
    defenses to allegations of sexual harassment, 168–171
    describing purpose of investigation, 162–163
    evasive behavior in, 166
    follow-up contact with respondent, 172
    general questions, 163

    during the interview process, 165
    maintaining focus on issues, 165–166
    not assuming guilt or innocence, 163
    obtaining specific information in, 167–168
    Peace Officer Bill of Rights and, 161
    preparation for, 160–162
    preparing necessary paperwork for, 161
    rapport in, 163–164
    representation during, 163
    reviewing respondent's personnel and investigation files, 162
    standard instructions for, 160–161
    start of, 162–164
    supervisor or manager as respondent, 162
    written statement signed by respondent, 172
Respondents
    following up with respondents, 196
    meeting with, 197
    reviewing personnel and investigative files of, 188
    summary of statements by, in final investigative report, 182
Responses to complaints, 106–109
    advising complainant, 108
    immediate safety and, 106
    informing immediate supervisors, 108
    informing respondent, 108
    investigative process, 108–109
    separating parties, 107–108
    by supervisors and managers, 93
Responses to sexual harassment by employees. *See* Employee responses to sexual harassment
Retaining women, 63–64
Retaliation, 8, 51–58
    complainant interviews and, 158–159
    against complainant or others, 94
    discipline and, 56–57
    elements to establish, 52–53
    explaining steps to be taken to prevent, 95
    failing to stop, 94–95
    federal protection against, 24
    investigation and, 122
    legal protection against, 51–53
    monitoring for, 197
    preventing and responding to, 55–58
    protecting complainant from, 195–196
    respondent interviews and, 164, 172
    social, 54–55
    triggers for, 55
    types of, 53–55
    work, 53–54

Robinson v. *Jacksonville Shipyards,* 27, 38
Rumors about the complainant, spreading, 55

S

Same-gender harassment, 198–199
Same-sex sexual harassment, 34
Screening investigators, 111–112
Severity of sexual harassment, 16–17
Sex discrimination (gender discrimination). *See also*
          Gender harassment and discrimination
     African-American women firefighters and, 14
     federal prohibitions against, 23–24
     sexual harassment as a form of, 23–24
     state and local prohibitions against, 24
Sexual behavior, hostile work environment and, 28
Sexual favoritism, 77
Sexual orientation, harassment based on, 199–200
Shunning, hostile work environment and, 29
Shunning the complainant, 54
Silva v. *Lucky Stores, Inc.,* 38
Social retaliation, 54–55
Stalking the complainant, 54
Standard of proof, 192
Standing committee to monitor prevention
          efforts, 66
Stereotypes
     complainant interviews and, 133–135
     in gender harassment/discrimination, 43
     hostile work environment and, 28
Supervisors and managers, 91–97
     complaints of harassment or discrimination
         against, 96–97
     additional sexual harassment training
         for, 82–83
     complainant interviews and, 156
     dating between subordinates and, 76–77
     definition of, 91
     employer liability for hostile work environment
         and behaviors of, 31–54
     holding accountable, 194–195
     inappropriate actions by, 93–95
     informing about allegations, 108
     legal responsibilities of, 91–92
     monitoring prevention and, 66
     prevention of retaliation by, 96
     prevention strategies of, 92–93
     reporting sexual harassment to, 128–129
     as respondents, 162
     responses to sexual harassment by, 95
     work retaliation by, 53

Surveys
     employee, importance of, 87
     of work environment (climate), 64–65, 103

T

Tangible job actions. *See also* Negative job actions;
         and *specific job actions*
     quid pro quo sexual harassment and, 25–27
Taping complainant interviews, 137–138
Third-party harassment, 34–35
Timely response by employers, 38
Title VII of the 1964 Civil Rights Act, 23, 24, 36,
         49, 130, 132, 200
     protection against retaliation under, 51, 52
Touching employees, 94
Training investigators, 112–113
Training program regarding sexual harassment,
         7, 79–90
     as response to informal complaint process, 102
     challenges in, 79–81
     content of, 81–83
     design of, 83–86
     evaluation of, 87–88
     experiential learning, 84
     gender difference in perceptions and, 81
     regularly scheduled training sessions, 83
     remedial training, 86
     respondent's attendance at training classes
         on sexual harassment, 168
     small workshops for different groups, 85
     strong agency leadership, 84
     strong facilitators, 84–85
     sufficient time for learning, 84
     victim's perspective and, 85

U

Ulterior motives of parties or witnesses, 191
Unwelcome sexual behavior, 5
     determination of, 32–33

V

Verbal behavior, hostile work environment and, 28
Victim dynamics, focus on, 2–3
Victims
     impact of retaliation on, 55
     impact of sexual harassment on, 14–17
     training program and perspective of, 85
Visual materials, hostile work environment and, 27–28
Volunteer investigative teams, 112

W

Websites for investigators, 39
Weeks v. *Baker & Mackenzie,* 35
Witnesses
    identifying potential, 157
    summary of witness statements, in final
        investigative report, 182
    types of, 173–174
    ulterior motives of, 191
Witness interviews, 173–180
    additional information to obtain from
        supervisors, 179
    code of silence and, 174–175
    concerns of witnesses and, 175–176
    concluding, 179

confidentiality and, 177, 179
eliciting names of other witnesses, 179
follow-up contact with witnesses, 180
general guidelines for, 177–178
process of, 175–180
protecting identity of complainant
    and, 176
standard instructions for, 178
types of information to obtain in, 178
Work culture, reporting sexual harassment and, 21–22
Work environment (climate). *See also* Hostile work
    environment
    other employees hurt by, 61
    professional, promoting a, 63
    surveys of, 64–65
Work retaliation, 53–54